Books on Bosnia

a critical bibliography
of works relating to
Bosnia-Herzegovina
published since 1990 in
West European languages

edited by
Quintin Hoare
and
Noel Malcolm

THE BOSNIAN INSTITUTE

Books on Bosnia

Published by The Bosnian Institute (Charity No.1064733)
14/16 St Mark's Road, London S11 1RQ
Tel: 0171 243 2900
e-mail: bosinst@globalnet.co.uk

Typeset in 10.5 Life by Sumner Type, London SE22
Printed by Trade Union Printing Services, Newcastle-upon-Tyne

A C.I.P. cataloque record for this book is available from the British Library

ISBN 1 901029 03 4

CONTENTS

Part Two

PREFACE

The war in Bosnia has been one of the most written-about events in modern history. Works of all kinds have been published: polemical, historical, sociological, philosophical, journalistic, autobiographical, literary. Almost 350 are listed here. However, although this bibliography is certainly the most thorough critical listing of its kind to be published so far, the first thing that needs to be said about it is that it makes no claim to be comprehensive. It is subject to limitations and exclusions of several kinds.

Most obviously, this listing is confined to works in English and other Western European languages. It excludes, therefore, a large number of books published in Bosnia and in other parts of the former Yugoslavia; this bibliography is directed primarily at British, American and Western European readers. (Even for those who also read Bosnian, a thorough listing of works published in Bosnia would be a frustrating thing, as so many of those works have not found their way into Western libraries.) The main focus of the bibliography is on English-language books, and the coverage of works in other Western languages is necessarily more selective; nevertheless, a total of ten languages is represented here.

This bibliography also excludes articles published in journals: some of the 'books' listed here may be fairly brief pamphlets, but all of the items in this list are separately published works. Since articles are omitted, so too are books of essays in which only one essay or article is about Bosnia.

Everything included in this bibliography relates in some way or other to the crisis which engulfed Bosnia in 1992. The year 1990 has been chosen as the chronological starting-point for the publications listed here, in order to include works on the breakdown of the old Yugoslavia. Many of these works are general studies of the Yugoslav débâcle, but all of them have some direct relevance to the Bosnian crisis: books which are concerned exclusively with the war in Croatia, for example, or with the internal politics of Serbia, have not been included. Also excluded are works which do relate to Bosnia, but are not linked in any direct way to the crisis of the

1990s — for instance, scholarly monographs on earlier periods of Bosnian history, or new English translations of literary works by Ivo Andrić.

The arrangement of the bibliography is as follows. Works have been put into three divisions: 'Essential Reading', 'Other Recommended Reading' and 'Other Reading'. Within each of these divisions, the books are grouped according to category: 'General background', 'Background to the war', 'War and genocide in Bosnia-Herzegovina', 'Personal testimony: the military', 'After the war', and so on. Several of these categories overlap, and there are inevitably some cases where a book could well have been assigned to a different one; overall, however, it is hoped that this system of categorization will serve the needs of the reader far better than a completely unsorted alphabetical listing would have done.

Similarly, the sorting of these works into the three divisions has required some awkward choices in marginal cases. Relevant criteria for our classification have included originality, scholarship, analytic power and coherence, historical and political grasp, value as a documentary or primary source, etc. It should be emphasized that although evaluative principles have been used in the selection of the first and second divisions, this does not mean that everything placed in the third division is judged to be of inferior (or even negative) value. Our aim in selecting 'Essential Reading' and 'Other Recommended Reading' has been not only to draw attention to the best works available, but also to present, as it were, two reading-lists — one short and made up exclusively of works available in English, the other longer — for anyone embarking on a study of the Bosnian crisis. It is in the nature of a reading-list that it tries to avoid duplication: accordingly, some works have been consigned to 'Other Reading', not because they are thought to be worthless, but because the valid points they make have been made already by the books listed in the first two divisions. The third division is thus something of a catch-all. It is true, on the other hand, that some of the things caught in it are works of very low value, or of no value at all. The critical comments made here on such works may sometimes strike the reader as peremptory: naturally, it is not possible to set out detailed arguments or counter-evidence in a critical appraisal of no more than a few sentences. For those readers who want a more substantial justification of the critical position adopted in this bibliography, the best thing to do would be to read the works listed in the first and second divisions, where they will find evidence and arguments in plenty. The next best thing, for those with less time to spare, would be to read the selection of full-length reviews printed in the second half of this publication. Some of these reviews make positive appraisals, while others make very negative ones; all, it is hoped, will both inform and stimulate the reader's own critical judgement. Works for which longer reviews are included have been asterisked in the main listing.

The editors of this bibliography are responsible for the assignment of works to the three divisions and their various categories. They also made the selection of full-length reviews: some of these were first published in *Bosnia Report*, the bulletin of The Bosnian Institute, while others appeared in other journals (as listed in each case), whose permission to reprint them here is gratefully acknowledged. The editors have also checked the publication details of all these books (including prices, where known, though the inclusion of a price here does not necessarily mean that the work is still in print). They are also responsible for the majority of the critical entries in the bibliography. Other entries have been contributed by Paul Garde and Attila Hoare, for whose assistance they are extremely grateful. They, like the authors of the full-length reviews reprinted here, are members or supporters of The Bosnian Institute; nevertheless, their comments are expressions of their own personal judgements. The Institute itself does not express a corporate opinion, but publishes this bibliography in the hope that it will be a useful research tool, and a stimulus to informed debate, among all those who care about the recent past, the present and the uncertain future of Bosnia-Herzegovina.

Quintin Hoare and Noel Malcolm
May 1999

Part One

ESSENTIAL READING

General background

Ali, Rabia, and Lawrence Lifschultz (ed.) **Why Bosnia? writings on the Balkan war**, Pamphleteer's Press, New Haven 1993 (UK distributor Central Books), 353 pp, £14.95

Important collection of essays, interviews and literary texts, providing a richly varied introduction to Bosnia's multi-national and multi-cultural society, while chronicling and analysing its internationally sanctioned destruction. An ideal starting-point. A portion of the proceeds go to a fund for the reconstruction of Sarajevo's National Library.

*Bringa, Tone **Being Muslim the Bosnian Way: identity and community in a Central Bosnian village**, Princeton University Press, Princeton and London 1995, 281 pp, £13.99

Detailed portrayal of the conditions of life, beliefs and customs of ordinary Bosnian Muslim and Catholic villagers, studied by the author (a social anthropologist) in a central Bosnian village a few years before the war.

Malcolm, Noel **Bosnia: a short history**, Macmillan, London 1994, 340 pp., £9.99

Covers the whole history of Bosnia, from the end of the Roman Empire to the Dayton Accords, in a single accessible volume; equally suited to the general reader or to the expert, it draws on a wide range of primary and secondary sources in all the relevant languages.

Pinson, Mark (ed.) **The Muslims of Bosnia-Herzegovina**, Harvard University Press, Cambridge Mass. and London 1994, 187 pp., £11.95

Valuable collection of essays by Balkan and Ottoman historians (John Fine, Colin Heywood, Justin McCarthy, Mark Pinson and Ivo Banac), arranged chronologically and providing an introduction to the history of Bosnia and its Muslim population from the middle ages to the present.

Background to the war

Magaš, Branka **The Destruction of Yugoslavia: tracking the break-up 1980-92**, Verso, London 1993, 366 pp., £12.95

Sequence of contemporaneous commentaries and analyses covering the political history of Yugoslavia's final decade, and concentrating particularly on Kosova, the Greater Serbia project, Milošević's destruction of the federal system, the Slovenian democratizing alternative, and the nature of the wars unleashed by Belgrade as the country broke up.

Silber, Laura, and Allan Little **The Death of Yugoslavia**, Penguin/BBC, London 1995, 400 pp., £6.99

Linked to the BBC documentary of the same name, provides a detailed account, based on exceptionally valuable and extensive interview material and on contemporary reportage, of the rise of Milošević and the dissolution of Yugoslavia.

Thompson, Mark **A Paper House: the ending of Yugoslavia**, Vintage, London 1992, 347 pp., £6.99

Combines travelogue, cultural history and political analysis to give an atmospheric and nuanced account of Yugoslavia at the point of its collapse.

War and genocide in Bosnia-Herzegovina

*Cigar, Norman **Genocide in Bosnia: the policy of 'ethnic cleansing'**, Texas A&M University Press, College Station 1995, 242 pp., £27.95

Rigorous and thoroughly documented analysis, demonstrating the planned and systematic nature of 'ethnic cleansing'. Especially valuable on the ideological preparation for this policy in Serbia, analysing the responsibility of senior academics and churchmen.

Dizdarević, Zlatko **Sarajevo — a War Journal,** preface by Joseph Brodsky, Henry Holt and Co., New York 1994, 208 pp., $19.95

Written in the first years of the siege by an editor at *Oslobođenje,* these poignant war stories, compelling descriptions, and perceptive reflections from a city under fire constitute one of the most authoritative testimonies of the entire Bosnian war. A powerful and often scathing articulation of Sarajevo's disillusionment with Western inaction and betrayal of international norms and values.

Gutman, Roy **Witness to Genocide,** Element, Longmead 1993, 180 pp., £8.99

Key collection of reports from Bosnia by the Pulitzer Prize-winning journalist, especially valuable for its revelations about the concentration camps of northern Bosnia in the summer of 1992.

Helsinki Watch **War Crimes in Bosnia,** New York 1992, 358 pp., £14.95; Vol. 2 1993, 422 pp., £14.95

The fullest published collection of dossiers on human-rights abuses committed during the war (although its date of publication precluded it from including later events such as the Srebrenica massacres) The long introduction to volume I, with a chronology of events, is also an important work of reference.

Kurspahić, Kemal **As Long As Sarajevo Exists**, Pamphleteers Press, Stony Creek Conn. 1997, xxxviii + 248 pp., £19.95

This memoir by the editor-in-chief of *Oslobođenje* from 1991 to 1995 bears unrivalled witness to the resilience and survival of an operative civil society in Sarajevo under siege. Under Kurspahić's editorship the paper came to symbolize the resistance of Bosnia-Herzegovina and its people to genocidal aggression and to terrible deprivation, while at the same time maintaining its journalistic integrity and critical independence when to do so was hard indeed.

Rieff, David **Slaughterhouse: Bosnia and the failure of the West**, Simon and Schuster, New York 1995, 240 pp., $22

After a somewhat rambling introduction, this provides a damning exposé of the UN's complicity in Bosnia's suffering, with a wealth of insights into the bureaucratism and callousness that characterized the UN mission in Bosnia, into its indulgence towards the forces of Pale and Belgrade, and into the petty prejudices and ignorance of many of its officials.

Rohde, David **A Safe Area [Endgame in USA], Srebrenica — Europe's worst massacre since the Second World War**, Simon and Schuster, London 1997, 440 pp., £8.99

Painstaking reconstruction of the events leading up to the fall of Srebrenica, and the massacres which followed it. Rohde was the first Western journalist to investigate mass burial sites in the Srebrenica area, and was awarded a Pulitzer Prize for his achievement.

Sudetić, Chuck **Blood and Vengeance: one family's story of the war in Bosnia**, W. W. Norton & Co., New York 1998, 393 pp., $26.95

Sudetić traces the story of an ordinary Bosniak family, from a mountain village just north of Višegrad, some of whose members fled to Srebrenica in the late summer of 1992. His account of the fate that befell them also includes quite a detailed analysis of the failures and stupidities of UN policy towards the Srebrenica 'safe area'. This is a very impressive book: unsentimental, unbiased, uncompromising in its assignment of blame (above all to Milošević, Karadžić, Arkan, Mladić, Rose, Janvier and Akashi) and, in places, very moving.

Vranić, Seada **Breaking the Wall of Silence: the voices of raped Bosnia**, English edition prepared with the assistance of Diane Conklin, Antibarbarus, Zagreb 1996, 343 pp., £10

Outstanding study by a Bosnian author of the mass rape perpetrated by Serbian forces in Bosnia-Herzegovina, consisting of interviews with victims, comments by experts and discussions of the key issues involved — social, political and legal. Full of original insights into the mental state of both perpetrators and victims, the character of Bosnia-Herzegovina's multi-ethnic society and the purpose of Serbian rape warfare, this book stands head and shoulders above others dealing with the subject.

*Vulliamy, Ed **Seasons in Hell: understanding Bosnia's war**, Simon and Schuster, New York and London 1994, 370 pp., £6.99

Powerful account of the nature of the war in Bosnia (especially central Bosnia) during 1992-3, by a leading correspondent. Of particular interest for its coverage of the Croat-Muslim conflict, though it is less reliable on the background to Yugoslavia's break-up and descent into war.

Williams, Paul, and Norman Cigar **War Crimes and Individual Responsibility: a prima facie case for the indictment of Slobodan Milošević**, Alliance to Defend Bosnia-Herzegovina, London 1996, 98 pp., £5

Written in the form of (and observing all the criteria for) a formal indictment, distinguishing carefully between different categories of legal responsibility and presenting a mass of detailed evidence in the notes.

The international response

*Almond, Mark **Europe's Backyard War**, Heinemann, London 1994, 432 pp., £20

Rigorous (but often richly entertaining) dissection of the ignorant assumptions and incompetent proceedings of Western policy, concentrating especially on Britain and the European Union.

*Cohen, Ben, and George Stamkoski (ed.), **With No Peace to Keep: UN peacekeeping and the war in the former Yugoslavia** (includes texts by Mark Almond, Lee Bryant, Roy Gutman, Drago Hedl, Tihomir Loza, Branka Magaš, Noel Malcolm, Vlastimir Mijović, Rosemary Righter, Michael Scharf, Ed Vulliamy, Ian Williams, Paul Williams and others), Media East West, London 1996, 184 pp., £10

Authoritative, well-constructed collection of essays containing a wealth of information on the whole record of the muddled, bureaucratic, ill-conceived UN missions to Croatia and Bosnia: what they were purportedly or actually sent to do (specific texts on British, French, Russian and US policy, preceded by a general overview); how they functioned, or did not function, in practice on the ground; how they were shaped by the UN's inherent weaknesses and prejudices; the compromises they made with the architects and executors of genocide.

Cushman, Thomas, and Stjepan Mestrović (ed.) **This Time We Knew: Western responses to genocide in Bosnia** (includes texts by Michael Barnett, Jean Baudrillard, Brad Blitz, Philip Cohen, Daniele Conversi, Sheri Fink, Liah Greenfeld, Daniel Kofman, Slaven Letica, David Riesman, James Sadkovich, Brendan Simms), New York University Press, New York and London 1996, 412 pp., $18.95

Valuable and wide-ranging collection of essays; of particular interest are those by Brad Blitz (on the activities of the Serb lobby in the United States), Daniele Conversi (on British Serbophilia) and Daniel Kofman (on the response in Israel to the war).

Holbrooke, Richard **To End a War,** Random House, New

York 1998, 408 pp., $27.95

Those who thought of Holbrooke as simply an amoral diplomatic fixer will be pleasantly surprised by this book: he had strong views about the essential rights and wrongs of the Bosnian war, and does not hide his contempt for pusillanimous UN officials and military men. There are some omissions: the weaknesses of Western military intelligence are only hinted at, and certain key assumptions (e.g. the need to proceed on the basis of a 49:51 territorial division) are never examined. Still, the vividness, intelligence and sheer detail of Holbrooke's account of the high-level diplomacy put this book in a class of its own.

OTHER RECOMMENDED READING

General background

Balić, Smail **Das unbekannte Bosnien: Europas Brücke zur islamischen Welt**, Böhlau Verlag, Cologne 1992, 526 pp., DM 88

A rich survey of Bosnian cultural history, concentrating especially on the Ottoman period and the heritage of Islam, by one of the foremost scholars of Ottoman Bosnian literature. Also discusses the tradition of religious coexistence, and the problems of defining 'Bosnian' and/or 'Bosniak' identity.

Donia, Robert, and John Fine **Bosnia-Hercegovina: a tradition betrayed**, C. Hurst & Co., London 1994, 316 pp., £9.50

Rejecting any idea that the current conflict in Bosnia is a result of 'ancient tribal hatreds', the authors — two of the foremost English-language historians of the area — argue that the reasons for Bosnia's agony are more contemporary and political in nature than historical and cultural. Their work traces the centuries-long traditions of statehood and pluralism in Bosnia from the arrival of Slavic tribes in the 6th century to the 1990s.

Friedman, Francine **The Bosnian Muslims: denial of a nation**, Westview Press, Boulder and Oxford 1996, 288 pp., $21.95

Study of the origins and evolution of the Muslim nation in Bosnia, from the middle ages to the outbreak of war. Usefully synthesizes a wealth of information unavailable elsewhere to the English-language reader.

Garde, Paul Vie et mort de la Yougoslavie, Fayard, Paris 1992, 465 pp., FF 140

This book, by a Slavic scholar who has known Yugoslavia for more than 40 years, combines three things in one: a brief historical sketch (from the middle ages to Tito); a 'panorama' describing each component territory in turn; and a 160-page account of the break-up and the international response to it. The writing is lively, almost conversational in style, but the judgements are sure and fortified by wide reading.

Grmek, Mirko, Marc Gjidara and Neven Simić (ed.) Le nettoyage ethnique: documents historiques sur une idéologie serbe, Fayard, Paris 1993, 340 pp., FF 120

This important collection includes all the major texts of Serb nationalist ideology, from Vuk Karadžić and Ilija Garašanin to the Memorandum of the Serbian Academy, together with a useful analysis of the different currents of that ideology (Šešelj, Jović, Karadžić, Drašković, etc.) active in the early 1990s.

Kappeler, Andreas, Gerhard Simon and Georg Brunner (ed. German edition, 1989) and Edward Allworth (ed. English edition) Muslim Communities Re-emerge: historical perspectives on nationality, politics and opposition in the former Soviet Union and Yugoslavia, translated by Caroline Sawyer, Duke University Press, Durham NC and London 1994, 365 pp., $24.95

This heavyweight historical collection contains three important texts on the former Yugoslavia — Sabrina Ramet on the national consciousness of the Muslims (Bosniaks), Georg Brunner comparing the status of Muslims in the Soviet Union and the former Yugoslavia, and Wolfgang Höpken on the evolution of Yugoslav Communist policy towards the Bosnian Muslims — together with one extremely thin and tendentious one by Alexandre Popović, arguing that recognition of Bosnian Muslims as a nation was simply a 'devious means to weaken once more the position of the Serbs'.

Klemenčić, Mladen **Territorial Proposals for the Settlement of the War in Bosnia-Hercegovina,** International Boundaries Research Unit, University of Durham, Durham 1994, 74 pp., £20

A very valuable and well illustrated survey of all the various plans (official and unofficial, domestic and international) put forward for the 'cantonization' or outright partition of Bosnia, from 1991 to mid 1994.

Lovrenović, Ivan **Bosnien und Herzegowina: eine Kulturgeschichte,** translated by Klaus Detlef Olof, Folio, Vienna 1998, 239 pp., DM 39

A rich and deeply knowledgeable survey of Bosnian cultural history, paying proper attention to the cultural legacy of all the religious communities, by one of Bosnia's best prose-writers and leading intellectuals.

Ramet, Sabrina, and Ljubiša Adamović (ed.) **Beyond Yugoslavia: politics, economics and culture in a shattered community,** Westview Press, Boulder Col. 1995, 501 pp., £60.95

Important collection of scholarly essays, originally planned in 1988 although not completed until the early nineties. In addition to interesting and wide-ranging contributions on cultural and social questions, there are solid texts by Ivo Banac on historiography, Dennis Rusinow on 'The avoidable catastrophe', Marko Milivojević on the JNA, Jasmina Kuzmanović on media, Sabrina Ramet on Macedonia, etc. The main essay directly on Bosnia, by Paul Shoup, although well researched and argued, is too indulgent to Karadžić's public justifications in 1990-92, and tends to obscure the scale, genocidal character, and purposiveness, of the assault on Bosnia-Herzegovina and, above all, its origins in Belgrade.

Background to the war

Bennett, Christopher **Yugoslavia's Bloody Collapse: causes, course and consequence**, C. Hurst & Co., London 1995, 272 pp., £ 9.95

A succinct textbook account of the break-up of Yugoslavia, including a brief introduction to the history of the country.

Bethlehem, Daniel and Marc Weller (ed.) **The Yugoslav Crisis in International Law: general issues, part one**, Cambridge University Press, New York and Cambridge 1997, 769 pp., £75

First in a projected series of volumes of documents now unfortunately discontinued, this book contains all the relevant general UN materials (Security Council resolutions and debates, Secretary-General's reports, etc.) pertaining to the crisis in the former Yugoslavia, up to 1994.

Bryant, Lee **The Betrayal of Bosnia**, University of Westminster Press, London 1993, 100 pp., £3.50

Outlining Bosnia's history and the causes of the war, then presenting with passion the case against the Western policy of partitioning the country, the author provides a wealth of information about the events of the first two-and-a-half years of war in the former Yugoslavia, including notably at the local level.

Fogelquist, Alan **Handbook of Facts on the Break-Up of Yugoslavia, international policy and the war in Bosnia-Herzegovina**, AEIOU Publishing 1993, 70 pp., $9.95

An incisive summary of events, and criticism of Western policy, by a scholarly author who had closely monitored the Bosnian and Croatian press.

Janigro, Nicole **L'esplosione delle nazioni: il caso jugoslavo**, Feltrinelli, Milan 1993, 215 pp., Lit. 23,000

Thoughtful, intelligent, knowledgeable, at times almost elegiac yet 'warts and all' portrayal of the ex-Yugoslavia in its final stages, viewed through the prism of its horrific break-up, by an Italian journalist born in Zagreb. The author is not simply at home in the language and culture of her foster country — from Krleža and Kiš to rock music — but is also informed by a wide selection of sources in English, French and German as well as Italian and Serbo-Croat. The essayistic approach she adopts provides an often perceptive phenomenology of Yugoslav culture, society and political life, illuminating in its details, even if offering little in the way of direct explanation.

Lukić, Reneo and Allen Lynch **Europe from the Balkans to the Urals: the disintegration of Yugoslavia and the Soviet Union**, OUP, Oxford and New York 1996, 436 pp., £35

A rich, well-researched and lucid comparative study of the dissolutions of Yugoslavia and the Soviet Union (with valuable comments also on the 'velvet divorce' of the Czechs and Slovaks). Central to the book is a powerful and detailed analysis of the role of Milošević in ensuring that the break-up of Yugoslavia took a violent form. The last part expertly covers the policy responses of the EU, UN, USA and Russia. It is strange that this study has received so little attention (in comparison with, say, the widely quoted and greatly over-rated work of Susan Woodward).

Meier, Viktor **Wie Jugoslawien verspielt wurde**, Verlag C.H.Beck, Munich 1995, 464 pp., DM 29.80

Important study of the break-up of Yugoslavia by a senior German journalist and Balkan specialist; concentrates on Serbia, Slovenia and Croatia in the period 1987-91, but also includes a valuable chapter on Bosnia, 1990-92.

Rogel, Carole **The Break-up of Yugoslavia and the War in Bosnia**, Greenwood Press, Westport and London 1998, 182 pp., £35.95

Despite being 'designed for secondary-school and college research', this is a serious, well-sourced and balanced work by a retired US academic historian of Slovene background. The first eighty pages contain a concise historical account of Yugoslavia's emergence and demise, from the Habsburg and Ottoman empires to the aftermath of Dayton. The next forty pages contain useful biographies of a score of major domestic and international players — from Arkan to

Zimmermann. There is then a selection of valuable primary sources, including extracts from the SANU Memorandum, a revealing 1981 text by Tudjman on Bosnia and all the most relevant UN resolutions. The book is topped off with a useful glossary and annotated bibliography.

War and genocide in Bosnia-Herzegovina

Boyle, Francis **The Bosnian People Charge Genocide: proceedings at the International Court of Justice concerning Bosnia v. Serbia on the prevention and punishment of the crime of genocide**, Aletheia Press, Amherst 1996, 373 pp., $20

An important documentary source-book, with full transcripts of the 1993 hearings which led to the International Court making a provisional court order demanding that the Federal Republic of Yugoslavia 'take all measures... to prevent commission of the crime of genocide' by forces it supported in Bosnia. Also containing important evidence of the negotiations over the Owen-Stoltenberg plan, which would have divided Bosnia into three quasi-states.

*Cohen, Roger **Hearts Grown Brutal: sagas of Sarajevo**, Random House, New York 1998, 523 pp., $27.95

A big, passionate book by the *New York Times* correspondent, who has tried to pack everything into it: the Bosnian experience of the war (told through several family histories), the Western response and UN policy, and the historical background. Cohen argues well against the 'ethnic hatreds' doctrine, but tends to substitute World War II hatreds instead. However, his analysis of UN failure, including evidence drawn from minutes of a high-level meeting held before the fall of Srebrenica, will be of lasting importance.

*Heller, Yves **Des brasiers mal éteints: un reporter dans les guerres yougoslaves 1991-95**, Le Monde, Paris 1997, 340 pp., FF 120

Collection of fine reports on the wars in Croatia and Bosnia first published in *Le Monde*.

Hukanović, Rezak **Tenth Circle of Hell: a memoir of life in the death camps of Bosnia**, Little Brown & Co., London 1997, 163 pp., £14.99

Heart-rending, unforgettable account of a survivor of the Serbian death camp at Omarska. The parallel extremes of sadism and degradation described by the author strikingly illustrate the dehumanizing purpose of that institution.

Kadrić, Jusuf **Brčko: genocide and testimony**, translated by Saba Risaluddin and Hasan Rončević, Institute for the Research of Crimes Against Humanity and International Law, Sarajevo 1999, 300 pp., £10

A serious and copiously documented account of the seizure by the JNA and its subordinate irregular units (notably those led by Arkan) of the majority-Bosniak town of Brčko in the spring of 1992, with unbearable testimony by survivors of the subsequent massacre, terror and ethnic cleansing. Amply illustrated, and with statistical tables, lists of known perpetrators, and the text of the Hague Tribunal's indictment against two of the most notorious for genocide and murder.

Lukić, Reneo **The Wars of South Slavic Succession: Yugoslavia 1991-93**, Graduate Institute of International Studies, Geneva 1993, 48 pp.

A brief but marvellously clear-headed pamphlet, accurately summarizing the key factors that led to the war and analysing the fundamental inadequacy of Vance-Owen-style 'peace plans'.

Maass, Peter **Love Thy Neighbour: a story of war**, Macmillan, London 1996, 305 pp., £10

This memorable book is more than just an autobiographical account by a journalist who covered Bosnia during 1992. It concentrates on the abnormalities and normalities of Bosnian wartime life, but also comments thoughtfully on the ethics and practice of journalism, the Yugoslav political background and the international response.

Mazower, Mark **The War in Bosnia: an analysis**, Action for Bosnia, London 1992, 32 pp.

Written only a few months after the start of the Bosnian war, this brief pamphlet displayed a remarkable ability to understand the real nature of what was happening: the strategic pattern of the initial Serb conquests, the system of co-operation between regular army units and paramilitaries, and the fact that the 'ethnic cleansing' of non-Serbs was an aim, not a by-product, of the fighting.

Mertus, Julie, Jasmina Tesanović, Habiba Metikos and Rada Borić (ed.) **The Suitcase: refugee voices from Bosnia and Croatia**, University of California Press, Berkeley, Los Angeles and London 1997, 238 pp., £13.95

The great value of this book lies in the refugee voices themselves, which take up two thirds of it. Drawn carefully from all national groups, and arranged in five sections — on the circumstances of leaving, on dreams of home, on everyday refugee life, on the child's view, and on starting life anew (i.e. giving up on ever going home) — the refugees evoke unforgettably, whether in unadorned prose or sometimes in moving poetry, the inhumanities visited upon ordinary people from all walks of life during the wars in Bosnia and Croatia. The editorial material that makes up the remaining third of the book — introductions, notes on the refugee contributors, afterwords — is for the most part sober and non-patronizing, although in places it suffers from a naive apoliticism that blurs the real contours of the war and its architects.

Neier, Aryeh **Brutality, Genocide, Terror, and the Struggle for Justice,** Times Books/Random House, New York 1998, 286 pp., $25

This impressive work, by an Auschwitz survivor and lifelong campaigner for human rights, first reviews earlier attempts since Nuremberg to devise international mechanisms to deal with crimes against humanity, then examines the events in Bosnia and Rwanda which led to the creation of the special tribunals at The Hague which, the author hopes, may lead to the establishment of a permanent International Criminal Court (although, in the former Yugoslav case, Neier argues that setting up the Tribunal was the right decision for the wrong reason, since it was in large part a substitute for decisive action to prevent the crimes). Specific chapters are devoted to concentration camps, siege warfare, rape, incitement to mass murder, and guilt, and the whole work constitutes a powerful argument in favour of the Tribunals, concluding that: 'for the first time in human history, those committing war crimes, crimes against humanity, or the ultimate crime, genocide, would have to reckon seriously with the possibility that they would be brought before the international bar to face truth, be held accountable, and serve justice.'

Prstojević, Miroslav **Sarajevo Survival Guide**, FAMA, Sarajevo 1993, 95 pp.

A sardonic mock-Michelin Guide to a city under siege, containing an extraordinary mixture of useful information, chilling factual statement, ironic observation and almost unbearable black humour.

*Sells, Michael **The Bridge Betrayed: religion and genocide in Bosnia**, University of California Press, Berkeley, Los Angeles and London 1996, 244 pp., £15.95

The author, an American Professor of Religious Studies with a partly Serb background, analyses with great thoroughness and understanding the part played by religion and myth in enabling Serbs, and Croats too, to be mobilized by nationalist leaders behind genocidal projects in Bosnia. He also examines how people in the West — politicians and church leaders alike — for the most part systematically closed their eyes to the greatest crime committed in post-Second-World-War Europe.

Sofri, Adriano **Lo specchio di Sarajevo,** Sellerio, Palermo 1997, 230 pp., Lit. 24,000

The main portion of this book, consisting of reports written from Sarajevo for *L'Unità* and other Italian papers between early 1994 and July 1996, contains some of the most eloquent, perceptive and sympathetic writing by any foreign journalist on the people and life of the city — articles that at their best attain genuine literary quality. An appendix contains a few rather different but equally valuable texts: polemical articles written in early 1993 against the ideological mantras trotted out by much of the Italian left to justify its passivity and indifference towards the fate of Bosnia; the spoken text of one of the five television documentaries on Bosnia Sofri made for RAI; and a thoughtful essay reflecting on the problems and inevitable ambiguities of filming in a war zone.

Stiglmayer, Alexandra (ed.) **Mass Rape: the war against women in Bosnia-Herzegovina,,** University of Nebraska Press, Lincoln and London 1994, 232 pp., $14.95

A valuable study of rape in the Bosnian War, with essays by Ruth Seifert, Catharine MacKinnon, Susan Brownmiller, Rhonda Copelon, and others, and interviews with rape victims and some of the rapists. An international and collaborative effort strong on sociological and legal analysis.

Welser, Maria von **Am Ende wünschst du dir nur noch den Tod: die Massenvergewaltigungen im Krieg auf dem Balkan,** Knaur, Munich 1993, 191 pp., DM 12.90

The first detailed account of organized rape in Serb-run concentration camps.

Zülch, Tilman (ed.) **'Ethnische Säuberung' — Völkermord für 'Grossserbien': eine Dokumentation der Gesellschaft für bedrohte Völker,** Luchterhand Literaturverlag, Hamburg 1993, 170 pp., DM 12

Important collection of articles chronicling ethnic cleansing in Bosnia (with shorter sections also on Croatia and the Vojvodina).

The international response

Benda, Marc, and François Crémieux, **Paris-Bihać,** *Les Temps Modernes* /Éditions Michalon, Paris 1995, 186 pp., FF 90

A fascinating account by two young men who did their military service with a French battalion serving in the Bihać enclave in the summer of 1994. Gives specific examples of anti-Muslim prejudice in the French military; also describes the extraordinary passivity of French operations (entire armoured columns turned back by three-man roadblocks, etc.).

Cigar, Norman **The Right to Defence: thoughts on the Bosnian arms embargo**, IEDSS, London 1995, 48 pp., £6.00

Cogent demolition of the arguments used in defence of the UN Security Council's arms embargo on Bosnia.

Conversi, Daniele **German-Bashing and the Break-up of Yugoslavia**, Donald W. Treadgold Papers, Seattle 1998, 82 pp., $6.45

Vigorous pamphlet exploding the myths surrounding Germany's role in the break-up of Yugoslavia and the outbreak of war in Bosnia. The author shows how anti-German prejudices were deliberately exploited by the British and French governments and their media spokesmen in order to hide their own culpable passivity in the face of Milošević's aggression.

Davies, John, Bob Myers and Geoff Robinson (ed.) **Taking Sides — against ethnic cleansing in Bosnia: the story of the Workers Aid convoys**, Workers Aid For Bosnia, Leeds 1998, 198 pp., £10

Well produced visual and documentary record of the work of the most effective British group to combine the provision of aid with political solidarity, from 1993 until the end of the war and beyond.

Dizdarević, Zlatko, and Gigi Riva **L'ONU è morta a Sarajevo**, Il Saggiatore, Milan 1996, 248 pp., Lit. 29,000

A powerful and well-researched account of the failings of the UN operation in Bosnia, with special chapters on General Morillon, Boutros Boutros-Ghali, General Rose, Yasushi Akashi, Goražde and Srebrenica. The book was also published in French as *J'Accuse l'ONU* (Calmann-Lévy, Paris 1995, 207 pp.); but this Italian edition includes a valuable extra chapter by Riva, analysing Italy's Bosnian policy.

Hastings, Adrian **SOS Bosnia**, 3rd edition 1994, 54 pp., £2.00.

This collection of articles and letters written by the author to the British press throughout the years of war in Croatia and Bosnia represents one of the most passionate, cogent and sustained individual challenges to the then British government's policy of active appeasement of Belgrade. The authentic voice of an unofficial Britain protesting against the bankruptcy of Western politicking in Bosnia-Herzegovina.

Libal, Michael **Limits of Persuasion: Germany and the Yugoslav crisis, 1991-1992**, Praeger, Westport 1997, 206 pp., £47.95

Highly valuable study of German policy towards the break-up of Yugoslavia and the beginning of the Bosnian war, arguing cogently against the 'premature recognition' thesis; the author was head of the German Foreign Ministry's Yugoslav Department, 1991-5.

Meštrović, Stjepan (ed.) **Genocide After Emotion: the postemotional Balkan war** (includes essays by Norman Cigar, Philip Cohen, Slaven Letica, Igor Primoratz, James Sadkovich), Routledge, London and New York 1996, 225 pp., £12.99

The editor develops the theme of 'post-emotionalism' (as an alternative to post-modernism), by which he means 'the culture industry's manipulation of emotionally charged historical events'. He contributes a stimulating essay on the Orwellian misrepresentation of the Bosnian war in the West, while other contributors range more widely. Especially valuable are the important analysis of the Serbian-Croatian war by Norman Cigar, and a searching study by Igor Primoratz of the way in which the war was misrepresented in Israel.

Nilsen, Kjell Arild **Europas svik: et oppgjor med vestlig unnfallenhet i Bosnia**, Spartacus Forlag, Oslo 1996, 93 pp.

Unfortunately available only in Norwegian, this is a carefully researched and very critical analysis of Western policy, paying special attention to the influence of propaganda on the shapers of that policy. Includes the complete text of the extraordinary speech by Stoltenberg in Oslo on 31 May 1995, which described all Bosnians as Serbs.

Sharp, Jane **Honest Broker or Perfidious Albion?** — **British policy in former Yugoslavia**, IPPR, London 1997, 94 pp., £7.50

A clear-sighted critical overview of British foreign policy in the former Yugoslavia from 1991 until the aftermath of Dayton, arguing that: 'Britain and its allies should have intervened on the side of the victims, or they should have stayed out altogether, lifted the embargo and let the Bosnian government forces defend themselves. Maintaining the necessary consent from the warring parties to allow the delivery of humanitarian aid became the figleaf for not addressing the issue of genocide.'

After the war

International Crisis Group **Elections in Bosnia and Herzegovina**, ICG Bosnia Report no. 16, London 1996, 61 pp.

A thorough and authoritative report, detailing the OSCE's railroading through of an electoral process in conditions that rendered genuinely free and fair voting impossible. It pays particular attention to the problem of 'electoral engineering' (through the manipulation of voter registration), and highlights serious discrepancies between the size of the electorate and the size of the recorded vote.

International Crisis Group **Going Nowhere Fast: refugees and internally displaced persons in Bosnia and Herzegovina**, ICG Bosnia Report no. 23, London 1997, 74 pp.

A highly valuable study, discussing the limited measures undertaken by the Office of the High Representative and other bodies to promote the return of refugees and displaced persons, analysing the main obstacles (forcible obstruction, media propaganda, 'ethnic engineering', etc.), and proposing a series of practical and political initiatives to break the deadlock.

International Crisis Group **Minority Return or Mass Relocation?**, ICG Bosnia Report no. 33, London 1998, 58 pp.

Another valuable report by the ICG, concentrating on the problem of people wishing to return to areas in which their 'ethnic group' would (now) be in the minority. Particularly useful are the case-studies of Konjic (an example of the 'Open Cities' initiative), Drvar, Central Bosnia and Sarajevo. The pamphlet ends with a set of recommendations for 'strategic breakthroughs'.

Magaš, Branka (ed.) **Question of Survival: a common education system for Bosnia-Herzegovina**, The Bosnian Institute, London 1998, 94 pp., £6

Edited and translated proceedings of a seminar organized by The Bosnian Institute in Sarajevo in April 1998; the participants include a roster of the most eminent Bosnian intellectuals, addressing a vital issue for their country's future.

O'Flaherty, Michael, and Gregory Gisvold **Post-War Protection of Human Rights in Bosnia and Herzegovina**, Martinus Nijhoff, The Hague 1998, 333 pp., £56

An important collection of essays on the human-rights provisions of Dayton and their patchy implementation. Papers by Zoran Paić and Neđo Milićević discuss the Dayton agreement and the mechanisms it set up — both complicated and inadequate — for the enforcement of human-rights claims; there is a valuable study of the problems surrounding the restitution of property (by Elena Popović), and a good account of the refugee's 'right to return' in international law (by Maria Stavropoulou). Gisvold contributes a more speculative paper on the idea of a 'Truth Commission' for Bosnia. The most depressing essays are by Dražen Petrović, on the War Crimes Tribunal, and Manfred Nowak, on the problem of 'the disappeared' and the exhumation of mass graves: both emphasize the foot-dragging or outright non-cooperation of IFOR (over which Nowak resigned in protest from his UN post in 1997).

Scharf, Michael **Balkan Justice: the story behind the first international war crimes tribunal since Nuremberg**, Carolina Academic Press, Durham NC 1997, 340 pp., $14.95

A valuable, detailed and lucid study, written by a legal expert but with the general reader in mind. More than half the book tells the story of the trial of Dušan Tadić; appendices give the Statute of the Tribunal, the Tadić indictment and a summary of the Tadić verdict.

Williams, Paul, et al. **Bringing War Criminals to Justice**, The Center for International Programs 1997, Dayton Ohio, 40 pp.

Cogent pamphlet, produced by a mainly legal working group assembled at the University of Dayton, which sets out the legal and political arguments for apprehending and prosecuting war criminals from the former Yugoslavia, and highlights the dangers of failing to do so.

Žilić, Ahmed, and Saba Risaluddin **The Case of the Zvornik Seven: ethnic cleansing of the legal system in Bosnia-Herzegovina,** The Bosnian Institute, London 1998, 36 pp., £5

An examination of the present chaotic and ineffectual state of the legal system in Bosnia-Herzegovina seen through an examination of the case of the Zvornik Seven, a group of Bosniaks from Srebrenica handed over by American NATO troops to the authorities in Republika Srpska.

Visual Representations

Huppen, Hermann **Sarajevo-Tango**, Éditions Dupuis, Brussels 1998, 64 pp., FF 79

Extraordinary homage — through the medium of comic strip — to an old Sarajevo friend of the artist who lives through the siege with his family, and through him to the bitter experience of an entire city and its population, this unforgettable work is motivated, as the introduction makes explicit, by indignation and obsession.

Kubert, Joe **Fax from Sarajevo: a story of survival**, Dark Horse Books, Milwaukie Or. 1996, 224 pp., $15

Brilliantly executed 'graphic novel' that has won a raft of prizes for its story of the author's friend Ervin Rustemagić, as he and his family struggle to preserve their lives and dignity during the siege of Sarajevo — a story communicated in hundreds of faxes to friends outside.

Sacco, Joe **Šoba**, Drawn & Quarterly Publications, Montreal 1998, 41 pp., $3.95

First in a projected series of comic-book 'Stories from Bosnia' by an award-winning Maltese-American graphic artist who spent several months in Sarajevo, Goražde and elsewhere in B-H in the aftermath of the war. Gritty, evocative, unromantic portrayal of the horrors, traumas and also the joys of life during and after the siege, through the experiences of the eponymous hero (based on a real-life original).

Stoddart, Tom, and Alastair Thain **Edge of Madness: Sarajevo, a city and its people under siege**, with an introduction by Martin Bell, Royal Festival Hall, London 1997, unpaged, £12.95

Produced as the catalogue of an exhibition at the Royal Festival Hall, this contains some of the most magnificently evocative photographs of Sarajevo and its population under siege. The mastery with which Thain captures the grandeur and misery of the ruined architecture is matched by that with which Stoddart catches the spirit and the tragedy of the tormented people.

Stover, Eric, and Gilles Peress **The Graves: Srebrenica and Vukovar**, with a foreword by Judge Richard Goldstone, Scalo, Zurich 1998, 334 pp., £16.95

The text (by Stover, a former director of Physicians For Human Rights) lucidly describes the discovery and investigation of the mass graves, with testimony also from survivors and relatives. Particularly chilling is the account of obstruction by a Belgian UN officer at Vukovar in 1993. But what makes this book exceptional and unforgettable is its 200 pages of photographs — of excavations, grieving relatives, and truly haunting mud-caked skulls — by Peress, a world-famous photographer.

Media

Gjelten, Tom **Sarajevo Daily: a city and its newspaper under siege**, HarperCollins, New York 1995, 278 pp., $13

Excellent history of wartime *Oslobođenje*, well researched and sensitive, based on a wealth of interviews with the paper's editors and journalists past and present, with whom the author clearly established not just a close rapport but also in many cases ties of friendship. Through the story of the paper, Gjelten also provides a portrait of the city under siege and of the complex and often very difficult political context within which independent-minded journalists loyal to Bosnia-Herzegovina had to operate.

Vollmer, Johannes (ed.) **'Dass wir in Bosnien zur Welt gehören': für ein multikulturelles Zusammenleben**, Benziger, Solothurn and Dusseldorf 1995, 306 pp., DM 26.80

An important collection of essays, including interviews with Marko Vešović and Ljubomir Berberović. A long essay by the editor, entitled 'Medienlüge Bosnien? Eine Desinformationskampagne im Namen unparteiischer Information', offers one of the best analyses available of how propaganda and disinformation (for example, blaming the Bosnian Government for the marketplace massacre) circulated in the Western media.

Literary works

Agee, Chris (ed.) **Scar on the Stone: contemporary poetry from Bosnia**, Bloodaxe Books, Newcastle upon Tyne 1998, 208 pp., £8.95

Important anthology featuring the work of fourteen Bosnian poets (all living, with the exception of Mak Dizdar), supplemented by shorter selections from six younger poets and by a number of short prose extracts, edited and introduced by an American poet domiciled in Northern Ireland. The works are presented in translations by English-language poets, either (like Francis Jones and Charles Simić) themselves fluent in the source language, or working with Bosnian collaborators.

Brown, Kenneth, and Hannah Davis Taïeb **Bridges Destroyed: writings from Bosnia, Croatia, Kosovo, Macedonia, Serbia, Slovenia**, Special issue of *Mediterraneans,* Association Méditerranéens, Paris 1995, 288 pp., £8

Valuable selection of poetry, prose pieces and photographs by a wide range of artists from the former Yugoslavia (and elsewhere), including texts — many of them from, or inspired by, Bosnia — by Ivo Andrić, Bogdan Bogdanović, Stanko Cerović, Dževad Karahasan, Danilo Kiš, Mirko Kovač, Ivan Lovrenović, Predrag Matvejević, Semezdin Mehmedinović, Abdulah Sidran, Mark Thompson and others.

Jergović, Miljenko **Sarajevo Marlboro**, translated by Stela Tomašević, Penguin, London 1997, 154 pp., £6.99

Memorable collection of short pieces — variously sharp, eloquent, dark and poetic — written against the backdrop of wartime Sarajevo by one of the best young writers to emerge from Bosnia in the past decade.

Karahasan, Dževad **Sarajevo, Exodus of a City,** translated by Slobodan Drakulić, Kodansha International, New York, Tokyo and London 1994, 123 pp., $10

A powerful evocation of the unique quality of Sarajevo, a quietly savage dissection of the false perceptions of so many (even sympathetic) outside commentators, and an at times despairing elegy for what was continuing to be destroyed by the forces of barbarism even as this — beautifully translated — short book was being written.

Mehmedinović, Semezdin **Sarajevo Blues**, translated and with an introduction by Ammiel Alcalay, City Lights Books, San Francisco 1998, 122 pp., £12.95

Sarajevo Blues: pojmovnik opsjednutog grada was first published in Sarajevo in 1992: a brilliant, bitter collection of short verse and prose vignettes written during the siege by one of Bosnia's best younger poets, with such titles as 'grenade', 'wells', 'hero', 'ruins', 'living together', etc. This excellent English rendering is based on the expanded edition published in Zagreb in 1995; it contains as an appendix a substantial interview with the author, now living in the United States.

Smith, Ken, and Judi Benson (ed.) **Klaonica: poems for Bosnia**, Bloodaxe Books, London 1993, 128 pp., £7.95

Over one hundred poets from many countries contribute to this moving anthology of poems written, in the words of the editors, 'in whatever measure of solidarity is possible with the victims of this most vicious of wars' (the title means 'Slaughterhouse' in Bosnian/Croatian/Serbian).

OTHER READING

General background

Augustinos, Gerasimos **The National Idea in Eastern Europe: the politics of ethnic and civic community**, D.C. Heath and Co., Lexington Mass. and Toronto 1996, 211 pp., £9.95

Enjoyable collection of short readings — albeit of uneven intrinsic merit — from authors as various as Thomas Masaryk, Václav Havel or Milan Kundera, Alfred Cobban, Hugh Seton-Watson or Adam Michnik, and from a number of post-Communist constitutions, accompanied by a very useful bibliographical appendix.

Bax, Mart **Medjugorje: religion, politics and violence in rural Bosnia**, VU Uitgeverij, Amsterdam 1995, 139 pp., $25

This short book by a Dutch anthropologist, who has studied the Medjugorje district since the early 1980s, is really a group of essays on different themes. The best are those related to the development of the Marian cult and its local political ramifications. The weakest is the last in the book, which generalizes wildly on the basis of some local disputes between Croat nationalists and Serb Communists, concluding that the entire war in Bosnia was merely the product of simmering long-term ethno-nationalist feuds.

Begić, Midhat **La Bosnie, carrefour d'identités culturelles**, L'esprit des péninsules, Paris 1994, 251 pp., FF 95

A collection of essays by the Bosniak literary scholar Begić

(1911-83), published under a thoroughly misleading title. There is one short essay on Bosniak literature, and one on Andrić; all the rest are on Krleža, Skerlić, Baudelaire, Gide, Malraux, Sartre and Bachelard. Of very limited relevance to Bosnia.

Bell-Fialkoff, Andrew **Ethnic Cleansing**, St Martin's Press, New York, and Macmillan, London 1996, 346 pp., £37.50

A sprawling survey of ethnic cleansing in world history, followed by a large number of contemporary case studies, including one on Bosnia. The author recommends organized 'population transfers' (in place of violent expulsions), and offers two possible schemes for Bosnia. The first involves moving all Bosniaks to the western half, all Serbs to the east, and all Croats to the Bihać pocket (!); the second scheme is simply to transport all 2 million Bosniaks to Turkey. With an insouciance which some readers will find childish and others simply disgusting, he recommends the second as the best 'solution'.

Bianchini, Stefano **La questione jugoslavo**, Giunti, Florence 1996, 190 pp., Lit. 16,000

Competent brief résumé of the Yugoslav project and its various incarnations over the past century and a half (up to Dayton), by a leading Italian academic authority on the region.

Bianchini, Stefano **Sarajevo, le radici dell'odio. Identità e destino dei popoli balcanici**, 2nd (expanded) edition, Edizioni Associate, Rome 1996, 420 pp., Lit. 36,000

Somewhat misleadingly titled, this is a quite ambitious attempt by a leading Italian academic authority on South-Eastern Europe to set the break-up of Yugoslavia in a wider historical and regional context. The book has well-researched and well-organized material on state formation, the development of national consciousness, and the revival of sometimes exacerbated forms of nationalism after the collapse of Communism, not just in Yugoslavia itself and among its constituent peoples, but also in Albania, Bulgaria, Macedonia, Romania, etc. It suffers, however, from a tendency to obscure the role of conscious decisions taken in Belgrade when discussing Yugoslavia's break-up and subsequent wars, so that the genocidal character of the assault on Bosnia is not given due emphasis.

Bokovoy, Melissa, Jill Irvine and Carol Lilly **State-Society Relations in Yugoslavia 1945-1992**, St Martin's Press, New York 1997, 375 pp., £35

Papers from an academic conference held in mid 1994, including a rather general survey of the development of Bosnian Muslim nationhood by Francine Friedman, a good essay on Milošević and Serbian nationalism by Lenard J. Cohen, and an interesting study by Wolfgang Höpken of the history textbooks used in different Yugoslav republics in the Tito period.

Bugajski, Janusz **Ethnic Politics in Eastern Europe: a guide to nationality policies, organizations and parties**, Sharpe, Armonk NY 1994, 493 pp., £24

The first chapter of this well-sourced and informative political handbook is devoted to Bosnia-Herzegovina, the first six (almost half the entire work) to the former Yugoslav republics. Events since 1989 are summarized in considerable detail, making the work a useful reference tool (those prior to that date are presented only in rudimentary outline). The material on B-H is better than that on e.g. Serbia (while Kosova gets only the most cursory treatment); it includes figures, thumbnail sketches of political organizations, and (in the appendices) acronyms, both English and for the regional languages, and parties listed by country and national affiliation.

Bugajski, Janusz **Nations in Turmoil: conflict and cooperation in Eastern Europe**, 2nd edition, Westview Press, Boulder Col. 1995, 265 pp., £16

About one quarter of this book, lightly updated from the original 1993 edition, is devoted to the former Yugoslavia, in the form of two well-informed and balanced chapters summarizing the internal and external dimensions of the Yugoslav crisis. The author, director of East European Studies at the Center for Strategic and International Studies in Washington DC, is one of the best informed academic commentators on contemporary political developments in Eastern Europe.

Carley, Patricia **Self-Determination: sovereignty, territorial integrity, and the right to secession**, United States Institute of Peace, Washington DC 1996, x + 20 pp.

Basically a report-back from a high-level seminar, jointly organized by USIP and the policy planning staff of the State Department, this short pamphlet examines the confused state of general perceptions, international law and US policy in relation to 'the right of self-determination', and concludes that for the US government there is little alternative to continuing with a pragmatic policy, opposed to the creation of new states by secessionist movements without excluding it on principle.

Carter, F.W., and H.T. Norris (ed.) **The Changing Shape of the Balkans**, UCL Press, London 1996, 180 pp., £14.95

Includes a short but valuable essay by Cornelia Sorabji on the role of Islam in modern Bosniak identity, and two very general essays on the break-up of Yugoslavia, by John Allcock and Michael Foucher.

Chamberland, Paul, Alain Horic, France Théoret and Pierre Vallières (ed.) **La Bosnie nous regarde**, Quartier Libre, Montreal 1995, 175 pp., $19.95

An interesting collection of articles and literary materials by members of the 'Solidarité Québec-Bosnie' committee, including a valuable study by Stephen Albert of Canada's diplomatic and military role.

Cohen, Lenard **Broken Bonds**, Westview Press, Boulder Col. and Oxford 1995, 396 pp., £13.50

Detailed and generally reliable academic account of the disintegration of the second Yugoslavia (preceded by a short historical introduction on the evolution of the 'Yugoslav idea' from 1830 to 1989), its main drawbacks are a somewhat bureaucratic approach to political developments, and a tendency to ascribe them to impersonal processes rather than to human actors. The result is a version of events that is too indulgent to political leaders; too euphemistic about the responsibility for — and scale of — the wars in Croatia and Bosnia (no aggression or genocide here); too prone to entertain a version of the 'ancient ethnic hatreds' explanation.

Čuvalo, Ante **Historical Dictionary of Bosnia-Herzegovina**, Scarecrow, Lanham Md and London 1997, 355 pp., $45

A serious reference work, containing also a useful chronology and a rich bibliography. The author's Croat sympathies are apparent (e.g.

in the rather defensive entry on 'Herceg-Bosna'); but his treatment of Muslim subjects is generally fair and objective. The main fault of the book is that its heavy concentration on the war and recent politics leaves far too little room for a proper coverage of Bosnian history: there are entries for minor government ministers of the 1990s and for Scott O'Grady, but no entries for Gazi Husref-beg, Husein of Gradačac or even Gavrilo Princip.

Cviić, Christopher **Remaking the Balkans**, RIIA/Pinter, London 1991, 113 pp., £9.75

The first half of the book is a general outline of the post-1945 political and economic history of all the Balkan countries; the second concentrates on the wars in the former Yugoslavia, coolly surveying the background to the conflict and the Western response. A few final pages, suggesting possible future 'confederations' of states in the region, reveal a surprisingly fanciful strain of thought in this otherwise resolutely realistic analyst.

Dawisha, Karen, and Bruce Parrott (ed.) **Politics, Power and the Struggle for Democracy in SE Europe**, Cambridge University Press, Cambridge and New York 1997, 472 pp., £19.95

Almost half of this serious academic collection, with its copious tables and footnotes, is devoted to the former Yugoslavia, with informative if uneven essays by Lenard Cohen (a particularly judicious text on 'Postcommunist Croatia in transition'); Steven Burg ('Bosnia-Herzegovina: a case of failed democratization' — an oddly constructed but useful contribution that proceeds backwards, as it were, from an inappropriate title to the right conclusion that the country never had a chance to democratize, since it was attacked first); Nicholas Miller ('A failed transition: the case of Serbia' — a well-documented account, correctly identifying the impasse into which the Milošević regime has led the country and the need for a 'complete transformation of political culture'); Sabrina Ramet (a characteristically challenging and well-sourced text on 'Democratization in Slovenia'); and Duncan Perry (well-informed on 'Macedonia: finding its way', but insufficiently aware of the unviability of a Macedonia that does not accord its minorities, above all its large Albanian minority, very concrete and substantial national rights).

Debeljak, Aleš **Twilight of the Idols: reflections of a lost Yugoslavia: an essay**, translated by Michael Biggins, White Pine Press, Fredonia NY 1994, 85 pp., $8.99

An elegiac essay, by an American-educated Slovene poet, on the heterogeneity of the old Yugoslavia, denying that ethnic violence was inevitable.

Dragnich, Alex **Yugoslavia's Disintegration and the Struggle for Truth**, Columbia University Press, New York 1995, 278 pp., £28

Collection of journalistic pieces, many never actually published, written between 1989 and 1995 by an indefatigable veteran American Serb campaigner for the nationalist cause.

Duncan, W. Raymond, and G. Paul Holman Jr (ed.) **Ethnic Nationalism and Regional Conflict: the former Soviet Union and Yugoslavia**, Westview Press, Boulder Col. 1994, 218 pp.

In this volume (based on an April 1993 conference at the Naval War College in Newport, RI), only the editors' introduction and conclusion, and one fairly uninspiring chapter by Duncan, relate to the former Yugoslavia. Sources drawn upon include 'John' Zametica, Aleksa Djilas and particularly Misha Glenny, and blame for the country's bloody demise is allocated to such impersonal factors as ethnic tensions, or even mere ethnic diversity, rather than, for example, to Slobodan Milošević and his policies.

Hille, Saskia **Völkerrechtliche Probleme der Staatenanerkennung bei den ehemaligen jugoslawischen Teilrepubliken**, Florentz, Munich 1996, 219 pp.

Useful work reviewing the legal doctrines of state recognition and succession in the context of the post-1945 Yugoslav federation's dissolution, and seeking to identify new legal trends in relation to them.

Hupchick, Dennis **Conflict and Chaos in Eastern Europe**, St Martins Press, New York 1995, 303 pp., £35

This book of essays on various areas of eastern and central Europe includes a 60-page study giving a general summary of Bosnian history from the middle ages to 1992.

*Ignatieff, Michael **Warrior's Honor: ethnic war and the modern conscience,** Chatto, London 1997, 224 pp., £10.99

Attempt to argue the philosophical case for liberal universalism as against nationalist particularism that, unfortunately, fails to confront the most difficult issues and in addition, when discussing the case of the former Yugoslavia, fails to base its arguments on an accurate factual foundation.

Ivanović, Vane **Yugoslav Democracy on Hold**, Dodir, Rijeka 1996, 185 pp.

Collection of texts, spanning the period from 1949 to 1992, by a Yugoslav long resident in Britain, who obtained political asylum in 1945 rather than accept the new Communist order in Yugoslavia; who in 1963 helped to found what became the 'Democratic Alternative'; and who in 1990 became a citizen of the Republic of Croatia. In two of the most recent, a 1992 interview published in *Borba* (Belgrade) and the book's epilogue, the author provides an eloquent refutation of Serb and Croat nationalist denials of the Bosniak national identity, and a critique of 'the "Yugoslav" cover they [Serb nationalists] provided for Serb domination over others in Yugoslavia' that is all the more devastating since it comes from someone who continued until his death in 1999 to think of himself as a Yugoslav.

Judah, Tim **The Serbs: history, myth and the destruction of Yugoslavia**, Yale University Press, New Haven and London 1997, 350 pp., £19.95

Vivid account of the gangsterism and corruption permeating all levels of state and society in contemporary Serbia, set alongside an introduction to the ideology and mythology of Serb nationalism, with its juxtaposition of romantic escapism with cold-blooded cynicism.

Julliard, Jacques **Ce fascisme qui vient...**, Éditions du Seuil, Paris 1994, 202 pp., FF 89

A passionately argued essay on the significance of the fascistic ideology underlying the policy of ethnic cleansing and partition, by a leading French historian and commentator.

Kennan, George (ed.) **The Other Balkan Wars** (a 1913 Carnegie Endowment inquiry in retrospect, with a new introduction and reflections on the present conflict by George F. Kennan), Carnegie Endowment, Washington DC 1993, 410 pp., $16

The then president of the Carnegie Endowment for International Peace, Morton Abramowitz, was stimulated first to read and then to reprint this remarkable report into the Balkan Wars when he saw it quoted in an article in 1992 on the horrors of the current war in Bosnia. Unfortunately, however, the 'new introduction and reflections on the present conflict' by George Kennan represent a wasted opportunity, since the author has little evident knowledge of the area and does not go beyond commonplace generalities about 'aggressive nationalism' drawing on 'deeper traits of character inherited, presumably, from a distant tribal past'; about 'the undue predominance among the Balkan peoples' of 'non-European characteristics' deriving from 'the Turkish domination' and 'earlier ones as well'; or about 'the distracted Balkan region' with 'its excited peoples'.

*Lampe, John **Yugoslavia as History: twice there was a country**, CUP, Cambridge 1996, 421 pp., £14.95

Readers of this sloppy and unimaginative textbook history of Yugoslavia will learn nothing about the origins of the break-up of the country that could not have been learned from textbooks written before it had even happened.

McGarry, John, and Brendan O'Leary (ed.) **The Politics of Ethnic Conflict Regulation: case studies of protracted ethnic conflicts**, Routledge, New York and London 1993, 321 pp., £14.99

Contains only one contribution specifically on the former Yugoslavia — a perceptive and judicious historico-political essay by George Schöpflin — but also has a substantial and challenging introduction that makes a rare serious attempt at a taxonomic approach. This classifies genocide, forced population transfers, partition and/or secession, and integration and/or assimilation, as 'methods for eliminating differences'; while 'methods for managing differences' include hegemonic control, arbitration, federalization and/or cantonalization, and power-sharing.

Meštrović, Stjepan, Slaven Letica and Miroslav Goreta **Habits of the Balkan Heart: social character and the fall of communism**, Texas A & M University Press, College Station 1993, 181 pp., $18.95

Extended essay that attempts an interpretation of the collapse of Communist Yugoslavia in terms of psycho-sociological theories of personality and culture, especially those of Dinko Tomašić on the 'Dinaric type'.

Meštrović, Stjepan, Slaven Letica and Miroslav Goreta **The Road from Paradise: prospects for democracy in Eastern Europe**, University Press of Kentucky, Lexington 1993, 204 pp., $28

Extended essay that attempts an interpretation of the 1991 Balkan war, the fall of Communism, the democratization of Eastern Europe and the former Soviet Union, and 'the consequences of post-Communism', in terms of classical (Durkheim, de Tocqueville, Veblen, Simmel, Freud) and contemporary (Baudrillard, Riesman) sociological theory. The work polemicizes with Brzezinski and Fukuyama, within the context of a critique of Western policies that first sought to preserve the 'artificial' state of Yugoslavia, then appeased the Greater Serbia project.

Neweklowsky, Gerhard **Die bosnisch-herzegowinischen Muslime: Geschichte, Brauche, Alltagskultur**, Wieser-Verlag, Klagenfurt 1996, 242 pp.

An attractive and sympathetic book, containing a miscellany of information (much of it gleaned from refugees) about Bosniak religious and social customs, food, folk-medicine, etc., together with a brief survey of Bosnian history.

Norris, H.T. **Islam in the Balkans**, C. Hurst & Co., London 1994, 304 pp., £27.50

A rich miscellany of information about Islamic culture, dervish orders, folk poetry, etc., concentrating more on the Albanian lands than on Bosnia, but including some fascinating details on Bosnian subjects, especially on Bosnia's religious and cultural links with the Middle East.

Pavković, Aleksandar **The Fragmentation of Yugoslavia: nationalism in a multinational state**, Macmillan, London 1997, 222 pp., £40

In the first half of this book surveying Yugoslav history up to 1990, the author tries hard to be balanced and objective, and more or less succeeds. But thereafter his narrative turns into little more than a distillation of Serb nationalist themes and accusations, both against Croatia and against the Bosnian government.

Peroche, Gregory **Histoire de la Croatie et des nations slaves du Sud, 395-1992,** F.X. de Guibert, Paris 1992, 560 pp., FF 175

General survey of the history of the Yugoslav lands, written in encyclopaedia-like prose, with lists of names, dates, etc., but no references or bibliography. The tendency of the book is to defend Croatia whenever possible.

Popović, Alexandre **Les Musulmans yougoslaves, 1945-1989: médiateurs et métaphores**, L'âge d'homme, Lausanne 1990, 67 pp., FF 90

A very thin tract, which says little about Bosnia and is in places almost hysterical in tone (e.g. when denouncing acts of 'terror' by Albanians in Kosova, whom Popović describes as having been 'implanted' there by a 'foreign occupier' — the Ottomans — because of their Muslim faith). Popović is a distinguished scholar who has done important work on the history of dervish orders and Islamic institutions in the former Yugoslavia; but this publication does him no credit at all.

Poulton, Hugh **The Balkans: minorities and states in conflict**, Minority Right Publications, London 1993, 166 pp., £9.95

A well-researched, objective and useful study, covering minority-related disputes in every Balkan state.

Ramet, Sabrina **Nationalism and Federalism in Yugoslavia 1962-1991**, 2nd edition, Indiana University Press, Bloomington 1994, 346 pp., $18.95

Perhaps the best English-language textbook history of Titoist Yugoslavia. In the first edition published in 1984, Ramet highlighted the importance of inter-republican contradictions within the Yugoslav Federation and the trend towards confederalization. A somewhat rigid theoretical framework gives the added chapters on the road to war a tacked-on feel.

Rupnik, Jacques (ed.) **De Sarajevo à Sarajevo: l'échec yougoslave**, Éditions Complexe, Brussels 1992, 150 pp., FF 59

Brief, general essays on Yugoslavism (Nataša Rajaković), Titoism (Stevan Pavlowitch), the break-up (a weak piece by Joseph Krulić, presenting the war in Bosnia as a spontaneous Serb reaction to an out-of-the-blue declaration of sovereignty by Bosniaks and Croats) and international attitudes and policies (Rupnik).

Shah-Kazemi, Reza (ed.) **Bosnia: destruction of a nation**, Islamic World Report, London 1996, 78 pp., £10

Includes essays by Asim Zubčević (on the Islamization of Bosnia), H.T.Norris (on Bosnian Sufism), Noel Malcolm (on the Bosniaks in the post-Ottoman period), Branka Magaš (a general survey of the war), Hasan Rončević (on the final phase of the fighting), Rusmir Mahmutćehajić (a Sufi perspective on the suffering of the war), and a final paper by Noel Malcolm on the Western response to the war.

Stefanov, Nenad, and Michael Werz (ed.) **Bosnien und Europa: die Ethnisierung der Gesellschaft**, Fischer Taschenbuch Verlag, Frankfurt 1994, 207 pp., DM 18.90

Mainly rather abstract essays by political scientists influenced by the

Frankfurt School in Germany and the *Praxis* Group in the former Yugoslavia; contains some strong pleas for the survival of Bosnia as a multi-ethnic society, and one powerful essay by the Swiss writer Paul Parin, entitled 'Das Lügenarsenal des Westens'.

Stern, Brigitte (ed.) **Dissolution, Continuation and Succession in Eastern Europe**, Martinus Nijhoff, Boston 1998, 220 pp., £46

Proceedings of a conference addressing legal issues of state succession generated by the post-cold-war changes in Eastern Europe, with panels devoted to general aspects of the law on succession; to succession and international organizations; and to economic consequences of succession.

Tanner, Marcus **Croatia: a nation forged in war**, Yale University Press, New Haven and London 1997, 338 pp., £19.95

History of Croatia from the middle ages to the present day, summarizing a wealth of information unavailable elsewhere to the English-language reader. Readable, succinct and often intelligent, it is weakest on World War II and the period since, failing adequately to challenge the assumptions of contemporary Croat nationalism.

Tertsch, Hermann **La venganza de la historia,** Ediciones El País, Madrid 1993, 272 pp., Ptas 2,180

A sequence of mini-chapters, of only a few pages each, darting from one part of the former Communist Eastern Europe to another. Several chapters are on Bosnia, but the butterfly approach prevents Tertsch from developing any proper analysis or argument.

Trifunovska, Snežana (ed.) **Yugoslavia Through Documents: from its creation to its dissolution**, Martinus Nijhoff, Dordrecht and London 1994, 1,074 pp., £189

Despite the title, this book is essentially a collection of documents relating to the break-up of Yugoslavia and the wars in Croatia and Bosnia. Otherwise its coverage of Yugoslav history is skimpy: the first 233 pages are on the period 1809-1990, including some extracts from the constitutions of 1946 and 1974, but nothing else from the entire Titoist period. The rest of the book (841 pp.) is a compilation of Security Council resolutions, EC declarations, letters, communiqués, etc., most of them emanating from outside the former Yugoslavia.

Tvrtković, Paul **Bosnia-Hercegovina — back to the future**, London 1993, 64 pp., £6.50

This eccentric pamphlet, by a man who claims direct descent from the mediaeval King Tvrtko, ends with a policy proposal but consists mainly of a very slanted account of Bosnian history, designed to link Bosnia and its population as closely as possible to Croatia. The policy proposal is to turn Bosnia into a weak cluster of nine provinces with no proper central government at all. It must be a comfort to Lord Owen to know that, however bad his own plans were, it was always possible to devise an even worse one.

Veiga, Francesco **Els Balcans: le desfeta d'un somni, 1945-91**, translated by Francesca Bartrina and Jordi Sala, 2nd edition, Eumo Editorial, Vic (Osona) 1993, 194 pp., Ptas 2,060

A disappointingly superficial study, attempting to summarize the whole history of the Balkans since 1945. Milošević is presented merely as a typical 'nationalist-conservative', and the account given of the origins of the wars in Croatia and Bosnia is thin and patchy. Veiga is apparently a specialist on Romania; the reader's confidence, however, is not strengthened by his mis-spelling of 'Ceauşescu' throughout the book.

Vucinich, Wayne (ed.) **Ivo Andrić Revisited: the bridge still stands**, IAS, Berkeley Ca. 1995, 239 pp., $18.95

Essays on Andrić and his legacy; two are of more general Bosnian interest. 'Bosnian cultural identity in the works of Andrić', by Tomislav Longinović, discusses the elements of 'Orientalism' (in the Edward Said sense) in his work; a paper by John Loud discusses Andrić's fiercely anti-Ottoman (and anti-Muslim) doctoral dissertation and its echoes in his other writings.

Wachtel, Andrew **Making a Nation, Breaking a Nation: literature and cultural politics in Yugoslavia,** Stanford University Press, Stanford Ca. 1998, 302 pp., £11.95

The author's thesis is that Yugoslavia's break-up was due to the failure to develop a unified Yugoslav national culture capable of providing all the country's peoples with a robust identity that could have kept them united in the face of economic and political storms. Although he provides interesting commentaries on the works and ideas of Yugoslavist artists and writers, his argument is tautological, begging questions that can be answered only in terms of the economic and political factors he dismisses as secondary.

Background to the war

Akhavan, Payam, and Robert Howse (ed.) **Yugoslavia the Former and the Future**, Brookings Institute and UNRISD, Geneva 1995, 188 pp., $13.56

Essays mainly by liberal Serb intellectuals, praising civil society, dialogue, etc., and tending to blame all the fighting on a rather abstract thing called nationalism.

*Barratt Brown, Michael **The Yugoslav Tragedy: lessons for socialists**, Socialist Renewal, Nottingham 1996, 82 pp.

This staggeringly ill-informed pamphlet shows how blind faith in the laws of economic determinism can lead a 'socialist' to shift the blame for the Yugoslav tragedy away from the real culprits onto the shoulders of favoured (especially German) bogeys.

Bookman: *see* Žarković Bookman

Borden, Anthony, Ben Cohen, Marisa Crevatin and Davorka Zmiarević (ed.) **Breakdown: war and reconstruction in Yugoslavia** (with articles by Paul Beaver, Ivan Ćolović, Vojin Dimitrijević, Misha Glenny, Dušan Janjić, Mary Kaldor, Sonja Licht, Tihomir Loza, Vladimir Milčin, Žarko Puhovski, Milorad Pupovac, Miloš Vasić, and others), special issue of *Yugofax*, published by War Report/Helsinki Citizens' Assembly, London 1992, 80 pp., £5

A collection of brief reports and commentaries published in March 1992, surveying the situation in the whole of the former Yugoslavia after the end of the Croatian war. The dominant view here is that of the Helsinki Citizens' Assembly, which claimed that Yugoslavia's political problems could be solved by 'building politics from below', sending 'peace caravans', etc.

Burg, Steven, and Paul Shoup **The War in Bosnia-Herzegovina: ethnic conflict and international intervention,** Eurospan, London 1998, 512 pp., £39.95

This substantial book by two prominent US academic specialists in Balkan studies provides a good example of inability to see the wood for the trees. There is plenty of useful information: maps, figures, detailed accounts of events (e.g. what the authors rightly term 'negotiating partition 1993-4'). But the sources used are seriously inadequate: fewer than half the works listed by us as 'essential reading' are included in a bibliography of over two hundred. And altogether too much space is devoted to studiously neutral exposition of competing nationalist arguments, or of claims and counter-claims over responsibility for bomb massacres, where the reader might reasonably expect an authoritative judgement on such issues. Above all, the authors' chosen title and initial statement of purpose — to 'examine the dynamics of ethnic conflict in Bosnia-Herzegovina' — reflect an interpretive paradigm that makes it only too predictable that throughout the book they will radically downplay the factor of external aggression.

Calic, Marie-Janine **Der Krieg in Bosnien-Hercegovina: Ursachen, Konfliktstrukturen, internationale Lösungsversuche,** Suhrkamp, Frankfurt 1995, 257 pp., DM 19.80

A factual and well-sourced account of the war — up to early 1995 — and of international policy towards it (with useful maps of the various Western plans for cantonization and/or partition). However, the role of Milošević and the JNA is systematically understated, and the war is thus reduced to the product of 'structural' causes, à la Susan Woodward.

Crnobrnja, Mihailo **The Yugoslav Drama**, I.B.Tauris, London 1994, 281 pp., £12.95

Although written by a former Yugoslav diplomat, this book unfortunately offers little in the way of direct testimony or eyewitness insights. Cast in the form of an impersonal attempt to present a 'balanced' explanation for the break-up, it nevertheless expresses the theoretical stance of a moderate Serb nationalist: albeit identifying Serbia as the greatest culprit in the conflict, the author ends up by calling for border changes in Serbia's favour.

Denitch, Bogdan **Ethnic Nationalism: the tragic death of Yugoslavia**, 3rd edition, University of Minnesota Press, Minneapolis and London 1996, 259 pp., £13.95

The US-educated son of Serb émigré parents, Denitch published sociological studies of the former Yugoslavia from a 'democratic socialist' perspective before partially relocating to Croatia in 1990. Since then he has been attacked both by Serb nationalists (for his forthright denunciations of Milošević and support for the rights of Kosova) and by Croat nationalists (for his equally trenchant criticisms of Tudjman and the HDZ). This text is not so much a historical analysis (though there are elements of that) as a sequence of essays on democracy, nationalism and the use and misuse of 'ethnic' categories.

Dragnich, Alex **Serbs and Croats: the struggle in Yugoslavia**, Harcourt Brace Jovanovich, New York 1992, 202 pp., £8.27

Shallow, inaccurate Serb-nationalist summary of Yugoslav history, which describes the autonomy of Kosova and Vojvodina as an 'insult' and Stjepan Radić as having died of diabetes.

Dyker, David, and Ivan Vejvoda (ed.) **Yugoslavia and After** (includes texts by Christopher Cviić, Shkelzen Maliqi, Miloš Vasić), Longman, London and New York 1996, 268 pp., £16.99

A collection of essays, some on general themes, others covering individual republics and provinces before and during the fighting. The general essays tend towards 'structural', sociological explanations; the best of the particular studies are those on Kosova (by Shkelzen Maliqi) and Serbia-Montenegro (by Jovan Teokarević). There is also a valuable study of the JNA and post-Yugoslav armies by Miloš Vasić. The long essay on Bosnia by Xavier Bougarel contains useful information, but concentrates in a very misleading way on purely internal factors, attributing the 'dismantling' of Bosnia to the rise of 'communitarian politics' there. When the term 'communitarian' is used equally for the SDS and the Serb Civic Council, readers must wonder what analytic value it can possibly have.

*Glenny, Misha **The Fall of Yugoslavia: the third Balkan war**, Penguin, London 1992, 194 pp., £5.99

Combines shameless ethnic stereotyping of the former Yugoslavs as brutal and treacherous with repeated calls for a Western policy more conciliatory to Belgrade. A colourful but shallow journalistic account of Yugoslavia's break-up, suited to readers with no serious desire to understand it. Praised highly by David Owen.

Gligorov, Vladimir **Why Do Countries Break Up?: the case of Yugoslavia**, Uppsala 1994, 128 pp., $37.50

A very theoretical study by a liberal intellectual. Rejects economic determinism and the idea that 'the Balkans are different', but reduces everything to 'ethnic strategies' and 'power structures', and seems not to notice any difference between a peaceful 'break-up' and a war of territorial conquest.

Gow, James **Legitimacy and the Military: the Yugoslav crisis**, St Martin's Press, London 1992, 208 pp., $49.95

A detailed analysis of the decay of the Titoist political system in the 1980s, focusing on the increasing concentration of legitimacy at republican level, and on the counter-productive attempts of the Yugoslav Army to restore the legitimacy of the federal regime. Central to the book is a valuable study of the shift in public opinion and politics in Slovenia in the late 1980s.

Hall, Brian **The Impossible Country: a journey through the last days of Yugoslavia**, Secker & Warburg, London 1994, 422 pp., £18.99

A well-written and intelligent travelogue (with some passages of historical and political background), describing a journey in the summer of 1991. Hall mastered Serbo-Croat well enough to catch the nuances of what people say; his pages are filled with conversations with ordinary people, who reveal their prejudices, fears and hopes.

Heuvel, Martin van den, and Jan G. Siccama (ed.) **The Disintegration of Yugoslavia**, Rodopi, Amsterdam 1992, 218 pp., $22

General essays on such subjects as the idea of Yugoslavia (a valuable summary by Ivo Banac), Titoism (a routine article by Paul Shoup) and EC policy in 1991 (a short and dim piece by Maarten Lak); this is not a sharply focused book, and contains little of direct relevance to the war in Bosnia.

Johnsen, William **Deciphering the Balkan Enigma: using history to inform policy** (2nd edition), Strategic Studies Institute, US Army War College, Carlisle Penn. 1995, 125 pp.

A better subtitle would have been: 'misusing history to misinform policy'. Depends heavily on claims about 'ancient ethnic hatreds', dismisses Bosnia as 'largely ... a geographical-political expression', and recommends partition, with ethnic separation, as the best 'solution'. It is dismaying to think that this work was taken seriously by a US Army think-tank.

Kuzmanić, Tonči, and Arno Truger (ed.) **Yugoslavia War**, Austrian Study Centre for Peace and Conflict Resolution, Ljubljana 1993, 200 pp.

A collection based on three 'peace studies' conferences held as Yugoslavia was disintegrating, this makes dispiriting reading today, shot through as most of the contributions are with ideological, political or national *parti pris*, inaccurate prediction and/or ponderous moralizing. The only bright spots are a perceptive little warning text by Muhamed Filipović and a deeply pessimistic essay by Srđan Vrcan, discussing the possible relevance of the Lebanese model.

Libal, Wolfgang **Das Ende Jugoslawiens: Selbstzerstörung, Krieg und Ohnmacht der Welt**, Europaverlag, Vienna 1993, 214 pp., DM 34

This enlarged edition of a book first published in 1991 contains a brief section on the war in Bosnia. Wolfgang Libal is one of the elder statesmen of Balkan journalists in the German-speaking world; this is a clear and authoritative work written for the general reader.

Mojzes, Paul (ed.) **Religion and the War in Bosnia**, Scholars Press, Atlanta Ga 1998, 294 pp., £12.20

A useful, albeit uneven, collection including valuable texts, notably by Francine Friedman on 'The Bosnian Muslim national question', by Srđan Vrcan on 'The religious factor in the war in B-H', by Michael Sells on 'Serbian religious nationalism and the genocide in Bosnia, 1992-1995', and by Gerard Powers on 'Religion, conflict, and prospects for peace in Bosnia, Croatia and Yugoslavia'. But some of the texts have no place in a scholarly volume, however ecumenical. This is particularly true for 'The Serbian Orthodox Church's view of the role of religion in the war in B-H' by Dimitrije Kalezić, whose dismissal of reports of 'Muslim casualties' at Srebrenica as 'montage and deceit' might almost have come from the pen of Radovan Karadžić.

Mojzes, Paul **Yugoslavian Inferno: ethnoreligious warfare in the Balkans**, Continuum, New York 1994, 248 pp., £18.99

A well-intentioned but seriously flawed book for the general reader, by a Yugoslav American of unusual background (his parents were both Protestant ministers in Vojvodina). Tries to spread the blame for the war as widely as possible; ends by recommending Western military intervention, against all sides, in order to effect a partition of Bosnia.

Pešić, Vesna **Serbian Nationalism and the Origins of the Yugoslav Crisis**, USIP, Washington DC 1996, 41 pp.

Thoughtful extended essay by a founder of the Belgrade anti-war movement and the most liberal of the main Serbian opposition leaders, written during a visiting fellowship to the United States in 1994-5. The text is good in characterizing the role of Serb 'ressentiment' — deliberately stoked — in undermining the federal order during the eighties, but nevertheless reflects a primarily Serbian view of things, e.g. in its negative interpretation of the 1974 constitution, and is sometimes cavalier with figures (most blatantly in relation to Serb representation in the federation).

Ramet, Sabrina **Balkan Babel**, Westview Press, Boulder Col. and Oxford 1996, 354 pp., £13.50

Originally a collection of six previously published articles (some first issued under the author's former name Pedro Ramet), plus three additional ones, this second edition contains a further four new chapters and updates earlier ones. Topics include political developments of the 1980s, the press, rock music, the Catholic and Serbian Orthodox churches, Islam, the run-up to war in Croatia, the emergence of an independent Slovenia and Macedonia, the Bosnian war and international responses to it, and the repercussions of war in religion, gender relations and culture. All carry the Ramet hallmark of valuably detailed references to contemporary sources.

Rezun, Miron **Europe and War in the Balkans: towards a new Yugoslav identity**, Praeger, Westport and London 1995, 241 pp., £37.93

This book by a Canadian academic, written in 1993 and hardly updated at all for publication two years later, consists mainly of a routine summary of 20th-century Yugoslav history; it ends by presenting the war in Bosnia as essentially a 'civil war'. Includes a defence of General Lewis MacKenzie.

Samary, Catharine **Yugoslavia Dismembered**, translated by Peter Drucker, Monthly Review, New York 1995, 185 pp., $16

Samary, a French economist specializing in planning and 'workers' self-management' in the former Yugoslavia, has for many years been the Fourth International's main 'expert' on the area. Unwilling either to take sides in Yugoslavia's wars of succession or, on the other hand, to equate the victims entirely with their oppressors, Samary's rambling, incoherent book manages to conceal rather than make manifest her views on the conflict.

Šekelj, Laslo **Yugoslavia: the process of disintegration**, translated by Vera Vukelić, Westview Press, Boulder Col. 1993, 234 pp.

The author is a researcher at the University of Belgrade, and seems unable to extricate himself from the intellectual constraints of his position. The first half of the book deals with 'self-management' and the bureaucratization of the Communist Party: valid themes, no doubt, but hardly key elements of an explanation of the war. When he finally turns to the break-up of Yugoslavia, he begins with a grossly Serb-nationalist account of the Kosova question; thereafter all blame is placed on Slovenes, Croats, etc.

Stark, Hans **Les Balkans: le retour de la guerre en Europe**, La découverte, Paris 1991, expanded edition IFRI/Dunod, Paris 1993, 238 pp., FF92

Despite its somewhat misleading title, this book (apart from one chapter) is about the former Yugoslavia only. It provides a competent account of the federation's progressive breakdown during the eighties and the growing strength of republican and regional centres, followed by war, genocide and an ineffective international response.

Stojanović, Svetozar **The Fall of Yugoslavia,** Prometheus Books, New York 1997, 341 pp., $34.95

Cumbersome self-serving attempt by this former 'humanist Marxist dissident' to justify his transmogrification into a nationalist sufficiently red-blooded to become chief adviser to Dobrica Ćosić, during the period when the latter was president of FRY, and subsequently to attack Milošević for abandoning the Serbs across the Drina.

Taibo, Carlos, and José Carlos Lechado, **Los conflictos yugoslavos: una introducción**, 3rd edition, Editorial Fundamentos, Madrid 1995, 239 pp., Ptas 1,200

A useful summary of the political background to the war, and of events up to October 1995; also discusses briefly the problems of other parts of the former Yugoslavia, such as Kosova and Macedonia. In their treatment of the Bosnian war, the authors argue explicitly against the doctrine of moral equivalence between aggressors and victims.

Thomas, Raju, and Richard Friman (ed.) **The South Slav Conflict: history, religion, ethnicity and nationalism**, Garland, New York and London 1996, 427 pp., £65

A very mixed bag of essays. The best is a paper by Janusz Bugajski on the development of the Bosnian war and its misreading by Western commentators. Also valuable is a study of Germany's policy by Wolfgang Schloer. One of the feebler papers is by Thomas, containing many uncritical repetitions of Serb nationalist claims. But the worst by a long way is Carl Jacobsen's essay, ostensibly on 'War Crimes and Media Manipulation', which consists of almost unadulterated pro-Pale propaganda: 'Bosnia was historically Serb', 'Serbs held title to about 65% of Bosnia', etc., etc.

*Udovički, Jasminka, and James Ridgway **Yugoslavia's Ethni Nightmare**, Lawrence Hill, New York 1995, 252 pp.

Collection of essays by Belgrade-based writers claiming to be representative of the anti-war opposition throughout the former Yugoslavia. The contributors' partisan airing of Serb-nationalist grievances makes them more representative, however, of (most of) the non-régime intelligentsia in Serbia alone.

Udovički, Jasminka, and James Ridgway **Burn this House: the making and unmaking of Yugoslavia**, Duke University Press, Durham NC 1997, 337 pp., £11.50

Somewhat expanded and revised version of the previous entry, subject to the same comment.

Volcic, Demetrio **Sarajevo: quando la storia uccide**, Mondadori, Milan 1993, 230 pp.

Rambling, essayistic and insubstantial account of the various conflicting national ideologies and historical myths of the peoples of the former Yugoslavia.

Vuckovié, Gojko **Ethnic Cleavages and Conflict — the sources of national cohesion and disintegration: the case of Yugoslavia**, Ashgate, Brookfield Vt and Aldershot 1997, 170 pp., £35

In terms of intellectual substance, this study is anorexically thin; but it comes dressed up in thick layers of theoretical clothing, with a long opening section on 'structures', 'variables', etc. After that there is a potted history of the Yugoslav peoples, then a slanted account of the 'secession' of Slovenia and Croatia, and finally an account of the 'secession' of Bosnia in which it appears that the only people responsible for the war were the German government, Izetbegović and Mate Boban.

*Woodward, Susan **Balkan Tragedy**, Brookings Institution, Washington DC 1995, 536 pp., $15.16

Interpretation of the Yugoslav crisis resting on wholly economic determinants, in which the persistent championing of Serbian claims is hidden behind a dense screen of political-science jargon.

Zametica, 'John' **The Yugoslav Conflict**, International Institute for Strategic Studies, London 1992, 87 pp., £9.50

A sophisticated apologia for the destruction of Bosnia, which exerted some influence (notably on the work of Susan Woodward, where it is cited respectfully). Mr Zametica concluded: 'frontiers can and do collapse, but the will of a nation to build a state can only be temporarily repressed.' He later went off to Pale to help 'build' a state, on land from which hundreds of thousands of the original inhabitants had conveniently been removed by his friend Mr Karadžić.

Žarković Bookman, Milica **Economic Decline and Nationalism in the Balkans**, Macmillan, Basingstoke 1994, 214 pp., £42.50

Padded out with much general stuff about the Balkans, this is essentially a presentation of the pro-Pale case: the war in Bosnia was just a civil war, caused by the West's unfair refusal to recognize the right to self-determination of the Bosnian Serbs, who 'had property rights to some 60 per cent of the territory', etc. The authority most frequently cited here is 'John' Zametica.

War and genocide in Bosnia-Herzegovina

Allen, Beverly **Rape Warfare: the hidden genocide in Bosnia-Herzegovina and Croatia**, University of Minnesota Press, Minneapolis and London 1996, 181 pp., £13.95

Albeit personalized and sketchy in places, this is an accessible introduction to many of the terms and issues associated with mass rape during the Bosnian war, including genocidal rape, rape camps and their relationship to the Serb-nationalist ideology.

Babić, Marko **Bosnian Posavina: international diplomatic legitimization of Serbian occupation and atrocities in Dayton**, translated by Anthony Dawe, Vidovice, Zagreb 1996, 402 pp.

Despite the title, only the last 30 pp. discuss the implications of Dayton for the Posavina region. Most of the book is a detailed study of the pre-war population of the region, the ethnic cleansing and destruction it suffered during the war, and the treatment of it in various international peace plans (especially Owen-Stoltenberg). Includes many maps, photos and statistical tables.

Backmann, René (ed.) **Le livre noir de l'ex-Yougoslavie: purification ethnique et crimes de guerre**, with a preface by Paul Bouchet, Arléa, Paris 1993, 486 pp., FF 130

An important collection of reports by human-rights organizations, gathering and translating texts first published between June 1992 and January 1993: these include ones by Helsinki Watch, Amnesty, the CSCE and Médecins sans frontières, as well as the first three reports issued by UN human-rights rapporteur Tadeusz Mazowiecki.

Barros-Duchêne, Laurence de **Srebrenica: histoire d'un crime international**, L'Harmattan, Paris 1996, 138 pp., FF 80

Concise account of the Srebrenica massacre and its antecedents, by French journalist who spent 1993 and 1994 as a bureau chief for the former Yugoslavia.

Baumgartner, Ilse, and Wolfgang Baumgartner **Der Balkan-Krieg der 90er: Fakten, Hintergründe, Analysen, Zukunftperspektiven**, Verlag für Wissenschaft und Forschung, Berlin 1997, 249 pp., DM 38

A sensible book, saying little that is not said elsewhere, but offering a good summary of the chronology of the war, the nature of the war crimes, the international intervention and the Dayton Accord.

Čekić, Smail **The Aggression on Bosnia and Genocide against Bosniaks: 1991-93**, Institute for Research into Crimes against Humanity and International Law, Sarajevo 1995, 439 pp.

Compiled by Bosnia's most prominent specialist on genocide, this important work catalogues in great detail the organization and arming of the Bosnian Serb population by the Yugoslav People's Army and the Serbian Democratic Party, for the purpose of destroying Bosnia-Herzegovina and its Muslim population.

Chaslin, François **Une haine monumentale: essai sur la destruction des villes en ex-Yougoslavie**, Descartes, Paris 1997, 95 pp., FF 80

Five eloquent texts by an architect whose professional horror at the spectacle of destroyed cities in Croatia and Bosnia provides the starting-point for sombre reflections — buttressed by a wealth of historical detail — on siege warfare, ethnic cleansing and hatred.

Danopoulos, Constantine, and K. Messas (ed.) **Crises in the Balkans: views from the participants**, with a foreword by George Kenney, Westview Press, Boulder Col. 1996, 389 pp., £40.95

A disappointing collection, with only one interesting paper: an essay by Francine Friedman and Robin Remington on the changes of strategy of the Bosniak political leadership during the war. Other contributions include a routine survey of EU policy on the war (by K. Messas), and a paper on Milošević's policies and the Western response, by Obrad Kesić, which sneers at those Western 'moralists' who placed the primary blame for the war on Milošević.

Ercegovac-Jambrović, Božica **Genocide: ethnic cleansing in north-western Bosnia. Genozid: ethnische säuberung im Nordwesten Bosniens. Génocide: le nettoyage ethnique dans le nord-ouest de la Bosnie**, Croatian Information Centre, Zagreb 1993, 382 pp.

This publication, which prints the same material in English, German and French, contains detailed testimonies by victims of ethnic cleansing in the Prijedor region.

Finkielkraut, Alain **The Crime of Being Born,** translated by
Graham McMaster, Ceres, Zagreb 1997, 247 pp., Kn 165

Collection of essays, speeches and interviews spanning the years
from 1991 to 1996, by a French philosopher prominent in
combating the indifference and the misconceptions so often
characteristic of reactions in France (as elsewhere) to the wars
unleashed by Belgrade since 1991 (he is particularly good on the
hypocrisy of Mitterrand). His stance — rejecting catch-all
denunciations of 'nationalism' and 'secessionism', or the lumping
together of victims and aggressors as warring 'tribes' — took shape
mainly in the wake of the aggression against Slovenia and Croatia,
but as these texts demonstrate he has also been a vigorous defender
of Bosnia-Herzegovina.

Harris, Paul **Somebody Else's War: frontline reports from
the Balkan wars 1991-92**, Spa Books, Stevenage (Herts)
1992, 164 pp., £10.95

A well-written account by a photographer and reporter; mostly
about the war in Croatia, but including also a brief description of
the fighting at Bosanski Brod and other places on the Sava in the
first two months of the Bosnian war.

Hatzfeld, Jean **L'air de Guerre, sur les routes de Croatie
et de Bosnie-Herzégovine**, L'Olivier, Paris 1994, 345 pp.,
FF 130

Collection of fine reportage by the correspondent of *Libération*, who
covered a year of warfare in Croatia and B-H before being wounded
in Sarajevo in late June 1992. He was one of the first Western
journalists to report on the massacres in eastern Bosnia in May.

*Honig, Jan Willem, and Norbert Both, **Srebrenica: record
of a war crime**, Penguin, London 1996, 204 pp., £6.99

Impressive analysis of the circumstances and extent of the 1995
Srebrenica massacre, unfortunately compromised by the authors'
desire to explain and exculpate the behaviour of their Dutch
compatriots and by their pious attitude to the whole UN mediation
effort in the former Yugoslavia.

Köpf, Peter **Karadžić: die Schande Europas**, Econ Taschenbuch Verlag, Dusseldorf 1995, 160 pp., DM 12.90

An instant book, with its material largely drawn from press cuttings. It therefore contains some useful information; its limitations are that it tries at the same time to give a general history of the Bosnian war, that it has almost nothing about Karadžić before 1990, and that the author uses only German-language sources.

Kovač, Nikola **Bosnie, le prix de la paix**, Michalon, Paris 1995, 170 pp., FF 80

Eloquent extended essay, written in French by this distinguished Bosnian Serb academic who has served since early in the war as Bosnian ambassador in Paris. Includes discussions of Bosnian culture, the war and the international response to it; argues with great cogency that ethnic partition is alien to the nature of Bosnian history and culture.

Laerhoven, Bob van **Srebrenica: getuigen van een massamoord**, Icarus, Antwerp 1996, 194 pp., Fl 29.90

Detailed account of events in Srebrenica before and during its conquest, based on interviews with survivors.

Mian, Marzio **Karadžić: carnefice, psichiatra, poeta**, Mursia, Milan 1996, 133 pp., Lit. 18,000

A rather lightweight study of Radovan Karadžić, more an extended profile than a biography, but containing a few interesting anecdotes. Also prints fourteen of Karadžić's poems (in Italian translation by Dragan Mraović).

O'Ballance, Edgar **Civil War in Bosnia, 1992-94**, Macmillan, London 1995, 269 pp., £17.95

A dismally unintelligent book, compiled apparently from press-cuttings, but supplying no references, so that it lacks even the slightest documentary value. Blames EC recognition of Croatia and Slovenia for the break-up of Yugoslavia, and puts the primary blame for the war in Bosnia on 'Izetbegović's determination to govern a unitary republic'. Another typical judgement from this superannuated military analyst: 'The USA desperately wanted to pound the Serbs with air-strikes (and seemingly still does), but fortunately Britain and France did not and carried the day.'

O'Shea, Brendan **Crisis at Bihać: Bosnia's bloody battlefield**, with a Foreword by Robert Fisk, Sutton Publishing, Thrupp 1998, 245 pp., £19.99

This book, by a member of the EU Monitoring Mission, contains much valuably detailed information about events in the Bihać pocket (mainly covering the period between late 1993 and the end of the war). However, O'Shea operates at best in peacekeeper-as-football-referee mode, and at worst in a Rose-like frenzy of denouncing the Bosnian Government, and/or the Americans, as the real war-mongers. A statement by a White House spokesman that the Serbs were the aggressors in the war is described as 'despicable'. Robert Fisk contributes a suitably cock-eyed Foreword.

Plisson, Gabriel **Mourir pour Sarajevo**, Éditions In Fine, Paris 1994, 319 pp., FF 300

A rag-bag of a book, consisting first of a general historical narrative, then of a sequence of mini-articles in alphabetical order (Arkan, Armées, Boban, etc.). Contains snippets of useful information, but also some errors. Plisson, a former journalist who speaks Bosnian and worked as an adviser to General Morillon, argues strongly that the West should have intervened in July 1991.

Power, Samantha **Breakdown in the Balkans: a chronicle of events January 1989 to May 1993**, Carnegie Endowment, Washington DC 1993, 148 pp.

This detailed chronology prepared for the Carnegie Endowment is a useful reference tool, despite the fact that the narrow range of English-language press sources on which it is mainly based makes for too many gaps, inaccuracies and failures to discriminate between fact and propaganda claim.

Reissmüller, Johann Georg **Die bosnische Tragödie**, Deutsche Verlags-Anstalt, Stuttgart 1993, 189 pp., DM 24

A collection of commentaries by the distinguished columnist of the *Frankfurter Allgemeine Zeitung*, from January 1992 to April 1993. Because of the uncompromising stance he took from the outset, blaming the real instigators and perpetrators of the war, Reissmüller became a particular hate-figure for the Serb lobby in Germany.

Rojo, Alfonso **Yugoslavia: holocausto en los Balcanes**, Planeta, Barcelona 1992, 259 pp.

Rojo is one of Spain's leading foreign correspondents; this book is largely compiled from his reports from Croatia and Bosnia in 1991-2. Not factually detailed, but includes some useful information about events in Sarajevo in March and April 1992.

Ryan, Geoff (ed.) **Armageddon in Europe: why socialists support multi-ethnic Bosnia against Serbia's war**, Socialist Outlook, London 1994, 42 pp., £1.50

Collection of articles by members of International Workers Aid, which organized solidarity aid convoys to Tuzla during the war in Bosnia, presenting the movement's views, goals and activities.

Scott, Noll, and Derek Jones (ed.) **Bloody Bosnia: a European tragedy**, *The Guardian*, Channel 4 TV and SSEES, London 1994, 50 pp., £3.99

Produced to accompany a Channel 4 fortnight of programmes on Bosnia, this short illustrated booklet contains some eloquent visual images, some deplorably inaccurate and misleading maps, competent historical background essays by Mark Wheeler and Mark Thompson, graphic reportage by Maggie O'Kane and Ed Vulliamy, a thoughtful comment on Western failures by Martin Woollacott, and one real curiosity: a sympathetic profile of Captain 'Mike Stanley' (aka Miloš Stanković), who was to be accused in early 1998 of having passed Nato secrets to the Bosnian Serbs while working as an interpreter for UNPROFOR.

Stage, Jan **Asken braender: en forfatter i krig**, Informations Forlag, Copenhagen 1994, 168 pp.

A collection of reports from Bosnia by the leading Danish war correspondent, from June 1992 to August 1993. Mainly Sarajevo-based, but includes reports from Mostar and Travnik.

Tica, Ranko, and Jasminko Mulaomerović (ed.) **Conference on Reconstruction and Long-term Development of the City of Sarajevo: abstracts**, Sarajevo 1994, 125 pp.

Summaries of technical papers on subjects such as energy supplies, communications, water and sewerage, and other requirements for survival and reconstruction: unfortunately the summaries are so brief that they record very little factual detail at all.

Todorović, Goran **Sarajevo: cronaca delle illusioni perdute**, Ediesse, Rome 1996, 228 pp., Lit. 28,000

A translation of *Sarajevo: dani spaljenih iluzija*, a collection of journalism from the years 1992-5 by the former editor of *Valter* magazine. Includes interviews with leading Bosnian politicians.

Vernet, Daniel, and Jean-Marc Gonin **Guerre dans les Balkans — le miroir brisé yougoslave**, Odile Jacob, Paris 1994, 285 pp., FF 130

Reportage from the capitals of the former Yugoslavia's successor states during the first two years of war by two journalists, one from *Le Monde*, the other from *L'Express*, concentrating on the international-relations dimension of the conflict.

Volkan, Varnik **Blood Lines: from ethnic pride to ethnic terrorism,** Farrar Straus and Giroux, New York 1997, 280 pp., $15

Quirky attempt, by a US professor of psychiatry of Turkish Cypriot background, to apply Freudian psychoanalytic concepts to the study of ethnic identity and conflict. There is a chapter on Bosnia, but its disjointed, episodic structure — moving from the Field of Blackbirds to the family history of Milošević and Karadžić — does not illuminate greatly, and the book will hardly fulfil the author's ambition to complement diplomacy by shedding light on deeper realms of the individual and collective mind.

The international response

Albert, Sophie **Les réfugiés bosniaques en Europe**, Éditions Montchrestien, Paris 1995, 200 pp., FF 70

A well-researched, factual study of the different conditions prevailing in all the main countries of Europe, comparing those states' administrative systems for dealing with refugees and asylum-seekers, and their divergent interpretations of the relevant provisions of international law.

Barollier, Pascal, and Xavier Gautier **Main basse sur Sarajevo: la guerre secrète pour reconstruire la Bosnie**, Édition °1, Paris 1994, 137 pp., FF 75

Presented as an investigation into the way Western (and Muslim) governments were inveigling their way into the Bosnia economy to pick up lucrative reconstruction contracts after the war, this book is a great disappointment: while the thesis is not implausible, the authors just do not have enough hard facts to back it up.

Bert, Wayne **The Reluctant Superpower: United States policy in Bosnia, 1991-95**, Macmillan, London 1997, 296 pp., £45

Detailed, well-researched study of US policy-making. Somewhat limited in its understanding of the nature of the Bosnian war; the author is not a Balkan specialist and does not read Bosnian. But his general conclusion, that US policy-makers had a mistaken belief that intervention must be 'all or nothing', is well argued.

Bodansky, Yossef **Offensive in the Balkans: the potential for a wider war as a result of foreign intervention in Bosnia-Herzegovina**, International Media Corporation, London 1995, 117 pp.

This unusually shrill piece of pro-Pale polemics claims that the February 1994 market-place mortar shell, like the one in August 1995, was 'a self-inflicted act of terrorism by the Sarajevo regime'; contains much flesh-creeping rhetoric on the subject of 'Mujahedin'; and solemnly warns that any Western military intervention in Bosnia will lead to 'a new world war'. Curiously, the text was produced in November 1995: anyone can get predictions wrong in advance of the event, but it requires a special talent to make false predictions about events that have already happened.

Boidevaix, Francine **Une diplomatie informelle pour l'Europe, le groupe de contacte Bosnie**, Fondation pour les études de défense, Seuil, Paris 1997, 210 pp., FF 140

Detailed account, by a political scientist close to the Quai d'Orsay, of the Contact Group's activities before and after Dayton, providing useful insight into informal diplomatic activity away from the public gaze.

Burg, Steven **War or Peace: nationalism, democracy and American foreign policy in post-communist Europe**, New York University Press, New York 1996, 258 pp., $35

A general study of the problems faced by policy-makers and international organizations when dealing with 'ethnic' and territorial conflicts in many parts of the former Communist world. Argues well against ethnic partition as a 'solution', but gives a slanted account of the origins of the Bosnian war, seeing Bosnian Serb secessionism merely as a reaction to Izetbegović's policies in the spring of 1992.

Callahan, David **Unwinnable Wars: American power and ethnic conflict,** Hill and Wang, New York 1997, 271 pp., $13

This book is a plea for a rethinking of US foreign policy along more consistently internationalist lines, adapted to the post-cold-war world. Its main thrust is sensible and plausible — for example, in arguing for a case by case approach to issues of self-determination, eschewing sweeping edicts supporting or opposing any secession from existing states — but excessively indulgent in its discussion of past policies. This is especially true for those relating to Bosnia, which are frequently referred to, but with little evidence of much knowledge or understanding of realities there.

Campbell, David **National Deconstruction: violence, identity and justice in Bosnia**, University of Minnesota Press, Minneapolis and London 1998, 304 pp., £17.95

General readers will find this book very heavy going: the author is an unrepentant 'deconstructionist', and the text is littered with references to Derrida, Levinas, 'narrativizations' and something called 'ontopology'. But those who persist (and/or skip judiciously) will be rewarded by some penetrating, politically alert discussions of the mental categories and misrepresentations used by Western academics, journalists and politicians in their treatment of the Bosnian war. The notes also provide a rich mine of references, especially to news reports and commentaries (though in English only).

Caplan, Richard **Post-Mortem on UNPROFOR**, Brassey's London Defence Studies No.33, London 1996, 64 pp., £12

A valuable analysis of the ambiguities of UNPROFOR's mandate and the inadequacies of its performance.

Cot, General Jean, and Cécile Monnot (ed.) **Dernière guerre balkanique? — ex-Yougoslavie: témoignages, analyses, perspectives**, L'Harmattan, Paris 1996, 253 pp., FF 150

A stimulating collection of essays, edited by the French general who commanded UNPROFOR from July 1993 to March 1994; Cot was forced to resign after publicly criticizing the UN for its cumbersome system of bureaucratic approval for air-strikes. His bitterness is expressed here, but clouded also by anti-Americanism and hostility to NATO. There are valuable essays on the sequence of international peace-plans (by Franck Debié) and on French policy (by Patrice Canivez).

Cushman, Thomas **Critical Theory and the War in Croatia and Bosnia**, Jackson School of International Studies, Seattle 1997, 50 pp.

Perceptive essay on the relativist assumptions that allowed so many Western intellectuals, commentators and politicians to misunderstand the reality of the wars in Croatia and Bosnia, equalizing the responsibility for them and the crimes committed during them. Three representative articles published in prestigious journals — by Bette Denich, Milica Bakić-Hayden and Robert Hayden, and Charles Boyd — are analysed as case studies of a kind of ideological construction that in important ways mirrored the propaganda emanating from Belgrade and that was widely disseminated in political and academic circles.

Cviić, Christopher **An Awful Warning: the war in ex-Yugoslavia**, Centre for Policy Studies, London 1994, 46 pp., £6.95

Pithy analysis of the origins and nature of the conflict, focussing on the lost opportunities of Western diplomacy: Cviić argues that more robust policies by the West could have stopped the war in Croatia and prevented the one in Bosnia.

Danchev, Alex, and Thomas Halverson (ed.) **International Perspectives on the Yugoslav Conflict**, Macmillan, London 1996, 212 pp., £16.99

These papers, delivered at a conference in September 1994, seem not to have been updated in any way for their publication in 1996. They include routine summaries of the Bosnian policies of the USA (Halverson), Russia (Andrei Erdemskii) and Germany (Marie-Jeanne Calic), and a somewhat defensive account of British policy (James Gow).

Esman, Milton, and Shibley Telhami (ed.) **International Organizations and Ethnic Conflict**, Cornell University Press, Ithaca NY 1995, 343 pp., £13.95

This collection of essays on intervention by organizations such as the UN includes three papers on the former Yugoslavia: a basic background paper by V.P. Gagnon, an efficient but routine account of the international response by Steven Burg, and a paper by Susan Woodward. This last is useful because it gives her interpretation in a nutshell, thus obviating the need to read her long and turgid book. She blames only Slovenia and Croatia for 'the use of force to change borders'; dismisses out of hand the idea that 'the conflict was a result of the ambitions for a Greater Serbia of Milošević'; explains that the federal army was 'pushed by international action to ally with Serbs... in Bosnia'; and makes the grossly false claim that Izetbegović refused to sign the Vance-Owen Plan.

Freedman, Lawrence (ed.) **Military Intervention in European Conflicts**, Blackwell, Oxford 1994, 195 pp., £12.99

A collection of papers, mainly focused on the issue of intervention in the former Yugoslavia, including useful surveys of the policy debates in France (by Jolyon Howorth) and Germany (by Harald Müller). There are three general papers on intervention in Bosnia: a mainly historical summary of Western policy failures and hesitancies by James Gow, a strongly analytical and critical paper by Jane Sharp, and a weaselly anti-intervention piece by Ken Booth, which tries hard to relativize every aspect of the conflict, rejecting the word 'aggressor' and declaring that Milošević's attack on Bosnia was motivated by 'fear'.

Fyson, George, Argiris Malapanis and Jonathan Silberman **The Truth about Yugoslavia: why working people should oppose intervention**, Pathfinder, New York 1993, 89 pp., £5.95

This grotesquely titled pamphlet features the opinions of the editor (Fyson) and managing editor (Malapanis) of *Militant*, magazine of a US sect calling itself the Socialist Workers Party. While people were being shot and shelled on a daily basis, these authors solemnly concluded: 'Rather than imperialist intervention, what working people in Yugoslavia need above all is time to engage in politics — to test out leaderships, organizations and programs... Out of these experiences, a new vanguard can be formed. This vanguard will lead the struggle to overthrow the bureaucratic regime.' As the Duke of Wellington said: Madam, if you believe that, you'll believe anything.

Gow, James **Triumph of the Lack of Will: international diplomacy and the Yugoslav war**, C. Hurst & Co., London 1997, 343 pp., £14.95

Written very slowly (though its coverage ends at Dayton, the book appeared in May 1997) but proof-read in a great hurry, this book presents much important information and argument, albeit in a somewhat uneven way. The issue of recognition, and of the dissolution of Yugoslavia, is well handled (refuting Susan Woodward); the nature of the UNPROFOR mandate is thoroughly analysed; so are the shifting policies of London, Paris, Moscow and Washington. But coverage of the second half of the war is weak: the hostage crisis, Srebrenica, Holbrooke's diplomacy and the military end-game are treated quite perfunctorily. At the heart of the book is a curiously wistful defence of the Vance-Owen Plan, despite Gow's own acknowledgement that the Serbs rejected it and the West had no will to impose it by force.

Grulich, Rudolf, and Adolf Hampel, **Maastricht starb in Sarajevo: gegen die Totengräber Europas,** Fachbereich 07 der Justus-Liebig-Universität, Giessen 1993, 148 pp.

Collection of anguished short articles and appeals written under the impact of war in Croatia and Bosnia by two German Catholic theologians outraged by the failure of Western political and Church leaders to make any adequate response.

Handke, Peter **Eine winterliche Reise zu den Flüssen Donau, Save, Morawa und Drina: oder Gerechtigkeit für Serbien**, Suhrkamp, Frankfurt 1996, 135 pp., DM 24.80

First published as two long articles in the *Süddeutsche Zeitung* (5/6 and 13/14 January 1996), this bizarre text attempts to portray Milošević's Serbian state, and by implication the forces of Karadžić and Mladić in Bosnia, as innocent victims of Western prejudice. Handke employs a jumble of familiar propaganda ploys, plus one novel argument of his own: he visits a village inside Serbia, is entertained with plum brandy, and concludes that since the Serbs he has met are friendly and peaceful, all accusations against any Serbs anywhere are necessarily false. Because (but only because) of Handke's fame as a writer, this text attracted huge publicity in the German-speaking lands; for an important collection of replies to it, see the entry under Zülch on p.67 below.

Hedegard, Lars (ed.) **Bosnia and the West: a hearing (15-16 January 1996)**, The Danish Foreign Policy Society, Copenhagen 1996, 126 pp., DnKr. 80

Papers given at a conference in Copenhagen; contributors include Peter Galbraith (defending US policy), Hans Koschnick (warning of the long-term dangers of ethnic separation), Uffe Ellemann-Jensen (somewhat ruefully considering the weakness of European policy), Jovan Divjak (calling eloquently for a united, democratic Bosnian state), and Noel Malcolm (discussing the distorted analysis of the situation provided by UNPROFOR commanders, and arguing that military men, far from being automatically 'objective' observers, are influenced by their own quasi-political interests).

Hoare, Attila **Yugoslavia — the acid test**, Idolrare Ltd, London 1993, 32 pp., £1.50

Polemic against the virulently anti-Bosnian and anti-Croatian stance of Britain's largest Trotskyist groups, whose 'even-handed' anti-interventionism closely resembled that of John Major's Conservative government.

Jopp, Matthias (ed.) **The Implications of the Yugoslav Crisis for Western Europe's Foreign Relations**, Western European Union — Institute for Security Studies, Paris 1994, 91 pp.

Collection of short essays on the way in which the Yugoslav crisis has been perceived, or the impact it has had at the foreign-policy level, in Russia (Pavel Baev), Egypt (Ali Hillal Dessouki), the USA (F. Stephen Larrabee), Turkey (Duygu Bazoğlu Sezer) and Central Europe (Monika Wohlfeld). The authors are all international-relations specialists who appear relatively uninformed about, and indeed uninterested in, former Yugoslav realities, but who have some interesting things to say about policy formation in the countries in question.

Kelly, Mary Pat **'Good to Go': the rescue of Scott O'Grady from Bosnia**, Naval Institute Press, Annapolis Md and Airlife, Shrewsbury 1997, 355 pp., £24.95

An excessively detailed account of a minor incident: the rescue of the downed US F-16 pilot from Pale-held territory in June 1995. The author has interviewed everyone who took part in any way, and the text is filled with long extracts from their statements to her.

Kumar, Radha **Divide and Fall? — Bosnia in the annals of partition**, Verso, London 1998, 207 pp., £14

A frustrating book that wastes a potentially important theme. Despite intelligence and a proper scepticism towards Western policies, the author is undone by the muddled and inappropriate ideological schema into which she tries to force a Bosnian reality of which she anyway has too often an unsure grasp (gross mistakes include thinking that Dayton makes formal provision for the secession of Republika Srpska, and claiming that the notion of a 'constituent people' is inherently partitionist — tell that to the Serb Civic Council!) The idea of looking at partitionist reflexes and assumptions among Western politicians is a good one; examining their actions in India, Ireland, Cyprus or Palestine may indeed throw light on how they viewed Bosnia (though partition has never been the only option for them, as the history of decolonization makes immediately obvious). But to try to fit the partitionist policies

of Milošević and Tudjman into the same explanatory framework is
absurd, possible only if you ignore entirely the specific historical and
political context of the region, which has nothing to do with
post-colonialism.

Laplace, Yves **L'âge d'homme en Bosnie: petit guide d'une nausée suisse**, Éditions d'en bas, Lausanne 1997, 95 pp.

A spirited attack on the chief publisher of Serb nationalist
propaganda in the French-speaking world, the director of the Swiss
publishing house 'L'âge d'homme', Vladimir Dimitrijević. Laplace (a
well-known Swiss novelist) concentrates on an episode in April-May
1995 when two Swiss citizens were seized (from an UNPROFOR
armoured car) by Serb soldiers and held prisoner for 34 days:
Dimitrijević claimed to be negotiating for their release, while telling
the media their 'arrest' was justifiable because of their pro-Bosnian
views.

Meštrović, Stjepan **The Balkanization of the West: the confluence of postmodernism and postcommunism**, Routledge, London 1994, 226 pp., $18.95

The constant references to sociological theorists (Durkheim,
Veblen, Sorokin) and to debates about post-modernism will make
this an off-putting book for many readers; but it does contain some
valuable discussions of the misrepresentations of the Croatian and
Bosnian wars in Western politics and debate.

Meštrovic, Stjepan (ed.) **The Conceit of Innocence: losing the conscience of the West in the war against Bosnia**, A&M University Press, College Station Tex. 1997, 259 pp., $30

A collection of papers on Western responses, intellectual and
political, to the war. Particularly stimulating are the Introduction by
the editor; a detailed study by Brad Blitz of the indifference, and/or
relativism and revisionism, that characterized the US academic
world's response; an incisive analysis by Richard Johnson of US
'appeasement' of both Serbia and Russia (over Chechnya), pointing
out parallels and connections; and a withering account of Clinton's
Bosnia policy by Marshall Freeman Harris.

Mousavizadeh, Nader (ed.) **The Black Book of Bosnia** (authors include Joseph Brodsky, Zbigniew Brzezinski, Zlatko Dizdarević, Anna Husarska, Anthony Lewis, Arthur Miller, Czesław Miłosz, David Rieff), Basic Books, New York 1996, 219 pp., $10

This collection of articles from *The New Republic* is a mixed bag. On the one hand there is Aleksa Djilas, arguing for the partition of Bosnia and declaring that 'Bosnian Islam was unusually harsh', together with Misha Glenny, predicting the imminent collapse of Macedonia (in early 1994) and opining that 'Greece's fear of Macedonia is understandable.' On the other hand the book contains some fine reporting by Charles Lane, powerful essays by Fouad Ajami and Patrick Glynn, and a sequence of editorials incisively criticizing Western policy.

Paulsen, Thomas **Die Jugoslawienpolitik der USA 1989-1994: begrenztes Engagement und Konfliktdynamik**, Nomos Verlagsgesellschaft, Baden-Baden 1995, 190 pp., DM 35

A fine, very well-sourced, factual (and resolutely non-judgemental) account of the development of US policy, up to the end of 1994.

Ramcharan, B.G. (ed.) **The International Conference on the Former Yugoslavia: official papers**, Kluwer Law International, Dordrecht 1997, 2 volumes: 1,174 and 500 pp., £324

Volume 1 includes texts of the preceding 'London Conference' of August 1992, a chronology of the activities of the Geneva-based International Conference on the Former Yugoslavia (ICFY), texts of the Vance-Owen, Owen-Stoltenberg and other plans, and the ICFY's reports to the UN Security Council (which alone take up 630 pages). Volume 2 continues with the documents produced by the various 'working groups' (on Bosnia, humanitarian issues, etc.).

Rossanet, Bertrand de **Peacemaking and Peacekeeping in Yugoslavia**, Kluwer Law International, The Hague and London 1996, 127 pp., £56.50

This grotesquely over-priced paperback is a polemical work in defence of the Geneva-based, Owen-run International Conference on the Former Yugoslavia. The author blames the Bosnian 'factions' for failing to accept the various enlightened peace plans that were devised for them (Vance-Owen, Owen-Stoltenberg, etc.); and, just like Owen, he reserves special vituperation and all-round blame for the USA.

Sharp, Jane **Bankrupt in the Balkans: British policy in Bosnia,** Institute for Public Policy Research, London 1993, 24 pp., £2.95

An incisive pamphlet by a leading defence analyst, calling for military intervention and the setting up of a UN Trusteeship over Bosnia.

Sonyel, Salahi Ramadan **The Muslims of Bosnia: genocide of a people**, The Islamic Foundation, Leicester 1994, 72 pp., £2.75

An eloquent pamphlet by a Turkish Cypriot historian, quoting and amplifying many of the criticisms of Western policy which had appeared in the British media.

Turković, Bisera **Bosnia and Hercegovina in the Changing World Order,** Saraj-Invest, Sarajevo 1996, 150 pp.

The author is a Bosnian who returned home in 1992 from residence in Australia to work in the SDA party headquarters, and who then became Bosnia's ambassador first to Croatia (in 1993) and later to Hungary. In this extended essay, she discusses the geo-political position of her country and the ambivalent response of the Western powers when it came under attack from its neighbours.

Ullman, Richard (ed.) **The World and Yugoslavia's Wars**, Council on Foreign Relations, New York 1996, 227 pp., $18.95

This collection contains several very good essays and one strikingly bad one. Stanley Hoffmann's study of European diplomatic mismanagement, David Gompert's account of US policy and Paul Goble's important study of the Moscow-Belgrade relationship are all worth reading. But the essay by Jean Manas on the theory of self-determination and international recognition could have been written by a lobbyist for Republika Srpska: Manas dismisses the borders of Bosnia as arbitrary administrative inventions, and says there is no significant difference between defending Bosnian citizenship and defending a citizenship based on exclusive 'ethnic' criteria.

Various Authors **L'ex-Yougoslavie en Europe: de la faillite des démocraties au processus de paix**, L'Harmattan, Paris 1997, 340 pp., FF 180

Proceedings of a conference held in Paris soon after Dayton, to draw up a balance-sheet on 'the strange failure of the democracies' and consider 'the perspectives opened up by Dayton'. Participants included almost the full range of French specialists on the region, together with a number of foreign ones, and the volume includes a useful chronology and bibliography.

Zülch, Tilman (ed.) **Die Angst des Dichters vor der Wirklichkeit: 16 Antworten auf Peter Handkes Winterreise nach Serbien**, Steidl Verlag, Göttingen 1996, 139 pp., DM 10

A very valuable collection of replies to Peter Handke's *Eine winterliche Reise* (see the entry on p. 62 above); authors include Dževad Karahasan and Marcel Ophuls, as well as leading German and Swiss journalists.

Juvenile and primers

Beck, Paul, Edward Mast, Perry Tapper **The History of Eastern Europe for Beginners**, Writers and Readers, New York 1997, 186 pp., $11

The treatment of Bosnia and the 1992-5 war is quite sympathetic, in this lively comic-book by three American authors: a graphic artist of Hungarian descent, a playwright, and a popular historian domiciled in the Czech Republic. However, the subject is far too big for fewer than 15,000 words of text — not just the region's history since the Romans and before, but also such concepts as nation, nationalism, fascism, communism, Stalinism, capitalism, imperialism and so on.

The resulting simplifications, and even the book's characteristic brand of half-baked populism, would be more forgivable, moreover, if there were fewer sloppy mistakes: e.g. Serbia was never 'under Habsburg/Holy Roman rule', Tito was not a Serb, Bosnia was not an 'autonomous region' under communism, and the image of 'predominantly lower and lower-middle-class Serbs ... easily stirred up against the predominantly upper and upper-middle-class Muslims' is ludicrous.

Buckley, Richard **The Troubled Balkans: history's dangerous legacy**, Understanding Global Issues, Cheltenham 1996, 18 pp., £2.50

Moderately informative digest-type pamphlet, part of a series 'based on a concept developed as *Aktuelle Cornelsen Landkarte*' (Berlin). Contains four maps of varying utility, a historical introduction, a summary of twentieth-century conflicts, texts on geography, culture, religion, regional economies, 'pressure points' and 'prospects for peace', together with a short critical bibliography — all in 18 pages!

Clark, Arthur **Bosnia: what every American should know**, Berkley Books, New York 1996, 235 pp., $6.99

A 'popular digest' type of handbook by a major in the US Marine Corps Reserves, packed with information — ranging from basic data on the successor states of former Yugoslavia (area, literacy, exports in 1993, manpower available for military service, etc.), and a summary of Dayton, to a classification of war crimes and list of indictees, not to speak of a roster of US military units and the bases from which they were deployed to Bosnia — accompanied by skimpy and not always accurate historical and political background material.

Flint, David **Bosnia** (for children 9-12), Watts, London 1994, 32 pp., £15.74

Doubtless this picture book was designed to help out all the people who used to complain about the impossibility of understanding what was really going on in Bosnia. Unfortunately, however, if their children read it they would be little the wiser.

Harris, Nathanael **The War in Former Yugoslavia**, Wayland, Hove 1997, 64 pp., £10.99

Pity the 'young people' subjected to this kind of dumbing down, where everything is relativized, facts are few and far between, explanation is perfunctory, and Western politicians like international bodies are above criticism.

Isaac, John, and Keith Greenberg **Bosnia: civil war in Europe**, Blackbirch Press, Woodbridge Conn. 1997, 31 pp., $15

Intolerably sentimental and inaccurate (Bosnian Muslims are the descendants of Turks; the only real difference between Bosnia's national groups is religion, which is what has made them all hate each other, and so on) little epistle by a UN photographer, guaranteed to misinform any children unlucky enough to have it imposed upon them. The photographs are banal.

Rady, Martin **The Break-up of Yugoslavia**, Wayland, Hove 1994, 48 pp., £9.50

Better than most books designed for the juvenile market and surely benefiting from the role of Mark Wheeler as 'Consultant', this work is nevertheless not free from misleading if not downright mystificatory over-simplifications. From the first page, for example, we already encounter 'ill-feelings between [Yugoslavia's] separate peoples', which 'began to grow in the late 1980s, and suddenly exploded into violence in 1991' — like some natural phenomenon.

Ricchiardi, Sherry **Bosnia: the struggle for peace**, Milbrook Press, Brookfield Conn. 1996, 64 pp., $22.50

This short picture book, in a series whose intention is to 'explain the stories behind the headlines', contains few explanations that go beyond media clichés — from a 'region ... plagued by religious and cultural turmoil for more than 1,500 years' to the 'warring parties' who had to be forced to sign at Dayton. A whole page is devoted to the 'daring rescue of Captain O'Grady', and the concluding chronology starts by getting the date when the Yugoslav Communist Party collapsed wrong by five years.

Ricciuti, Edward **War in Yugoslavia: the breakup of a nation**, Evans Brothers, London 1993, 64 pp., £9.95

A picture-book, apparently produced for schoolchildren or dim students, who will emerge a little dimmer after reading it. Manages to discuss the origins of the war without blaming anyone or anything (except '1,500 years of history', which gets it in the neck). Contains some remarkable *aperçus* nonetheless — e.g. 'Some political groups in Kosovo favoured Bulgaria, making Bulgarian intervention another possibility.'

Humanitarian, pacifist and religious perspectives

Bašić, Nedžad **Children in Bosnian Tragedy**, translated by Jennifer McKenzie-Pellegrini, BCR Inc., St Catherine's (Canada) 1994, 116 pp.

Written for the Canadian charity Bosnian Children Relief, this book focuses on the specific fate of children in the war in Bosnia, through photographs, poems, and above all graphic accounts taken from a wide range of sources. An appendix brings together some of the international legal provisions relating to children.

Feed the Children **An Idea of Bosnia**, with a foreword by Jeremy Irons, Autumn House/Feed the Children, Grantham 1996, 281 pp., £7.95

A miscellany, including autobiographical pieces by Bosnians, field reports by Feed the Children personnel, and poems by British writers. By far the longest contribution is a 95-page memoir by a Bosniak woman from Mostar, Nerma Dizdarević.

Hastie, Rachel **Disabled Children in a Society at War: a casebook from Bosnia**, Oxfam, Oxford 1997, £7.95

This book, by Oxfam's deputy representative in Bosnia, 1995-6, presents the lessons learned from Oxfam's involvement in helping to run a centre for disabled children in Tuzla (from 1994). Problems discussed include organizational ones and the traditional attitudes in the region towards physical and mental handicap.

Kelly, Gerard, and Lowell Sheppard **Miracle in Mostar**, Lion, Oxford 1995, 157 pp., £4.99

An account (by two members of 'British Youth for Christ') of the setting up of an evangelical Protestant church in West Mostar by two Croatian Baptists/Pentecostalists.

Mercier, Michèle **Crimes Without Punishment: humanitarian action in former Yugoslavia**, with a foreword by Cyrus Vance, Pluto Press, London 1995, 236 pp., £12.99 (first published as *Crimes sans châtiment*, Brussels 1994)

Commissioned by the International Committee of the Red Cross (ICRC), this book has some of the hallmarks of an official history: it puts great emphasis on policy and organizational issues, and seems mainly aimed at defending the ICRC from criticisms made of it during the war by some politicians and journalists.

Scott Davis, G. (ed.) **Religion and Justice in the War over Bosnia**, Routledge, New York 1996, 181 pp., £15.99

An interesting book, different from the standard run of academic essay-collections. Each paper looks at one aspect of the war, and/or the Western response, in a religious or ethical perspective: Michael Sells discusses the ideological manipulation of religion, James Turner Johnson the laws of war in relation to sieges, and G. Scott Davis the 'just war' tradition and intervention. Necessarily inconclusive, but occasionally thought-provoking.

Personal testimony — Bosnian voices

Boulanger, Claire, Bernard Jacquemart and Philippe Granjon **L'enfer yougoslave: les victimes de la guerre témoignent**, Belfond, Paris 1995, 376 pp., FF 120

Serious study of ethnic cleansing, by members of 'Médecins du Monde'; contains numerous testimonies by victims.

Cataldi, Anna **Letters From Sarajevo: voices of a besieged city**, translated by Avril Bardoni, Element, Shaftesbury 1994, 195 pp., £12.99

A moving collection of personal letters, written by ordinary citizens of Sarajevo to friends and relatives between April 1992 and September 1993, interspersed with a chronicle of events.

Ceh, Nick, and Jeff Harder (ed.) **The Golden Apple: war and democracy in Croatia and Bosnia**, East European Monographs, Boulder Col. 1996, 135 pp., £16

A set of interviews, made originally for the documentary film *The Golden Apple*. Interviews with Croatians predominate, but there are also some moving testimonies by Bosnian refugees, including survivors of the Omarska death-camp.

*Filipović, Zlata **Zlata's Diary**, Viking, London 1994, 185 pp., £7.95

Ingenuous memoir by a well-to-do Sarajevo family's model teenage daughter during the first years of the siege.

Lešić, Zdenko (ed.) **Children of Atlantis: voices from the former Yugoslavia**, Central European University Press, Budapest 1995, 183 pp., £9.99

Brief essays by refugee students from all parts of the former Yugoslavia, including many Bosnians, describing their experiences during the war and their reasons for leaving.

Lieman, Baukje **Exit: het vluchtverhaal van Ibro Mensuri**, Globe Pockets, Amsterdam 1993, 155 pp.

This is the story of a Bosniak, 'Ibro Mensuri' (not his real name), as told to the Dutch writer Baukje Lieman. In late May 1992 his village, near Kozarac, was attacked by Serb extremists; he then spent a week in Omarska and a month in Trnopolje.

Manojlović Žarković, Radmila (ed.) **I Remember — sjećam se: writings by Bosnian women refugees**, Aunt Lute Books, San Francisco 1966, unnumbered pages, £13.75

A touching but very insubstantial work, produced originally by the Women in Black organization in Belgrade: it consists of 32 brief (one-page) texts by refugees, each printed here in Bosnian with English, Italian and Spanish translations.

Puljić, Vinko **Suffering with Hope: appeals, addresses, interviews**, HKD Napredak, Zagreb 1995, 189 pp., Kn 44

A selection of Cardinal Puljić's public pronouncements in the first two years of the war in Bosnia, in which he expresses eloquently his own and his Church's commitment to an integral multi-ethnic and religiously pluralist Bosnia-Herzegovina, and in which he does not spare his criticisms of policies emanating either from Zagreb or from Sarajevo that he sees as endangering this cause.

Simić, Elvira **The Cry of Bosnia: a personal diary of the Bosnian war**, Genie Quest, London 1998, 85 pp., £6.99

A short, very personal memoir describing the plight of a Bosniak woman, married to a Bosnian Serb and with a baby son, who spent the first nine months of the war in a village north of Tuzla. Her narrative captures especially well the sheer bewilderment of the opening weeks of the war.

Softić, Elma **Sarajevo Days, Sarajevo Nights**, translated by Nada Conić, Key Porter Books, Toronto 1995, 200 pp., £16.95

Vivid, clear-headed letters and diaries, sometimes despairing but never self-pitying, describing day-to-day conditions in Sarajevo from April 1992 to June 1995.

Vuksanović, Mladen **Pale: im Herzen der Finsternis (Tagebuch 5/4/1992 — 15/7/1992)**, translated by Detlef I. Olof, Folio, Vienna 1997, 150 pp., DM 36

A harrowing personal diary by a former worker for Sarajevo television, who refused to join Karadžić's broadcasting station and found himself trapped in Pale for the first three months of the war.

Zulfikarpašić, Adil, with Milovan Djilas and Nadežda Gace **The Bosniak**, with an introduction by Ivo Banac, C. Hurst & Co., London 1998, 194 pp., £30

This book (first published in Bosnian as *Bošnjak*, Zurich 1994) is essentially the autobiography of the prominent émigré businessman and politician Zulfikarpašić, told in the form of a conversation with Djilas and a Belgrade journalist. It contains a fascinating account of his family background and childhood (his father, aged 89 when Adil was born in 1921, was a leading member of the old Ottoman Bosnian aristocracy), and much about World War II. It also describes the politics of the early 1990s, criticizing Izetbegović and expressing perhaps exaggerated trust in the feasibility of an agreement with Milošević in 1991.

Personal testimony — journalists

Bell, Martin **In Harm's Way: reflections of a war-zone thug** (revised edition), Penguin, London 1996, 301 pp., £6.99

The cool-toned prose of the white-suited TV journalist conveys some useful information about the war, including details of General Rose's behaviour concerning Goražde and Bihać. Most useful, perhaps, are Bell's comments on the nature and constraints of TV reporting (and editing). And yet, for all his heart-searching about 'balance' and self-censorship, Bell has a streak of indomitable naivety. 'It also occurred to me ... to wonder why the Serbs were shelling this city': this bright thought occurs to him after no fewer than 100 pages.

Demick, Barbara **Logavina Street: life and death in a Sarajevo neighbourhood**, Andrews and McMeel, Kansas City 1996, 182 pp., $19.95

A well-written and well-informed 'human interest' book by a reporter for the *Philadelphia Inquirer* who lived in Sarajevo in 1994 and 1995. Demick describes the conditions of life, work, education and death of various families living in a typical 'Old Town' street.

Di Giovanni, Janine **The Quick and the Dead: under siege in Sarajevo**, Phoenix, London 1994, 178 pp., £5.99

A vivid account of experiences (the author's and those of ordinary people she got to know) in Bosnia from 1992 to 1994, by a *Sunday Times* correspondent. Despite the title, the book also includes descriptions of visits to Mostar, Travnik, Maglaj and Tuzla, as well as a chilling interview with Karadžić's 'Minister of Information' in Pale.

Morgan, Peter **A Barrel of Stones: in search of Serbia**, Planet, Aberystwyth 1997, 176 pp., £6.75

A thoughtful, well-informed and, in places, entertaining book by a British journalist who visited Serbia in 1995 and tried to assess the political and social mood there in relation to the war in Bosnia. Telling interviews (with propagandists, refugees from Knin, old Communists, intellectuals and others) alternate with accounts of city life, gangsterism, 'turbo-folk' and Šešelj's party. Morgan comments shrewdly on the role of the media and on the psychological strategies adopted by Serbs to deal with what they knew, and what they did not want to know, about the Bosnian war.

Nicholson, Michael **Natasha's Story**, Macmillan, London 1994, 182 pp., £14.99

A touching account of Nicholson's impulsive rescue of an eight-year-old girl from a Bosnian orphanage, and her subsequent experiences in England. But the story, as told here, sheds little light on Bosnia, and when Nicholson does discuss the war he repeats all the standard mantras (ancient ethnic hatreds, all sides guilty, etc., etc.).

Rathfelder, Erich **Sarajevo und danach: sechs Jahre Reporter in ehemaligen Jugoslawien**, Beck, Munich 1998, 297 pp., DM 24

A collection of reports by a well-known German journalist; of particular interest for its coverage of the two years after the Dayton accord.

Rumiz, Paolo **Maschere per un massacro: quello che non abbiamo voluto sapere della guerra in Jugoslavia**, introduction by Claudio Magris, Riuniti, Rome 1996, 166 pp., Lit. 15,000

A powerful critical essay by one of the best Italian reporters to have covered the war. Rumiz concentrates on the mistaken nature of a Western policy which proceeded from the assumption (or the pretext) that this was merely a 'tribal' conflict.

Russell, Alec **Prejudice and Plum Brandy: tales of a Balkan stringer**, Michael Joseph, London 1993, 302 pp., £15.99

Only the second half of this book is on the former Yugoslavia (the first is on Romania); there are chapters on the war in Slavonia and the bombardment of Dubrovnik, and one brief but dramatic account of a visit to the besieged town of Goražde in the late summer of 1992.

Personal testimony — military men

Briquemont, Francis **Do Something, General! chronique de Bosnie-Herzégovine, 12 juillet 1993 — 24 janvier 1994**, Labot, Brussels 1998, 376 pp., FF 140

Belgian general who commanded UNPROFOR in B-H in 1993-4 recounts the frustrations of his brief tour of duty in Bosnia — at a time when the West was pursuing a series of de facto partition plans and David Owen was doing his best to deter any recourse to air strikes, e.g. against Mladić's forces on Mount Igman — and advises the country's inhabitants to 'rely on themselves'.

Cory-Jones, Keith **War dogs: British mercenaries in Bosnia tell their own story**, Century, London 1996, 261 pp., £15.99

Despite its subtitle and first-person narrative form, this work does not consist of accounts by mercenaries; it is, rather, a novelistic telling of their 'story', as if by someone accompanying them on their adventures. Other aspects of the book have apparently also been fictionalized. The chronology is bizarre, with the war raging simultaneously in Bosnia and the Osijek region; conversations are reproduced in *extenso*, even in the middle of battles; and the lurid blood-and-guts combat descriptions seem aimed at the popular SAS memoir market. Although based on some factual material, the book thus has virtually no documentary value.

Franchet, Commandant (with Sébastien Fontenelle) **Casque bleu pour rien: ce que j'ai vraiment vu en Bosnie**, Lattès, Paris 1995, 139 pp., FF 79

A classic specimen of UNPROFOR in-house doctrine, larded with extra helpings of French military contempt towards those naive Parisian intellectuals who distinguished between aggressor and victim in the war. All the emphasis is on Muslim provocations, Mujahedin, Muslim propaganda, etc. Includes an account of the assassination of Turajlić (the deputy prime minister who was shot by a Serb soldier while in an UNPROFOR armoured car) which puts the blame on the Bosnian government for failing to follow correct procedures. But there are some scraps of useful information: comments on the use of medical services as 'cover' by British military intelligence, for example, and a brief account of the wooing of Abdić by Lord Owen.

Goisque, Thomas **Bosnie hiver 95: journal de marche d'un casque bleu appelé**, Addim, Paris 1996, 96 pp.

This volume, by a 20-year-old who did his military service with the French infantry battalion on Mount Igman in the winter of 1994-5, is little more than a picture-book, with atmospheric photographs of mountain-top scenery, vehicles stuck in snow, etc. The brief journal-style text which accompanies it tells us little, though when commenting on the Serb and Bosnian Army outposts he visits the author does notice the relatively low morale of the Serb forces. A brief 'historical' introduction serves up a new variety of cod history: apparently Serbs have always hated Croats because the latter failed to turn up at the Battle of Kosovo.

Kent-Payne, Major Vaughan **Bosnia Warriors: living on the front line**, Robert Hale, London 1998, 368 pp., £25

Vivid operational account by a British Army infantry officer who was based in Vitez for seven months in 1993, during the bitter conflict between Croat and Bosnian Government forces in central Bosnia.

MacKenzie, General Lewis **Peacekeeper: the road to Sarajevo**, Douglas and McIntyre, Vancouver 1993, 345 pp., £18.95

These self-regarding memoirs of the former UN commander in Sarajevo reveal his indulgence towards the Karadžić Serbs and belief that the Bosnian government was his principal opponent. His description of how he manipulated the French President's visit to Sarajevo in June 1992 should be read by anyone viewing the UN as a passive executor of muddled Western policies.

Morillon, General Philippe **Croire et oser: chronique de Sarajevo**, Grasset, Paris 1993, 215 pp., FF 95

Memoirs of French UN commander revealing a classic colonialist mind-set. Compares the Yugoslav People's Army in Bosnia with the French Army in Algeria (against whose independence he himself conspired); claims that Nigerian UN troops were at home in Bosnia because they were 'used to the ravages of tribal conflicts'.

*Rose, General Sir Michael **Fighting For Peace: Bosnia 1994**, Harvill, London 1998, 320 pp., £18

This book is of real historical interest — but not as a work of history. Rose's account of the origins and outbreak of the war is a parade of ignorance: names, dates and simple facts are garbled on page after page; and when he ends with a military 'analysis' of the 'new' factors that made possible the ending of the war by NATO in 1995, he grossly contradicts his own earlier statements in the book, when he pointed out that the same key factors were already in place in early 1994. But the historical value of this book lies in its nature as evidence, not analysis. What it offers to posterity is damning evidence of the mentality of a senior British UN commander at a crucial stage in the Bosnian war — of his cultural sympathies and antipathies, his historical and political ignorance, and his systematic suspicion and hostility towards the Bosnian Government and its forces.

Stewart, Colonel Bob **Broken Lives: a personal view of the Bosnian conflict**, HarperCollins, London 1994, 336 pp., £18.00

A detailed operational account by the commander of British forces in central Bosnia, from October 1992 to May 1993. It illustrates the extraordinary lack of background knowledge (let alone military intelligence) with which these soldiers entered Bosnia; the only briefing Stewart and his men had on the nature of the war was from Martin Bell, who assured them it was just a continuation of centuries-old fighting. However, Stewart did learn something while he was there: he explicitly describes the role of the Vance-Owen Plan in stirring up the Bosnian-Croatian (and often Bosniak-Croat) war in central Bosnia.

Veenhof, Herman (ed.) **Srebrenica: oorlogsdagboek van Piet Hein Both**, De Vuurbaak, Barneveld 1995, 107 pp., Fl 19.75

An edition of the diary (and occasional letters home) of a Dutch soldier serving in Srebrenica from January to July 1995. Unfortunately the diary contains only one, undated entry for the days 11, 12 and 13 July, a brief entry which ends: 'I can't write it down. I stop writing.'

Wolfe Murray, Rupert (ed.) **IFOR on IFOR: NATO peacekeepers in Bosnia-Herzegovina**, with a foreword by Richard Holbrooke, Connect, Edinburgh 1996, 163 pp., £20

A sequence of first-person statements by men and women of the international military, from all ranks and countries, with good-quality photos. Mainly illustrates what a world of their own these army units inhabit. But some unusual figures do emerge: Bosnian-speaking Gurkhas, for example, or Romanian army engineers building the long-awaited 'corridor' road to Goražde. ('A lot of it we do by hand', they say; this long-awaited hand-made road is still awaited.)

Personal testimony — diplomats and politicians

Bildt, Carl **Uppdrag fred,** Norstedts Förlag, Stockholm 1997, 552 pp. (available in an abridged translation as: **Peace Journey: the struggle for peace in Bosnia**, Weidenfeld, London 1998, 256 pp., £25)

Bildt replaced Lord Owen in June 1995. Although this memoir

therefore covers the final months of the war, it yields little new information on that period — which is not surprising, since the real work was taken off the hands of Bildt and Stoltenberg by Holbrooke and NATO. Roughly half the book, however, is on the period after Dayton: here it has some historical value, as it describes such issues as the engineered Serb exodus from outer Sarajevo, the half-hearted Western policy on the removal of Karadžić, and the problems of economic reconstruction.

Christopher, Warren **In the Stream of History: shaping foreign policy for a new era**, Cambridge University Press, Cambridge 1998, 608 pp., £13

These leaden memoirs have a chapter entitled 'Bringing peace to Bosnia' (pp. 343-72), the main value of which is to illustrate how little understanding of the causes or nature of the Bosnian war Christopher had achieved after four years (1993-6) as US Secretary of State. One useful titbit is his observation that 'Though unscrupulous and suspected of war crimes, Milošević has a rough charm, and he appealed to some Western European leaders as a bulwark against an Islamic tide' — but Christopher is too diplomatic, unfortunately, to name names.

Genscher, Hans-Dietrich **Rebuilding a House Divided**, translated by Thomas Thornton, Broadway Books, New York 1997, 580 pp., £24.45 (abridged translation of **Erinnerungen**, Siedler, Berlin 1995, 1,086 pp., DM 29.90)

These memoirs by the former German foreign minister contain one chapter, of 34 pp., on the Yugoslav crisis, full of bureaucratese about meetings and communiqués. It illustrates the dismal obsession of the European ministers and diplomats with their own institutional turf wars, while shedding a little light in passing on who was pushing for (or against) what — e.g., (of the crucial meeting at The Hague on 19 September 1991): 'The British foreign secretary spoke out emphatically against even beginning to entertain the thought of peacekeeping forces.' Genscher also reveals that the main opponents of any preventive deployment in Bosnia were the Netherlands and Greece.

Koschnick, Hans, and Jens Schneider **Brücke über die Neretva: der Wiederaufbau von Mostar**, Deutscher Taschenbuch Verlag, Munich 1995, 240 pp., DM 32

A valuable account of Koschnick's attempt to organize rebuilding and reconciliation in Mostar, written in a series of alternating chapters by the city's former EU supremo himself and the German journalist Jens Schneider, covering the period July 1994 — July 1995.

Mendiluce, José María **Con rabia y esperanzas: retos y límites de la acción humanitaria**, Planeta, Barcelona 1997, 283 pp., Ptas 1,800

This is a general study of humanitarian activity in conflict situations, referring not only to the former Yugoslavia but also to Cambodia, Central America and many other areas. But Mendiluce, who was director of UNHCR operations in Bosnia, has some especially heartfelt pages on his Bosnian experience, not mincing his words when it comes to the 'idiots' in UNPROFOR headquarters.

Mock, Alois (ed.) **Das Balkan-Dossier: der Aggressionskrieg in Ex-Jugoslawien — Perspektiven für die Zukunft**, documentation by Herbert Vytiska, Signum, Vienna 1997, 244 pp., DM 40.80

This book, put together by the press spokesman (Vytiska) of the former Austrian foreign minister (Mock), surveys the wars in Croatia and Bosnia from the perspective of Austrian policy, quoting many of Mock's criticisms of international organizations such as the OSCE and the UN.

*Owen, David **Balkan Odyssey**, Indigo, London 1996, 436 pp., £8.99

The potential documentary value of this relentlessly detailed account by one of the key international representatives during the Bosnian war is largely vitiated, regrettably, by the author's overriding concern with self-justification and by his cavalier treatment of facts that do not fit his own preconceptions.

Stoltenberg, Thorvald, and Kai Eide **De tusen dagene: fredsmeklere på Balkan**, Gyldendal Norsk Forlag, Oslo 1996, 427 pp.

This book by the Norwegian UN negotiator and his assistant has not been published in English, and is unlikely ever to be translated, for several reasons. It is long and dull; it is padded out with descriptions of well known matters, while revealing little that is new (though there is an interesting account of Stoltenberg's frantic attempt to stop Croatia from re-taking the Krajina); and it contains predictable defences of Vance-Owen, Owen-Stoltenberg, etc. But Stoltenberg says nothing whatsoever about the scandal caused by his bizarre Oslo speech in which he declared that all Bosnians were Serbs.

Wynaendts, Henry **L'engrenage: chroniques yougoslaves juillet 1991-août 1992**, Denoel, Paris 1993, 195 pp., FF 115

This memoir, by the Dutch diplomat who worked first as EC representative in Yugoslavia, then as assistant to Lord Carrington, is mainly about the diplomatic efforts to end the war in Croatia. However, it also discusses the handling of the Bosnian issue in the six months before the outbreak of war there, sticking loyally to the Carrington line.

*Zimmermann, Warren **Origins of a Catastrophe**, Times Books, New York 1996, 269 pp., $25

Describing the three years the author spent as US ambassador in Belgrade from March 1989 to January 1992 and offering his views on why the postwar Yugoslav federation disintegrated, this book provides a valuable insight into the misconceptions that ruled US policy during the period in question, and for which Zimmermann himself shared responsibility: misconceptions that were to have disastrous consequences for Bosnia.

Personal testimony — NGOs

Becker, Sally **The Angel of Mostar: one woman's fight to rescue children in Bosnia**, Hutchinson, London 1994, 193 pp., £14.95

If there was ever a book designed to make one feel positively sympathetic towards devious UN officials and obstructive UNPROFOR soldiers, it must be this pushy memoir by Sally Becker, the have-a-go aid worker. But there is some cheerful honesty here about her own shortcomings; and the fact remains that she did save lives.

Blackman, Ellen **Harvest in the Snow: my crusade to rescue the lost children of Bosnia**, Brassey's, Washington and London 1997, 305 pp., £15.95

The author went to Bosnia in the summer of 1993 as a freelance reporter-cum-aid-worker. She helped to organize some aid shipments and other activities (though the subtitle here gives a very exaggerated impression) funded by a major American Jewish charity. Rather too much of the book is spent describing her personal life in Sarajevo; but there are a few pages of some historical interest, describing the chaos (and UN manipulation) surrounding the Serb withdrawal from the Sarajevo 'exclusion zone' in February 1994.

Hollingworth, Larry **Merry Christmas Mr Larry**, Mandarin, London 1997, 384 pp., £ 7.99

A lively, engaging and self-deprecating account of Hollingworth's experiences organizing UNHCR's operations from July 1992 to April 1994; includes vivid descriptions of visits to Goražde, Žepa and Srebrenica. But, as with all memoirs of this sort, the understanding of the nature and origins of the war is extremely scanty: the rights and wrongs of the belligerents are judged purely in terms of their behaviour as combatants or aid-recipients.

Personal testimony — visitors

Duroy, Lionel **Il ne m'est rien arrivé**, Mercure de France, Paris 1994, 180 pp., FF 89

In 1993 this French writer travelled alone with an interpreter on both sides of the Serb-Croat fronts in Croatia and northern Bosnia. The sober, dispassionate account of his journey and his conversations with ordinary people throws into sharp relief the tragic context.

Garde, Paul **Journal de voyage en Bosnie-Herzégovine**, La Nuée Bleue, Strasbourg 1995, 142 pp., FF 88

This distinguished French professor of Slavic studies travelled independently through Bosnia in October 1994, visiting Mostar, Zenica and Sarajevo, meeting many ordinary Bosnians as well as intellectuals and journalists. His brief account is knowledgeable, alert and thoroughly *sympathique*.

Goytisolo, Juan **Cuaderno de Sarajevo: annotaciones de un viaje a la barbarie**, El Pais/Aguilar, Madrid 1993, 136 pp.

Sympathetic and atmospheric 'diary' of a visit to Sarajevo in the summer of 1993 by this famous Spanish writer; includes brief essays on the psychology and politics of ethnic cleansing.

Lévy, Bernard-Henri **Le lys et la cendre: journal d'un écrivain au temps de la guerre en Bosnie 1992-1995**, Grasset, Paris 1996, 560 pp., FF 145

The philosopher who became the foremost defender in France of the Bosnian cause, with his promotion of an electoral list on the issue and his remarkable film, here provides not just a wealth of acute observations from his repeated visits to Sarajevo during the war, but also illuminating insights drawn from his meetings with Mitterrand, Chirac, Izetbegović, Tudjman, etc. and pertinent comments on French reactions to the Bosnian war.

Security and military issues

Bianchini, Stefano, and Paul Shoup (ed.) **The Yugoslav War, Europe and the Balkans: how to achieve security?**, Longo Editore, Ravenna 1995, 192 pp., Lit. 30,000

Proceedings of academic meetings held in Italy in 1993 and 1994. Mainly general essays, saying little new; but there is one interesting study of Russian-Serbian relations, by Ilya Levin, analysing the pro-Belgrade currents in Russian politics and listing the Russian fascist organizations which sent 'volunteers' to lend a hand with ethnic cleansing.

Brown, J.F. **Nationalism, Democracy and Security in the Balkans**, Dartmouth Publishing Co., Aldershot and Brookfield Vt 1992, 205 pp., £33

A very general and rather routine study, discussing six Balkan countries in turn. Brown has one brief (20-page) chapter on the former Yugoslavia up to 1990, and just 18 pages in a final chapter on the outbreak of war in Croatia and Bosnia. His attempts to be even-handed become, in places, simply crass: his considered opinion on the bombardments of Vukovar and Dubrovnik is that 'the truth was that neither side deserved much sympathy.'

Danopoulos, Constantine, and Daniel Zirker (ed.), **Civil-Military Relations in the Soviet and Yugoslav Successor States**, Westview Press, Boulder Col. and Oxford 1996, 279 pp., £53

This volume contains little of interest apart from a short but stimulating essay on civil-military relations in Croatia by Ozren Žunec. The paper on Bosnia, by Dimitrios Kyriakou, attributes key aspects of the war to 'folk tradition', and explains that the reason why a large number of Serbs remained in Sarajevo during the war was that they were 'systematically terrorized' there.

Eyal, Jonathan **Europe and Yugoslavia: lessons from a failure**, RUSI, London 1993, 80pp., £6.50

A sharply worded pamphlet which, however, promises rather more superior wisdom than it ever manages to deliver. Eyal comments shrewdly on the way that European governments allowed their Yugoslav policy to be dominated by their own concerns with constructing a 'security architecture' for Europe. He rejects the 'premature recognition' argument where Croatia and Slovenia are concerned, but accepts it as the explanation of the war in Bosnia. As this point illustrates, what the pamphlet lacks is any real understanding of intra-Yugoslav politics — above all, Milošević's strategy.

Griffiths, Stephen Iwan **Nationalism and Ethnic Conflict: threats to European security**, Oxford University Press, Oxford and New York 1993, 136 pp., £16.50

This book contains only a brief discussion of the former Yugoslavia, and this consists mainly of a faithful summary of the views of Misha Glenny, supplemented by those of 'John' Zametica.

Ripley, Tim **Air War Bosnia: UN and NATO Airpower**, Airlife, Shrewsbury 1996, 112 pp., £16.95

The glossy photos which fill this book make it look, at first glance, like something strictly for the military equivalent of train-spotters. But the text, although larded with uncritical repetitions of UNPROFOR doctrine about the nature of the war, does contain a mass of hard facts and statistics (especially on the NATO bombing campaign of August-September 1995), plus useful diagrams of the chains of command.

After the war

Amnesty International **All the Way Home: safe 'minority returns' as a just remedy and for a secure future**, Amnesty International, London 1998, 36 pp.

The main thrust of this report describing the situation of Bosnian refugees and the obstacles preventing their return to their homes is directed against governments like that of Germany which are pressing refugees to go back to B-H even where they will clearly have no option but to 'relocate' to areas where their own ethnic group (and, in practice, they are usually Bosniaks) is in a majority.

Amnesty International **'Who's Living in my House?':** **obstacles to the safe return of refugees and internally displaced people**, Amnesty International, London 1997, 27 pp.

Useful report on the overall situation of refugees from the war in Bosnia, highlighting the small number who have been able to return and the obstacles to their doing so. But the report is sometimes neutral when it should not be (for instance, why should a Sarajevo government pressing for refugee return in the name of a multi-ethnic Bosnia be criticized for 'manipulation', alongside a Republika Srpska government determined to consolidate mono-ethnic entities?), and its recommendations could be more concrete.

Aspen Institute **Unfinished Peace: report of the International Commission on the Balkans**, with a foreword by Leo Tindemanns, Aspen Institute, Berlin, and Carnegie Endowment for International Peace, Washington DC 1996, 178 pp., £14.95

Conceived as a contemporary reprise of the remarkable 1913 Carnegie International Commission report reprinted in *The Other Balkan Wars* (see page 34 above), this judicious and informative report by Leo Tindemans, Lloyd Cutler, Bronislaw Geremek, John Roper, Theo Sommer, Simone Veil and David Anderson analyses the violent break-up of postwar Yugoslavia and the international response to the war, before surveying the successor states today and, more briefly, also their southern neighbours Bulgaria, Greece and Turkey. It also makes a large number of mostly sensible recommendations for Western policy, about whose past failings it is fairly scathing.

Bertelsmann Cartographic Institute and *New York Times*. **Macmillan Atlas of War and Peace: Bosnia-Herzegovina**, Macmillan, New York and London 1996, 48 pp., $12.95

Very useful collection of clear, up-to-date and generally excellent maps not just of B-H but of all the former Yugoslavia (here called the Western Balkans), properly indexed and with a number of larger-scale regional and city maps too. The maps themselves are preceded by six short journalistic texts, by *New York Times* correspondents, of more uneven quality.

Cot, Général Jean **Demain la Bosnie,** L'Harmattan, Paris 1999, 175 pp., FF 95

General Cot commanded UNPROFOR from July 1993 to March 1994, since when he has maintained a serious interest in Bosnia-Herzegovina's prospects for a democratic future, demonstrated in this book which is the product of an extended visit to the country, when the General travelled round talking to a wide range of 'ordinary people' and recording their views. His own often perceptive accompanying comments are an eloquent plea for the country's survival as a common state.

Hodge, Carole, and Mladen Grbin, **Test for Europe,** IREES, University of Glasgow, Glasgow 1996, 174 pp., £7.95

This short book, by two of the most tireless campaigners against the ignorance and prejudice that has inspired so much of Western policy towards the former Yugoslavia over the past decade, is oddly constructed but contains valuable insights and analyses, particularly of the myths that have too often justified wrong policies. It also makes a number of useful recommendations for confidence-building, especially in relation to post-Dayton Bosnia.

Hoppe, Hans-Joachim **Das Dayton-Abkommen und die neue Führungselite in Bosnien-Hercegovina** [sic], Berichte des Bundesinstituts für ostwissenschaftliche und internationale Studien, no. 14, Cologne 1998, 37 pp.

A rather elementary survey of the Bosnian political landscape in early 1998, placing excessive trust in the 'liberal' and 'pro-Western' forces of Mrs Plavšić, but arguing sensibly enough that the future of Bosnia depends on thoroughly dismantling the power-structures controlled by extremists in Republika Srpska and 'Herceg-Bosna'.

Human Rights Watch **Bosnia and Hercegovina — 'A Closed, Dark Place': past and present human rights abuses in Foča,** New York 1998, 67 pp.

A valuable report, documenting not only the appalling crimes committed in Foča in 1992, but also the persistent non-compliance of the local Serb authorities with their obligations under Dayton. Examples given here of their recent behaviour include police harassment, prevention of the return of refugees and the blocking of inter-entity projects. Also described are the passivity of the IPTF in the face of a swaggering, unreconstructed Serb police force, and the abject failure of the (French) SFOR troops to arrest known War Crimes Tribunal indictees.

Kalmanowitz, Debra, and Bobby Lloyd **The Portable Studio: art therapy and political conflict, initiatives in former Yugoslavia and South Africa**, Health Education Authority, London 1997, 114 pp., £15

Drawing on their own personal experiences, the authors provide an illuminating and moving account of their art therapy work in the former Yugoslavia and Kwa-Zulu Natal, accompanied by material on the theory of art therapy and practical models for those wishing to establish services and workshops.

Rubin, Barnett (ed.) **Toward Comprehensive Peace in Southeast Europe: conflict prevention in the South Balkans** (report of the South Balkans working group of the Council on Foreign Relations Center for Preventive Action), Twentieth Century Fund, New York 1996, 135 pp., $9.95

This report from a prestigious US think-tank seeks to use the experience of Bosnia , where 'many delayed for too long the actions needed to end the slaughter', to work out preventive measures relating, in particular, to Kosova, Macedonia and Albania. Its recommendations, however, based on the notion that the Helsinki principles provide an alternative to 'nationalism', are mostly feeble pieties that do not address at all the nature of the threat posed to regional peace and stability by the character of the Milošević regime.

Schmeets, Hans, and Jeanet Exel **The 1996 Bosnia-Herzegovina Elections: an analysis of the observations**, Kluwer Academic Publishers, Dordrecht 1997, 152 pp., £59

This short, narrowly technical and hugely over-priced study extracts various statistics from the forms filled in by OSCE observers at the 1996 elections. It also prints the whole sequence of self-congràtulatory communiqués issued by the OSCE official in charge of the operation, while paying no attention whatsoever to the serious criticisms of the election published by organizations such as the International Crisis Group.

Sopta, Marin (ed.) **Bosnia-Hercegovina: beyond Dayton** (proceedings of a two-day international conference held in Zagreb, Croatia, 15-16 March 1997), Croatian Centre of Strategic Studies, Zagreb 1997, 240 pp.

Includes contributions by Muhamed Šaćirbey, Peter Galbraith and Christopher Bennett. An interesting paper by Janusz Bugajski discusses possible future political scenarios; a depressing contribution by Jonas Widgren (of the International Centre for Migration Policy Development, Vienna) discusses the policies of West European governments on the return of refugees, which make no serious provision for those refugees whose homes are in the 'wrong' entity. Many speakers (especially Bennett) emphasize that the civilian aspects of Dayton are not being implemented.

Žilić, Ahmed, and Saba Risaluddin **Dayton v. Attorneys**, Sarajevo 1997, 119 pp.

A very valuable documentary study of the 'Zvornik Seven' case and the post-Dayton legal system: its key section was reprinted as the pamphlet *The Case of the Zvornik Seven* (see above, p. 22)

Visual representations

Dizdarević, Zlatko, and Gérard Roudeau **Oslobođenje: le journal qui refuse à mourir, Sarajevo 1992-1996**, foreword by Tadeusz Mazowiecki, La Découverte/ Reporters sans frontières, Paris 1996, 160 pp., FF 149

Mainly visual tribute to *Oslobođenje* and its staff, with fine photographs by Roudeau interspersed with a number of short texts by the newspaper's best known journalist.

*Grant, James (ed.) **I Dream of Peace: images of war by children of former Yugoslavia**, UNICEF/HarperCollins, London 1994, unnumbered pages, £8.99

Memorable little book of pictures and prose from children who have lived through the war and seen some of the worst of it.

Matvejević, Predrag **Sarajevo**, with photographs by Tom Stoddart, Smithsonian Institute Press, Washington DC 1998, 60 pp.

Stoddart's photographic tribute to the people of besieged Sarajevo, reproduced in a larger format in *Edge of Madness* (see p. 23 above), provides some of the most memorable and eloquent visual images of their suffering, endurance and unquenchable humanity. Matvejević contributes a sombre and powerful introductory essay.

Serotta, Edward **Survival in Sarajevo: how a Jewish community came to the aid of its city**, Brandstätter, Vienna 1995, 128 pp., $29.95

Excellent black-and-white photographs, with a text giving a fine account of the Jewish community and the activities of the charity 'La Benevolencija' during the first two years of the war. Also follows the story of two young boys sent out of Sarajevo, to Israel, in 1994.

Media

Gow, James, Richard Paterson and Alison Preston (ed.) **Bosnia by Television,** British Film Institute, London 1996, 181 pp., £12.99

This collection includes some valuable accounts by TV journalists of the practical and ethical problems of covering the Bosnian war; the last 60 pages present the results of an international research exercise, comparing national TV news coverage in 12 countries during one week in May 1994. The book is marred, however, by a piece of gross propaganda by a John Burns (not the *New York Times* journalist of that name, but someone attached to St Cross College, Oxford), which could have come straight from the pages of *Living Marxism*: the marketplace massacre was self-inflicted, Fikret Alić (in the famous photograph at Trnopolje) was actually a Serb suffering from TB, etc., etc. The inclusion of this farrago must raise doubts about the judgement of the editors of the volume.

Sadkovich, James **The US Media and Yugoslavia 1991-1995**, Praeger, Westport Conn. and London 1998, 296 pp., $69.50

Based on voluminous research, this impassioned denunciation of the ignorance and bias of much of the reporting on the former Yugoslavia in the US media hits home on many richly merited targets, uncovering a veritable mine of misinformation, both deliberate and unwitting. Its value as a reference tool is diminished, however, by an awkward thematic arrangement of the material, which also perhaps contributes to some failures of discrimination: for example, a decent journalist who gets something wrong or misunderstands the historical background may find himself lumped together here with a propagandist setting out to deceive.

Thompson, Mark **Forging War: the media in Serbia, Croatia and Bosnia-Hercegovina**, Article 19, London 1994, 271 pp., £9.99

A well-researched survey of the functioning of the Serbian, Croatian and Bosnian media, and their manipulation for political and propaganda purposes, both before and during the war. Oddly, the anti-censorship organization which published this work removed the name of the author from the jacket and title page; it may therefore be listed in some library catalogues simply as the work of 'Article 19'. Has continuing value as a reference tool, but flawed by failure to compare how Western media have functioned in wartime, and by tendency to equalize aggressors and victims. And are the epithets 'chetnik' and 'ustasha' not preferable, when actually referring to the extremists, to the 'Serb' and 'Croat' favoured by Western media?

Literary works

Branković, Avram **Bosnia Revelation**, Gay Men's Press, Swaffham 1998, 106 pp., £7.95

Spiritual journey of a young gay painter, tormented by memory and by the surrounding horror, in besieged Sarajevo.

Čolić, Velibor **Les Bosniaques**, translated by Mireille Robin, Le Serpent à plumes, Paris 1993, 138 pp., FF 35

A collection of vignettes, often less than a page long, some horrific, some heartrending, some grimly humorous, illustrating war and defeat in Posavina in 1992.

Curtis, S.D. **So Like Fire**, KUD France Prešeren, Ljubljana 1998, 95 pp., £6

Touching, candid and at times poetic fictionalization of the refugee experience seen through the eyes of an emotionally involved aid worker, and through letters she receives from former refugees now returned home, intertwined with memories of a lost love affair.

Demirović, Vahida **Visages from the Wasteland: a collection of true war stories from Bosnia**, translated by Ralph Bogert Genie Quest Publishing, London 1999, 193 pp., £8.99

The author, an eminent psychotherapist who worked throughout the siege of Sarajevo as a volunteer doctor at the city's Orthopaedic Clinic, uses her unique vantage-point to record and retell the sufferings of the Bosnian people in literary form, because in her own words 'the torture, the rape, slaughtering and ethnic cleansing, which the Bosnian people were exposed to, must never be forgotten.'

Dhomhnaill, Nuala Ní, Chris Agee, Harry Clifton and Bernard O'Donoghue **In the Heart of Europe: poems for Bosnia**, with original prints by Alfonso López Monreal, Rushlight Editions, Belfast 1998, n.p., £5

This little book, published for the Amnesty International Irish Section (with all proceeds going to the Tuzla children's charity *Zemlja Djece*), contains a fine poem from each of the four authors — one of them in English and Gaelic versions — and a series of four powerful mezzotints by the Mexican artist Monreal.

Fullerton, John **The Monkey House**, Bantam Press, London 1996, 287 pp., £15.99

Work of detective fiction loosely based on the Bosnian police's showdown with criminal warlords in Sarajevo in 1993. Despite its implausible plot, this pacy novel captures something of the spirit of the besieged city at a decisive moment in its history.

Jančić, Miroslav **The Flying Bosnian: poems from limbo,** Hearing Eye, London 1996, 87 pp., £7.50

Seventy-odd short poems, grouped under the headings 'Closing in on oneself', 'Beside oneself' and 'Homecoming', written in English by a passionately anti-nationalist former Yugoslav ambassador from B-H, who was already the author — in Serbo-Croat, a 'language which does not exist any more' — of three novels, ten plays/film scripts and two works of non-fiction, and who as a refugee in London suffered 'an attack of poetry'.

Janković, Goran **As Clouds Pass By**, translated by Damjan Bojadžiev, Tomislav Vrečar and Tone Škrjanec, KUD France Prešeren, Ljubljana, 68 pp.

Fifty-one short and in most cases untitled poems, by a Bosnian writer born in Zenica and now living in Slovenia, presented in four languages: Bosnian, English, Italian and Slovenian.

Jergović, Miljenko **Karivani: ein Familienmosaik**, translated by Klaus Detlef Olof, Folio, Vienna 1997, 177 pp., DM 36

Second collection of short stories by the author of *Sarajevo Marlboro*, which through a sequence of tales of ordinary Bosnian people during the past 150 years adumbrates both a fragmentary history of the country and an outline of Jergović's own family history.

Melčić, Dunja (ed.) **Das Wort im Krieg: ein bosnisch-kroatisches Lesebuch**, Dipa-Verlag, Frankfurt 1995, 189 pp., DM 34

A valuable anthology of literary work relating to the war in Bosnia, by Bosnian (and some Croatian) writers, including Mehmedinović, Sidran, Lovrenović and Jergović.

Monnery, David **Soldier O: SAS: the Bosnian inferno**, 22 Books, Rochester 1994, 281 pp., £4.99 (later reissued as **The Bosnian Inferno**, Severn House, Sutton and New York 1994)

The plot of this sometimes gory adventure novel, involving an SAS team rescuing a Bosniak woman from a Serb-run brothel in Vogošča and then going to look for her husband (a renegade SAS man organizing the defence of an isolated Bosnian town), is improbable enough, but many of the local details are reasonably authentic.

Samardžić, Goran, and Damir Uzunović **The Best of Lica**, translated by Edin Balalić, Antonela Glavinić, Nevena Hadžović, Celia Hawkesworth, Maja Starčević and Ulvija Tanović, Buybook, Sarajevo 1998, 96 pp., DM 5

Valuable anthology, selected and translated from the first ten issues of the Sarajevo literary magazine *Lica* (May 1996 to June 1998), which presents a wide range of recent Bosnia poetry and prose writing, featuring no fewer than sixty-two authors.

Simić, Goran **Sprinting from the Graveyard**, translated by David Harsent, OUP, Oxford and New York 1997, 47 pp., £7.99

Twenty-nine short poems — variously striking notes of wry perception, irony, horror, desperate stoicism, tenderness — mostly written during the siege of Sarajevo, by one of Bosnia's best-known poets, now living in Canada.

Suško, Mario (ed.) **Contemporary Poetry of Bosnia and Herzegovina**, translated by the editor and William Tribe, Pen Club B-H, Sarajevo 1993, 202 pp.

Producing this ambitious anthology of Bosnian poetry in translation in wartime conditions was an impressive achievement. It features the work of 32 living writers — some well-known, established figures like Sidran, Sarajlić or Vuletić, others who emerged in the eighties and nineties — and includes valuable biographical and bibliographical information on all of them.

Mark Almond, **Europe's Backyard War: the war in the Balkans**, Heinemann, London 1994, 432 pp., £20

One of the most striking features of the West's calamitous failure in Bosnia-Herzegovina has been its persistent over-estimation of the viability of the 'Greater Serbia' project, and corresponding under-estimation of the human forces and material constraints arrayed against it. Mark Almond outlines two dominant interpretations of why Western policy should have been as it has. First, that the West (the British Foreign Office in particular) 'preferred an Ordnungsmacht to dominate the Balkans, and Serbia fitted the bill'. Secondly, 'the plausible alternative to the Machiavellian interpretation of the inefficacy of Western policy is that crass stupidity not cynical Realpolitik dictated its course throughout the crisis.' But whichever explanation is preferred, the miscalculation remains the same. A simple totting up of tanks, howitzers and air strength is a very poor guide to understanding the character of a war and forecasting its likely outcome (a rather more pertinent lesson of Vietnam than the absurd 'quagmire' analogies indulged in by armchair critics of a more active US intervention against aggression in Bosnia). The truth, as Almond exhaustively catalogues, is that Western policy has from the outset been predicated upon at least the inevitability, and. perhaps the desirability, of a victory for Belgrade's expansionist ambitions. Of all the books so far to have appeared on the breakup of Yugoslavia and its bloody aftermath, this furnishes the most devastating and well-documented portrayal of the West's response. Chapters 2 ('Countdown: the West and the Yugoslav crisis') and 13 ('Last chances for peace') in particular should be required reading for anyone, for example, who still believes the myth of Germany's 'premature' recognition of Slovenia and Croatia, or who cannot understand how Lord Owen came to pin all his hopes on a peace with terms dictated by Slobodan Milošević.

Almond shows how, when Western politicians swore they would 'never' recognize the independence of Yugoslavia's republics, they were thinking above all of the Soviet Union, and how, even when they were nevertheless compelled to recognize them, as with the former Soviet republics, they did so only reluctantly and half-heartedly. As a consequence, instead of pursuing policies designed to ensure the integrity and viability of all the new successor states, they hoped instead that Serbia—like Russia—would re-establish some simulacrum of the order that had so regrettably passed away. This is why they have tried so hard to redefine Serbia's wars of aggression as civil conflicts internal to Croatia and Bosnia: first to ignore, then quickly to forget, the genocidal nature of a war designed to acquire territory without its non-Serb population; to treat Bosnia's legitimate and multi-ethnic government as a purely Muslim 'warring party'; and to present the project of carving a racially pure Serb state out of areas where Serbs were for the most part only a minority, as being both the will of all Bosnian Serbs and, ultimately, acceptable to the new European order. But they did not reckon with the other side of the equation: the new successor states and their refusal to surrender, or, standing behind these, all those latent forces throughout the region (including in Serbia itself) in search of a democratic future.

Almond aptly concludes by quoting Aristotle on 'occasions when indignation is the only appropriate response and indifference is a sign of folly', and Louis MacNeice's 'contemptuous verdict in 1938 on the illusions of appeasement'.

Branka Magaš

This review first appeared in International Affairs *(London), April 1995*

Michael Barratt Brown, **The Yugoslav Tragedy: lessons for socialists,** Socialist Renewal, Nottingham 1996, 82 pp., £4.99

'Lessons for Socialists' is the subtitle of Michael Barratt Brown's new booklet on the war in the former Yugoslavia. His publishers 'Socialist Renewal' are perhaps more in need of lessons than most, having published in the past a tribute to Romania's Ceauşescu *(The Man, his Ideas, his Socialist Achievements)* by Labour MEP Stan Newens, as well as the work of Mihailo Marković, a 'Marxist humanist' who helped write the 1986 Memorandum of the Serbian Academy, served as Milošević's party ideologue throughout the war, and enunciated the principle that Serbia could become democratic only if it first became ethnically pure. British readers of Barratt Brown's booklet will learn nothing of the former Yugoslavia, but gain some disturbing insights into the state of our own intelligentsia, particularly on the left. Only for that reason is it worth attention.

Many Western commentators have exhibited gross ignorance of Yugoslav history, but in Barratt Brown this extends to history in general. He seems not to know that Napoleonic France was ultimately defeated on land not at sea; that the War of the Spanish Succession was fought over the succession in Spain not the Holy Roman Empire; that the Prussian destruction of France's armies preceded German unification in 1871, not vice versa; that by 1913 the Russian navy had not managed to break out of the Black Sea; that Italy was not 'newly liberated and unified' in 1913, but had been fully unified forty-three years earlier; that in 1913 Transylvania was owned not by Romania but by Hungary; that Austria and Hungary were then parts of the same state (he describes them as 'united by their fear of Russia'); that Archduke Franz Ferdinand was the nephew not the son of the Austrian Emperor; that the Treaty of Versailles concerned Germany but not Austria-Hungary; and so on. Bosnian place-names as well known as Tuzla and Cazin are wrongly spelled, while Foča is spelled wrongly in two different ways on page 56 and again on page 57. Most bizarre of all, for someone who mentions repeatedly his own presence in Yugoslavia in 1945, Barratt Brown seems unaware that the Partisan struggle against the Axis was fought primarily in Bosnia-Herzegovina, Croatia and Slovenia, claiming that because of the 'mountainous location of guerrilla warfare, it was mostly Montenegrins and south Serbs who were caught in the German offensives against the Partisan strongholds'.

Barratt Brown develops two main themes: that he aims 'not to blame or acclaim any one of the nationalist forces which broke up

Yugoslavia, but to condemn all forms of nationalism'; and that the West is responsible for the war, its responsibility lying 'first in the demand of the banks for debt repayment [from Yugoslavia], which as elsewhere led to rising inflation; and second, in Chancellor Kohl's recognition of the withdrawal from Yugoslavia of the two rich republics — Slovenia and then Croatia.' His stress on economic collapse leads him to conclude that for the average Yugoslav, 'when you are unemployed and others are doing well, then it must be your neighbour's fault', so that 'if his name is a Moslem one or a Croat one and yours is Serbian, it does not need a Radovan Karadžić to tell you what to do.' Yugoslavia's vulnerability to economic disruption is blamed on the decentralizing liberal policies imposed by the Republics of Slovenia and Croatia ('the North') against the interests of the rest of the country ('the South').

It is remarkable that someone calling himself a socialist should portray the unemployed as prone to murder and rape spontaneously. Such economic reductionism can, of course, explain neither the collapse of Yugoslavia nor the outbreak of war. Since 1966, 'poor' Macedonia and Kosova had aligned themselves with 'rich' Slovenia and Croatia in favour of political and economic decentralization and in opposition to Serbian centralism; the Kosova Albanians, the poorest Yugoslav people, were those who pushed hardest for greater self-government (well before the selfish 'rich' republics), leading to mass protests in 1968 and 1981. In1969-71 Serbia was the most liberal republic, while from 1971 to 1989 Croatia was among the most conservative. Talk of a rich north vs poor south divide is a misleading vulgarization: in the mid-1980s Croatia's per capita income was closer to Serbia's than to Slovenia's, whilst Serbia's was closer to Croatia's than to Macedonia's. In the late 1980s and early 1990s, Serbia's support for political and economic recentralization brought it into conflict with a coalition of those poorer than itself (Bosnia and Macedonia) as well as those richer (Slovenia and Croatia).

An economically reductionist approach does not explain, moreover, why mass killing has not taken place in Slovenia, north-west Croatia, the Bosnian cities of Tuzla and Sarajevo, Serbia itself, or Macedonia. If Barratt Brown were correct, the unemployed here should be as willing to kill their neighbours as elsewhere. Funnily enough, he misses the fact that mass killing and destruction took place primarily in areas occupied or attacked by the Yugoslav People's Army (JNA) or by paramilitaries from Serbia proper: Kijevo in August 1991; Vukovar in November 1991; Bijeljina,

Zvornik, Foča and Prijedor in spring 1992; Srebrenica and Žepa in July 1995. Violence between neighbours, unemployed or otherwise, was quite secondary. Barratt Brown does not condemn the JNA, however, since he sees it as 'the one remaining force representing Yugoslavia' after the Yugoslav Communist Party had crumbled, and describes its genocidal actions in support of Greater Serbia as 'a state-building project'.

This brings us to the crux of the matter, for despite his supposed condemnation of 'all nationalisms', Barratt Brown himself plays the role of apologist for three different species of the latter. First, he does not hide his preference for a Yugoslav state and identity over a Croatian or Serbian one, his hostility to 'nationalism' being in actuality a hostility to small nations. Despite lavish praise of the Communist-led Partisan struggle, he seems unaware that the Bosnian, Croatian and Serbian identities were of greater import for mobilization by Partisans than was 'Yugoslavia', the latter being until the final months of World War II little more than an umbrella for its component parts.

Secondly, behind this screen of what one could call Barratt Brown's 'Yugoslav nationalism' is concealed a marked bias in favour of Serbian nationalism over Croatian or Slovenian. Though the Serbian nationalist campaign began in 1986, four years before the election of President Tudjman in Croatia, Barratt Brown insists that 'nationalists in Serbia followed enthusiastically where Slovenes and Croats had led'. Milošević's campaign to recentralize Yugoslavia under Serbian leadership receives no attention whatsoever, all blame going to Croatia and Slovenia. Indeed, so unable is Barratt Brown to grasp the most basic principles of chronological sequence that he claims that 'once Croatia's independence was recognized, with no guarantees for the large Serbian minorities within Croatia's borders, war between Serbs and Croats was assured inside .Croatia' — whereas in fact recognition did not take place until after six months of war and the JNA's destruction of Vukovar and bombardment of Dubrovnik. At the same time, the absence of guarantees for the large Albanian minority within the borders of Yugoslavia does not lead him to oppose recognition of that state.

Thirdly and finally, such talk reveals Barratt Brown's own very British chauvinism. Abandoning completely the realm of reality for a fantasy world of his own making, he imagines a Papist-backed Germany recognizing Croatia and annexing Austria so as to gain access to the Adriatic en route to 'control over the oil supplies of the Middle East'. If former Communists are causing such havoc under

Tone Bringa, **Being Muslim the Bosnian Way: identity and community in a Central Bosnian village,** Princeton University Press, Princeton and London 1995, 281 pp., £13.99

Since the popular view of anthropology is that it investigates the behaviour of primitive tribal peoples, many must think that only an anthropologist could explain what has happened in Bosnia during the past four years. British newspapers have been full of punditry about 'warring tribes'; one distinguished military historian even announced, half-way through the Bosnian war, that he had found the key to the conflict when reading a book about Stone Age Indians in the Amazonian jungle. The truth is that the war in Bosnia was caused, like any other modern war, by politicians with telephones on their desks and armies at their command. Bosnian society was not tribal at all (not even in the technical sense in which northern Albania and Montenegro could be described as 'tribal' until this century). Nor was the way of life of Bosnian peasants so very different from that of other parts of rural southern Europe: southern Italy, say, or northern Portugal. Just two things made Bosnia unusual, in comparison with other southern European countries: its kaleidoscopic intermingling of three religious-ethnic communities, and the fact that one of those communities was Muslim. Perhaps those two factors help to explain the paralysis of Western understanding. Mental laziness on the part of Western commentators converted the communities into 'tribes'; and some residual prejudice may have inclined them to think that a partly Muslim country must be, ipso facto, more 'primitive'.

The only possible excuse for this style of fantasy-commentary is that, until now, there was almost nothing available in English that described the texture of ordinary life in rural Bosnia and the nature of Muslim identity there. William Lockwood's *European Moslems*, written more than twenty years ago, was the only serious study by a Western social anthropologist; but it concentrated on socio-economic relations, and said curiously little about Islam. Now, at long last, there is a book which captures both the quiddity of Bosnian village life and the peculiar nature of Muslimhood in that part of Europe. It is difficult to imagine these two tasks being better performed than they are in Tone Bringa's *Being Muslim the Bosnian Way*. For fifteen months in 1987, Bringa, a young Norwegian anthropologist, lived in a mixed Muslim-Catholic (but predominantly Muslim) village in central Bosnia. She had got permission to do this by telling the authorities in Sarajevo that she wanted to study 'women and modernization'; only when she had won the trust of the villagers did she tell them that her main interest was 'Muslim customs'. The result is a book containing a wealth of information not only about Muslim religious practices, but also about the social structures of village life, about women and, indeed, about modernization too.

Living as a kind of adoptive daughter in a Muslim household, Bringa learned about Bosnian Islam from a distinctly female perspective. Some key elements of Muslim life (circumcision, for example) are excluded by their maleness from this book. Instead, we learn about the *bula*, a figure on whom very little has been written in the West: this is the women whose duties include giving religious instruction and washing female corpses for burial. A *bula* will also preside at a *ženski tehvid*, a religious and social ceremony of prayers for the dead attended by women and held in an ordinary house. The connections between women, the household and Muslim religious identity form the main substance of this book. Bringa gives special attention to marriage and its socio-religious implications. Even when the marriage is contracted through the strange device of 'fictive elopement', she suggests, the union is never simply between two individuals: it is a bond between households and families, who are joined in a web of social and ritual practices.

Hence the resistance to 'mixed marriages' in such traditional communities. While Muslims can enjoy close friendship and neighbourliness with Catholics, the observance of small differences (in dress, household etiquette and so on) between the two groups is something that helps to constitute the sense of identity of each. Reluctance to engage in mixed marriage, therefore, is not a sign of some irreducible element of prejudice or 'ethnic hatred'; it reflects the difficulty of combining two different types of social identity in a single household. In the cities, where modern conditions have worn away those social and familial contexts, mixed marriages are common and quite unproblematical.

One other type of modernization discussed in this book also deserves special attention: the pressure from the educated and city-based Islamic authorities against those aspects of rural Muslim life which they regard as unorthodox. Divining, faith-healing, the use of amulets, prayers at the tombs of Sufi saints and other practices derived from the dervish orders: all these meet with official disapproval, in classic illustration of what the late Ernest Gellner called the eternal conflict between High Islam and Folk Islam. What this means is that the newspaper pundits who write about 'warring tribes' are no less wrong when they warn of the danger of 'fundamentalism' sweeping through the Bosnian Muslim population. The strict neo-orthodoxy of any Arab-trained 'fundamentalists', if they ever took charge of official Islam in Bosnia, would immediately set them at odds with the majority of those village Muslims who still practise their faith. That, perhaps, is not the least important of the lessons which this lucid and marvellously informative book can teach us.

Noel Malcolm

This review first appeared in The Times Literary Supplement *28 June 1996*

Norman Cigar, **Genocide in Bosnia: the policy of 'ethnic cleansing',** Texas A&M University Press, College Station 1995, 242 pp., £27.95

Of all the books I have read about the Bosnian war, none has been quite so lucidly presented, cogently argued and fully supported by a mass of carefully analysed details as Norman Cigar's *Genocide in Bosnia*. If you want just one work which explains the real nature of this war, you should read this one.

Professor Norman Cigar is a military analyst (he teaches at the Marine Corps Academy in Quantico, Virginia), but this is not a work of military history. It is, as the subtitle says, a study of 'ethnic cleansing' — of the ideological basis for expulsions and mass-murderers, of the way the policy was implemented, and, most crucially, of the way in which the outside world was persuaded, at one and the same time, that ethnic cleansing was inevitable and that it was not really happening.

This policy of wiping (or, at best, shifting) non-Serb populations off the map is not a by-product of the war; not a sideshow or an unfortunate detail. It is central to the aims of the people in Belgrade and Pale who made the war happen.

Strangely, though, the sheer enormity of these crimes has acted as a kind of alibi for the people who organized them. The outside world looks on and says: 'Nobody could just create this kind of mayhem from above; it must be the inevitable result of thousands of years of ancient ethnic hatreds.' And the more we witter on about these so-called ancient ethnic hatreds, the more we imply that the victims must be equally guilty, having presumably some ancient hatreds of their own.

Norman Cigar dispels all these myths. He shows how the ideology of an ethnically pure Serbian state was developed from above, by people who knew exactly what they were doing. Two categories of ideologists stand out in particular. One is the 'Orientalists' of Serbia, the academic specialists in Islamic affairs, who developed a kind of bogus ethnic anthropology in which the Muslims of Bosnia were classed as subhuman non-Europeans exhibiting a 'semi-Arab subculture'. Professor Cigar, who is himself a scholar of Arabic, has monitored their writings in detail; his exposé of their activities is quite devastating.

The other category, dismayingly, is the Serbian Orthodox Church. While some of the Church's priests and many of its ordinary members remained true to the basic principles of Christian charity, the same cannot be said of the most prominent men in its hierarchy, who helped to create an atmosphere of paranoid hostility towards non-Serbs and were quite happy to depict the Serb attacks on peaceful Muslim cities as desperate acts of self-defence.

The organizer of one of the most brutal paramilitary gangs, 'Arkan', has even boasted of the help he has received from the Serbian Orthodox Church in organizing, financing and arming his militia.

In the last part of the book, Norman Cigar gives a balanced and cool analysis of the policy options which are (or were) available to the West. He does not call for thousands of British or American soldiers to be sent to Bosnia, though he notes that Western air power could be a significant component of a wider strategy.

His main concern, expressed here with all the clear logic and marshalling of evidence that characterize his argument as a whole, is to show that the Bosnians could defend themselves, if only they were permitted by our politicians to obtain the weapons they so desperately need.

Noel Malcolm

A longer version of this review first appeared in
The Sunday Telegraph, *11 June 1995*

Ben Cohen and George Stamkoski, **With No Peace to Keep: UN peacekeeping and the war in the former Yugoslavia,** Media East West, London 1996, 184 pp., £10

This book provides first-class analysis of the United Nations' four-year attempt at 'peacekeeping' — a misnomer from the start but, unfortunately, a deliberate one. Its editors have got together an exceptionally well-informed team, mostly historians and journalists, including Rosemary Righter of *The Times*, Ed Vulliamy of the *Guardian*, Paul Williams, formerly an attorney-adviser in the US State Department, Roy Gutman, the American journalist winner of the Pulitzer Prize for his work on ethnic cleansing, and the British historians Noel Malcolm and Mark Almond, among others.

This analysis is multi-faceted, focusing in one section of the book on the different parts of ex-Yugoslavia, in another on different aspects of the 'humanitarian mission', in a third on the foreign countries principally involved — Britain, France, Russia and the United States. I found John Laughland's account of French policy particularly enlightening, but it would be impossible to single out every chapter in a book appropriately launched in the House of Commons.

There are gaps which should be noted and may be regretted. Despite the fact that UN activity provides the bond which holds the book together, there is no analysis offered of the attitude throughout the war of Boutros-Ghali, nor of his principal representatives, neither civilians like Akashi nor generals from Mackenzie to Smith, though they do, of course, come into the discussion in many places. There is also no section devoted to the parallel UN-sponsored activity, the negotiations in Geneva, largely controlled by David Owen. These are serious omissions. More understandably, the book does not attempt to describe the war itself, its causes, methods, course or leaders. It is an account, not of the war, but of external response to the war, and not a comprehensive analysis even of that. It does, nevertheless, provide an invaluable — and hitherto unrivalled — collection of building blocks towards a comprehensive analysis.

What it offers is indeed damning. It confirms that from early 1992 to late 1995 UN policy in Bosnia was determined almost entirely by Britain and France; moreover, it shows how Britain , France and Russia were in almost total agreement in their desire to ensure that Serbian ambitions were satisfied. The problem for the great powers was how to cling on to that policy in face of the scale of Serbian atrocities. The so-called 'humanitarian' mission was dreamed up to ensure that international clamour for something to be done was met, while ensuring that no effective political or military help would reach the Bosnian government. All three major powers wanted a strong and enlarged Serbia. None of them cared much about concentration camps, mass graves or blatant aggression, but public horror at these things required a publicized response. The dispatch of a considerable number of British and French troops to Bosnia could be used time and again to demonstrate that the powers were doing their best, while at the same time ensuring that nothing would be done — 'our boys' must not be endangered. It was a clever policy and, for a long time, it worked.

It did, however, require complementary explanation as to what was really happening and why a 'humanitarian' response alone was possible. This interpretation took the form of continual playing on the themes of civil war, ancient ethnic hatreds and a sharing of guilt by all sides. Any mention of genocide was strictly taboo. This was the line that Belgrade had always pushed to persuade the West not to intervene; it was almost avidly taken over by Western politicians.

It is easy now to see the long disastrous history of international involvement from 1992 to 1995 in terms of just another UN failure, followed finally by a NATO success; and in consequence to draw conclusions about the nature of the UN. NATO has, after all, done what the UN always refused to do — bomb Serb military targets effectively and impose a peace agreement (unfortunately an unnecessarily bad one). But the fair contrast is not between UN and NATO. Both are controlled by the same Western powers.

Earlier Security Council resolutions were, in fact, adequate for the protection of the Safe Areas and, in the end, no new resolution was added to make possible the NATO bombing campaign. The reason for UN failure was its consistent interpretation of its mandate in a minimalist way as 'peacekeeping' instead of 'peace-enforcement'; but in reality that interpretation was imposed on it by the same Western powers which had passed the resolutions in the Security Council. What actually changed in the summer of 1995 was the attitude of the American government. Where there had hitherto been no political will to bring Serb attacks to a halt, the will was now there. Anglo-French policy was replaced by American policy (assisted by Chirac's replacement of Mitterrand). US intervention has now brought peace, but it has not brought justice, and whether the one will last without the other must be questionable.

Roger Cohen, **Hearts Grown Brutal: sagas of Sarajevo,** Random House, New York 1998, 523 pp., $27.95.

On 5 June 1995, Roger Cohen was sitting in his room in the Holiday Inn, Sarajevo, when a sudden surge of electricity enabled him to switch on the television and watch Al Gore telling Larry King about Bosnian history. 'This is a tragedy that has been unfolding for some time,' observed the Vice President. 'Some would say for 500 years.'

Only 500? If developments in the political and military history of the 1990's can be traced so confidently all the way back to the 15th century, why stop there? President Clinton showed an obliging willingness to go the extra mile. 'It's tragic, it's terrible,' he empathized, 'but their enmities go back 500 years, some would say almost a thousand years.'

So there you have it: the origins of the Bosnian war can be found somewhere in the late 10th century, between, let us say, the death of Alfred the Great and the birth of Omar Khayyam. This theory, attributing the conflict to ancient ethnic hatreds, has become a matter of almost religious faith in the minds of many Western politicians and diplomats.

Cohen, who reported from Bosnia for *The New York Times* throughout the war, is too good a journalist to be satisfied for one moment with this sort of pseudo-historical flimflam. Having interviewed the local politicians and having met innumerable ordinary Bosnians, he can see that the conflict was essentially a product of modern political history, and he knows that for most people lethal hatred was the consequence of the war, not its cause. This is perhaps the most important lesson that readers will learn from *Hearts Grown Brutal*, his powerfully written, ambitious and many-layered study of the Bosnian war.

Like any journalist worth his salt, Cohen knows, too, that when Western politicians utter vague historical platitudes, they are not necessarily explaining the real reasons for their policies. The doctrine of 'ancient ethnic hatreds' was convenient for Western leaders; it lent an air of justifiability to a policy approach — of hesitancy, inaction and denial — that had already been adopted for other reasons.

Cohen is also too decent a human being to remain entirely dispassionate when considering the moral failure of the West's Bosnian policy. The last third of this book consists of a scathing catalogue of Western cowardice and hypocrisy: from the early reluctance to accept (still less to look for) evidence of concentration camps and massacres, to the final tragedy of the so-called 'safe area' of Srebrenica.

Much of this has been said before, of course. But at several key points, Cohen has important information to add. He sheds new light, for example, on the role played during the hostage crisis of June 1995 by President Jacques Chirac of France, who pushed hard (and successfully) for a policy of appeasement. And he quotes from the secret minutes of a crucial meeting between the United Nations civilian and military authorities on the ninth of that month, at which fatal misjudgments about the Serbs' plans for Srebrenica became fixed in official United Nations policy. These sections of the book alone would suffice to make it required reading for all future historians of the Bosnian war.

But what Cohen has set out to provide in this book is much more than just a catalogue of Western blunders. He is also trying to explain the meaning of the war at two different levels: in terms of human experience and at the level of longer-term Yugoslav history. The first of these tasks is accomplished by weaving into the narrative the stories of several ordinary Bosnian families.

What comes across most strongly from these personal histories is the sense of bewilderment most people felt. The outbreak of war took them by surprise, and the transformation of neighbours into enemies seemed to have no basis in their previous experience. Their favourite metaphor was that a whirlwind had come out of nowhere and blown their lives apart.

Where and why had that whirlwind been generated? Because it is hard to imagine how hatreds can be created out of nothing at all, Cohen naturally hunts around for pre-existing tensions and animosities. These he finds not in 'ancient ethnic hatreds,' but in unresolved, or unrecognized, conflicts of 20th-century Yugoslav history. He tells the story of the massacres of Serbs by extremist Ustasha Croats in World War II, of Muslim collaboration with the Nazis, and of atrocities committed by Serb Chetniks. Because this murky history was never properly confronted or acknowledged during the Communist period, he suggests, such hatreds could only intensify and fester.

Cohen's argument here is a little misleading on some points. It can hardly be claimed that the Communists swept the history of Jasenovac (the notorious Ustasha-run death camp) under the carpet, when they built a sky-high monument at the camp and bussed in schoolchildren to visit it. And the way in which Cohen has presented his material, devoting the first 100 pages of the book to the family story of a Muslim who served with the Nazi SS in the war, may give a skewed impression. Only 18,000 Muslims joined the SS, out of a population of nearly one million; most Muslims took no part in the war, though many did join the anti-Nazi Partisans during its final phase.

Sometimes Cohen comes close to suggesting that this 20th-century history caused the Bosnian war, by creating psychological pressures that found their natural release in violence. This argument would seem not so very different from the 'ancient ethnic hatreds' thesis, merely substituting modern political ones.

More often, however, Cohen presents the causal mechanism the other way around: low-level prejudices were transformed into red-hot hatreds quite deliberately (and, I would add, wounds of war that had genuinely healed were violently reopened), for modern political purposes. If Cohen had known Bosnia long before the war, he would be even more certain of the truth of this explanation.

As it is, the bewilderment of those ordinary Bosnians, caught up in Slobodan Milošević's (and, later, Franjo Tudjman's) whirlwind, must stand as sufficient testimony to the tragic non-inevitability of the Bosnian war. Readers of *Hearts Grown Brutal* may also be bewildered by the sheer intensity of the violence it describes; but at the same time they will be informed, challenged and moved by this powerful and richly human book.

Noel Malcolm

This review first appeared in The New York Times, *19 October 1998*

Zlata Filipović, **Zlata's Diary: a child's life in Sarajevo,**
Viking, London 1994, 185 pp., £7.95

James Grant (ed.) **I Dream of Peace: images of war by
children of former Yugoslavia,** UNICEF/HarperCollins,
London 1994, £8.99

In one celebrated dramatized production of Anne Frank's *Diaries* it
is said that the audience was so inflamed by the sheer creepiness of
the heroine, played by Pia Zadora, that, when the Gestapo broke
into the house, demanding 'Where is she?', the audience responded
lustily: 'She's upstairs'. It is a bit like that with *Zlata's Diary*.

There has been a lot lately about the possibility that the diary has
been given a few grown-up touches to lend it political verisimilitude.
I think that is perfectly plausible. But it is the undoctored passages
that cloy. Zlata is the only child of a well-off family in Sarajevo who
watches unlimited satellite television, and says things like: 'I've
finished studying and tomorrow I can go to school bravely, without
being afraid of getting a bad grade. I deserve a good grade because I
studied all weekend and I didn't even go out to play with my friends
in the park.'

Yet you would need a heart of stone not to sympathize with her
distress at her favourite trees being chopped down in the park for
fuel or the birthday party where she is given vitamin tablets and a
small bar of soap as a present.

Yes, there is a version of the war here. But rather than coming to
grips with a situation in Europe where borders have been changed
by force, and, from the start of the war in Croatia through the worst
of the war in Bosnia, either facing up to military intervention, or
refraining at least from intervening on the wrong side by the arms
embargo, we have allowed ourselves to be distracted by poignant
little girls like Irma and Zlata, and many other images of distress.
We have been captivated by the symptoms of the war, not its causes.
Zlata is not to blame for her ingenuous confessions. But it is
worrying that so much concern is lavished on one Zlata, while the
process whereby 200,000 of her fellow citizens died unjustly and
horribly in the heart of Europe goes uncorrected.

I have rather more time for another product of the war from the
hands of pathetic children who are among its victims. *I Dream of
Peace* is a little book of pictures and prose from the children who
have lived through the war and seen some of the worst of it. For an

idea of the psychological disturbance that has afflicted some of the most vulnerable of the ethnically cleansed, look no further. Take this, from Alik, 13, a refugee: 'From the group they chose the ones they were going to kill. They picked my uncle and a neighbour. Then they machine-gunned them to death. After that, the soldiers put the women in the front cars of the train and the men in the back. As the train started moving they disconnected the back cars and took the men off and to the camps. I saw it all.' Poor child.

Melanie McDonagh

This review first appeared in The Tablet, *7 May 1994*

Misha Glenny, **The Fall of Yugoslavia: the third Balkan war,** Penguin, London 1992, 194 pp., £5.99

Misha Glenny plays the sophisticate. He goes to great lengths to show his credentials as a linguist and historian, but always manages to trip himself up. For example, in the first eight pages of his narrative, he wallows in South Slavic exoticism, preferring terms influenced or used by the natives — like 'partizans', 'Slavonija', and 'Vojna Krajina' — to the standard English partisans, Slavonia, or military frontier. Such an appearance of erudition does not protect him from glaring errors. For example, the Knin area of northern Dalmatia was never part of the Hapsburg Military Frontier, or, more properly, of the Croatian-Slavonian Military Frontier; the inhabitants of the latter were predominantly Croats (60 per cent in 1857) and not Serbs as Glenny intimates; the situation in Knin was different, but even there Serbs had a threadbare majority (54 per cent in the Knin county in 1921). Similarly, the migration of Serbian patriarch Arsenije III Čarnojević to southern Hungary had virtually nothing to do with the Serb presence in Banija, Kordun, Lika, and the Knin area; hence, the objections to the importance of Čarnojević's migration for those areas are not 'disingenuous and unsubstantiated' but quite correct. Since it would take pages to cite and rebut all of Glenny's errors, I shall not harp on them any further. Suffice it to say that he is a far better reporter than a historian.

That is precisely the trouble with Glenny's book. He is reliable — or at least amusing — when he reports and not nearly as reliable when he analyses. His book provides a sort of camera view of developments in the former Yugoslavia. Action is where Glenny is, and he is all over the place. In fact, there is too much Glenny in the book. He keeps interjecting his persona by reminding us that he is a coward, that he does not know how to use arms, that this or that person pleases him or does not, that he has definite views on East European hotel architecture, that hot weather causes him to perspire, and so on. The question is why a reader would wish to know anything at all about a British journalist in his mid-30s. More important, would it not be more useful to know a great deal more about the sources of the Yugoslav meltdown? Insights into the mentality of Ratko Mladić might be telling, but they will not provide answers to the larger questions.

Glenny's book is charming and even skilful, but it is not a work of history or politics. It only scratches the surface. Something is missing from it. The missing part is the written word. Apart from a brief and obscure note on the Memorandum of the Serbian Academy of Sciences and Arts (1986), a key political document, as well as a few references to the press, there is no evidence that Glenny read anything at all about or from the former Yugoslavia. As a consummate insider, he does not read; he converses. As a cameraman, he does not analyse; he focuses his Cyclopean eye on individuals and their interactions. There is no ideology here. No church or religion, either. No economy. No society. No culture. No history, minus a few encyclopaedia references. What we have is a journey that started in Knin, but should have started in Belgrade. We have consequences, but not the sources. We also have a set of opinions, the two most important being: 1. that Tudjman is co-responsible for the outbreak of the war (only relatively true, and not necessarily for the reasons outlined by Glenny); and 2. that Germany's recognition of Slovenia and Croatia was disastrous and widened the conflict (by now an accepted myth, but untrue even in terms of Glenny's own evidence).

Ivo Banac

This review is taken from a longer review article in Foreign Policy, *Winter 1993-94*

Heller, Yves, **Des brasiers mal éteints: un reporter dans les guerres yougoslaves 1991-95,** Le Monde Éditions, Paris 1997, 340 pp., FF 120

There are two sorts of experts on the recent history of the wars in Yugoslavia. One consists of decision-makers, or people who regard themselves as such: diplomats and politicians. The memoirs of Lord Owen, for example, give the impression that the whole drama of the Balkans was played out in Geneva, London and Washington, in the form of discreet negotiations between civilized if somewhat Machiavellian characters.

The other sort are the people on the ground who, day after day and sometimes at the risk of their lives, have trudged through the battlefields and ruins, seeing and talking to the victims and front-line actors, whose fears and anxieties they have understood and reported. This approach enables them to grasp as it were from within the internal logic of the drama, and sometimes even to predict future developments.

Yves Heller, who died recently, was a representative of the second category: he followed the whole conflict as a senior reporter for *Le Monde,* and this book is a collection of the resulting articles. In fact the subtitle, setting the chronological limits as 1991-1995, does not really do justice to the scope of the work: the earliest pieces, dealing with the first Kosovo crisis, date from 1990, while the last ones, covering the post-Dayton Accords period, were written in 1996. Heller thus emerges as one of those who saw the crisis coming some time before it exploded into public awareness; as early as 7 February 1990 — a year and a half before the guns started to speak — his researches in Prishtina and Belgrade led him to warn of the threat posed to the stability of the Yugoslav federation by the 'Serbian daydreams' being stirred up by Milošević.

After Kosovo, Heller travelled widely through the former Yugoslavia. From Croatia in 1991, he gives a very concrete account of an atrocious war that passed almost unnoticed in France, with the sudden unleashing of Serbian military power and 'irregulars' against the unarmed and helpless population of Croatia, and the dramas of Dubrovnik and Vukovar; but also the mistakes and hesitations of the Zagreb government.

In 1992 he was in Bosnia, describing the confused beginnings of the war in that country and the horrors of the siege of Sarajevo. The following year, in central Bosnia, he witnessed at close quarters the birth of the Croatian-Bosnian conflict in all its complexity, reporting the disarray of both populations, the anxiety in Vitez and other Croatian enclaves, and massacres like the one carried out in the Muslim village of Ahmići by the Croatian HVO. Behind the factual reportage there is always political analysis, throwing light on the background to the conflict, the Croatian wish to seize territory by jumping the gun on the Vance-Owen plan, and the military reversal that led to the Croatian defeat in central Bosnia at the hands of Bosnian forces.

In 1994-95 he was again in Bosnia, producing numerous striking snapshots of Sarajevo, Mostar and other places, but also (on 23 June 1995) a premonitory analysis of the new tactics adopted by the Croatians and Bosnians (now reconciled, willingly or unwillingly, by American diplomacy), which were to lead to their victories later that summer. Then came Dayton, which brought the fighting to an end but included an 'extravagant constitutional arrangement concocted in the big capitals' whose bogus nature the author has no difficulty in exposing.

There are some events that Heller did not witness directly: the 'ethnic cleansing' of northern Bosnia in spring 1992, with large-scale massacres, concentration camps, rapes and expulsions, was carried out in regions to which journalists had no access. But this serious reporter brought it to his readers' attention very early on, citing statements collected from refugees. One example is the massacre committed by the Serbian police at Zaklopača, in the commune of Vlasenica, on 16 May 1992: 'Aida Hodić, aged sixty-three, recalls: "It was five in the afternoon when the policemen, accompanied by militia reservists, got out of their cars and started firing. Half an hour later a hundred and fifty villagers were dead or dying in pools of their own blood... the corpses of men, women and children lay where they had fallen for three days, until the Serbs buried them in a common grave".' This piece appeared in *Le Monde* of 10 June 1992, a fortnight before François Mitterrand's visit to Sarajevo. Is it possible that our President, who believed that the Bosnians' only urgent need was for humanitarian aid, was not a *Le Monde* reader? Heller notes elsewhere (30 November 1992) the opinion of the Serbian general Momir Talić that Mitterrand's visit 'prevented an international˙ military intervention against the Serbian forces'.

The author returns to the massacres in northern Bosnia in articles published on 21 June 1995, covering the report submitted to the UN in May 1994 by the commission of experts chaired by Cherif Bassiouni. He underlines the systematic and premeditated character of these massacres. His reading of this report also enables him to criticize the policy applied by the international community — promoted especially by diplomats like Lord Owen — consisting of being 'inflexible on the concept of impartiality' and treating all the 'warring parties' as morally equal.

Of the many concrete observations with which this work is crammed, I have a particular interest in experiences I share, more or less, with the author, whose accounts of them I find strikingly true: the long bus journey to Sarajevo in the winter of 1994-95 (*A bus called Sarajevo*, 15-16 February 1995); or the passage through Croatia's '*Krajina, accursed land*' (26 February 1995), a region twice 'cleansed' — by the Serbs in 1991 and the Croats in 1995 — and now utterly devastated and almost empty. The absolute and unarguable legitimacy of this Croatian reconquest certainly cannot justify the reprisals that followed it.

Humanity vividly sketched from life, and penetrating political analysis: the combination of these two approaches gives Yves Heller's book a special value.

Paul Garde

This review, translated here by John Howe, first appeared in
Le Monde *9 May 1997*

Jan Willem Honig and Norbert Both, **Srebrenica: record of a war crime,** Penguin, London 1996, 204 pp., £6.99

The fall of the Muslim enclave of Srebrenica to Bosnian Serb forces in July 1995 and the subsequent massacre of thousands of its male inhabitants — civilian and military — proved to be a turning point in the war. Flushed by their success in eastern Bosnia, Bosnian Serb and Croatian Serb forces turned their attention to the Bihać pocket in the northwest of Bosnia. It was an enclave too far. In early August 1995, Croatian forces — armed and trained with United States assistance — launched a lightning assault and smashed the 'Serb Republic of the Krajina', thus precipitating the flight, though not the massacre, of over 100,000 refugees. At about the same time, the Republican-dominated US Congress, stirred by the harrowing scenes of the survivors of Srebrenica clutching their pitifully antiquated weaponry, voted to repeal the arms embargo against the sovereign state of Bosnia-Herzegovina. It was not least this unprecedented challenge to executive control of US foreign policy which helped finally to propel President Clinton into a campaign of coordinated air strikes against Bosnian Serb communications and arms dumps.

Jan Willem Honig's and Norbert Both's study is an impressive analysis of the circumstances and extent of the massacre. They do not mince their words: Srebrenica is described as 'the largest single war crime in Europe since the second world war'. Moreover, the executions were not spontaneous but 'orchestrated'. As the authors painstakingly demonstrate, the efficient and ruthless rounding-up, deportation and murder of such a large number of victims was 'preplanned' by the Serb political and military leadership, particularly General Mladić, the supreme commander, who not only organized but oversaw the massacre. In support of their argument Honig and Both have marshaled an unanswerable case, using evidence from an array of witnesses: the Dutch UN troops stationed in the enclave, journalists, satellite photographs, radio intercepts, survivor and even perpetrator testimony.

They also effectively dispose of the notion that the men of Srebrenica were themselves 'war criminals' felled by the righteous wrath of the victorious Serbs. Certainly, the Bosnian garrison under Naser Orić had been guilty of atrocities, especially during the winter of 1992/3. But these crimes were reactive; they are in no sense comparable with the calculated campaign of aggression and ethnic displacement waged by the Serbs. Besides it was only the skill and ruthlessness of Orić which had saved Srebrenica from early extinction at the hands of its Serb neighbours in 1992. Moreover, Bosnian raiding parties violating the ceasefire were a direct result of Serb bad faith in blocking aid convoys, which compelled Orić to forage for food.

Most importantly, Honig and Both are sure about the aim of the massacre, which was part of a systematic programme to 'cleanse' the area of Muslims. Hence, they argue: 'The Serbs were also guilty of crimes against humanity', in particular genocide, as defined by the UN Convention of 1948, which covered any act 'committed with intent to destroy, in whole or in part, a national, ethnical, racial or religious group, as such.'

Unfortunately, the book is seriously compromised by two pieties. The first is the authors' desire to explain and exculpate the behaviour of their Dutch compatriots, whom the Serbs shrugged aside contemptuously during the assault and massacre. According to Honig and Both, the Dutch soldiers were 'not cowards', but victims of an impossible situation. Yet their own book provides enough evidence to the contrary. Doubtless there were many individual acts of courage, such as the superbly unflappable (female) fighter pilot who participated in the belated air strike. Doubtless, too, the position of the lightly armed Dutch forces was very difficult. But even the most sympathetic reader can easily discern a depressing blend of fear, cynicism, indifference, defeatism and simple racism among the Dutch troops, who had been unambiguously ordered by UN headquarters in Zagreb 'to take up blocking positions' against the advancing Serbs. Their battle morale is summed up by one sergeant's comment: 'Everybody got a fright. You could easily get killed in such an operation.' There were, in fact, no Dutch fatalities except the bolting private killed in desperation by the Bosnians. They ran away. And in their haste they refused to take many of their Bosnian employees with them, not least in order to avoid 'provoking the Serbs'; these were left to certain deportation and death. By contrast, other organizations such as Médecins Sans Frontières, and even the UN High Commission for Refugees, who were less frantically concerned to save their own skins, evacuated many of their Bosnian helpers. But perhaps most seriously, the Dutch forbore to raise a full-scale alarm about the continuing massacre until all their men had been brought to safety.

The second piety is to the whole UN mediation effort in the former Yugoslavia, and in particular Lord Owen, whom Both served as a research assistant. No harsh words are to be found concerning their performance. For example, a bumbling bureaucrat like Yasushi Akashi is described merely as 'cautious by nature... highly experienced... ever mindful of the importance of compromise' and so on. The Americans, by contrast, are singled out for sharp criticism. US 'Serb-bashers' are blamed for failing to secure a compromise settlement before the assault on Srebrenica; for insisting on a lifting of the arms embargo against the Bosnian government; for an unrealistic faith in air power; for failing to commit ground troops of their own; and for vetoing UN withdrawal from the 'safe areas'. Doubtless the Americans made mistakes, but they were to be proved right on the main points in August to October 1995. It was possible to deter attacks on a 'safe area' by air power; this had not only been obvious, as the authors concede, when it seemed a likelihood at Srebrenica, but was also demonstrated by the successful guarantee of Goražde, another Bosnian 'safe area', once the albatross of its British garrison had withdrawn. It was possible, *pace* Owen, to turn the military tide by arming the Croatians and Bosnians. And it was possible, *pace* a dismissive footnote by Honig and Both, to facilitate this by attacking ground targets.

In short, this book must be approached with caution. As a pioneering study of the execution and purpose of the massacre at Srebrenica it can hardly be bettered. But as an interpretation of the baleful role of the international community — and DutchBat's contribution — it will not do.

Brendan Simms

This review first appeared in The Times Higher Education Supplement, *17 January 1997*

Michael Ignatieff, **The Warrior's Honor: ethnic war and the modern conscience,** Chatto and Windus, London 1998, 224 pp., £10.99

Between 1993 and 1997 Michael Ignatieff travelled through what he calls the landscapes of modern ethnic war: the former Yugoslavia, central Africa and Afghanistan. Like all good travellers, he was using these journeys to explore not only the world outside him, but also that inner world of assumptions and beliefs that he carried around in his head. So it is no criticism of *The Warrior's Honor,* his resultant collection of essays about war, nationalism and Western intervention, to say that it tells us more about the author than about any (or all) of the places he visited.

His most basic assumption is his belief in the fundamental equality of human beings. He holds that all human differences are minor, when set against the things we have in common; and from those common features of mankind there springs a set of 'human rights' which belong equally to us all.

Once upon a time this was a subversive doctrine. Nowadays, the intellectual *avant-garde* sneers at it as part of a discredited 'Enlightenment project', and the whole idea of universal values is beginning to sound positively old-fashioned. So it is quite refreshing to read an unabashed defence of it here, especially a defence by someone who admits that this doctrine of universal human rights also depends on a kind of fiction, a deliberate ignoring of the real differences which we encounter in our day-to-day experience of other people.

Ignatieff has no difficulty in showing that, when it comes to organizing any particular state, the fictions of liberal universalism are preferable to the fictions of nationalism. A state based on the supremacy of one national or ethnic group (Hutus, say, or Serbs) will be a less pleasant place than a state based on the liberal doctrine of equal citizenship.

But the difficult question is: how can we believe in universal values, without also believing that we should take action to defend those values universally? If a citizen of Essex has the same rights as a citizen of Yorkshire not because he is British but because he is a human being, then why should the British Government confine its protection of those rights merely to the human beings who happen to live in Britain? Is it not equally obliged to defend all the human beings in Rwanda, Tibet and East Timor?

This is really the central question of the book; and yet Ignatieff never gives it a proper answer. Of course, when he visits places where the West (or the UN) has intervened on the ground, he does treat the intervention as deeply problematic. Many critics argue that intervention either has no effect, or makes things even worse; Ignatieff takes these arguments seriously, while coming down, in the end, against them. But his underlying assumption remains unexplored and unchallenged — that, if we can do more good than ill by intervening, we are under a positive duty to intervene.

Among those critics who say that intervention is a complete waste of time, one rather facile argument is especially popular: the claim that wars such as the one in Bosnia are just endemic 'ethnic' conflicts, the inevitable expressions of ancient ethnic or religious hatreds. Ignatieff deals well with this claim (and with its most fashionable exponent, Samuel 'Clash of Civilizations' Huntington), pointing out that these so-called ancient hatreds are modern creations, largely created by political processes from above.

The key development, he suggests, is the break-up of the state: that political event is generally the cause, not the consequence, of local nationalisms. And so, unusually for someone in the left-liberal tradition, Ignatieff ends up recommending that states should be strengthened, not undermined or disbanded. Surveying the wreckage of Rwanda and Afghanistan, he writes: 'More than aid or emergency relief, more than peacekeepers, these societies need states, with professional armies under the command of trained leaders.'

Again, this brings us to a difficult question which Ignatieff fails to answer. If a strong state is so desirable, can he really afford to reject the thing that binds most successful states together — the sense of national identity that comes from a shared language and culture? How strong is a state going to be if people are taught to think of it merely as a geographical area containing a certain number of human beings endowed with universal rights?

Again and again in this book, one gets the impression that Michael Ignatieff breaks off his argument when the questions get difficult. The things he says well (in thoughtful, finely turned prose, with the occasional arresting metaphor) are, on the whole, the things that are easy to say: about the 'seductiveness of moral disgust', the 'narcissism of minor differences', and so on.

Unfortunately, when he writes about the war in the former Yugoslavia (the main example referred to throughout the book), he fails to do one other easy thing — to check his facts. The war in Bosnia did not start in May 1992. The Serbs who fled from the

Krajina in 1995 did not number 600,000. It is not true that by 1990 'more than a quarter' of the population of Yugoslavia identified themselves as 'Yugoslavs' (the correct figure, from the 1991census, is three percent).

And it is simply grotesque to say, of the Serb-run concentration camps in northern Bosnia in 1992, that 'the camps that the media actually got to see were not death camps but transit camps for civilian detainees whom the Serbs hoped to send into exile'. The very first camp visited by a group of Western journalists was Omarska, where several thousand Muslim prisoners were shot or beaten to death.

It is quite false to say that the Bosnian Muslims failed to keep 'their part of the bargain', which was to demilitarize all the UN-declared 'safe areas': no such condition was imposed by the UN. And it is frustrating, to put it mildly, to reach the end of a book about intervention without having found a single discussion of the most important Western intervention actually carried out during the Bosnian war: the imposition of an arms embargo, which prevented the victims from defending themselves.

Noel Malcolm

This review first appeared in The Sunday Telegraph,
25 January 1998

John R. Lampe, **Yugoslavia as History — twice there was a country,** Cambridge University Press, Cambridge 1996, 421 pp., £14.95

The war that broke out in the former Yugoslavia in the 1990s is undoubtedly one of the most misunderstood of modern history. Beyond the disinformation of Western governments and the ignorance of journalists, the reason for this must be sought in the failure of historians and other intellectuals to explain the history of Yugoslavia that led to the war. Textbook histories of Socialist Yugoslavia written prior to its collapse are remarkable in their neglect of the national question; the authors preferring to concentrate on the Tito regime's handling of domestic and diplomatic crises and its economic achievements or failures. The need for a reevaluation of the history of Yugoslavia in light of the recent war is therefore pressing.

John R. Lampe's textbook *Yugoslavia as History — twice there was a country* at first appears promising. In his introduction, Lampe indicates some of the long-term structural and ideological contradictions that plagued the Yugoslav project from its birth to its demise, and stresses that a united Yugoslavia was viable only when political, economic and military conditions were favourable. His narrative is 'federalized' throughout, with different sections dealing with the different peoples and regions of Yugoslavia, an improvement on the 'unitary' structure of many earlier textbooks.

Unfortunately, however, Lampe does not appear qualified for his task, outside of the economic sphere in which he specializes. His text is riddled with startling omissions and factual errors. He gives an overview of the history of the Yugoslav peoples since the middle ages, but the Kosova Albanians do not enter the story until the Balkan Wars of 1912-13; his account of Yugoslav unification in 1918 omits any mention of Montenegro's union with Serbia; his account of the 1928 crisis in Yugoslavia makes no reference to the formation in Zagreb of a separate parliament by dissident Croatian and Croatian Serb deputies; his account of World War II treats each region separately but leaves out Macedonia; and the watershed 1981 demonstrations in Kosova (or their violent suppression) might as well not have taken place. He states that the borders of Ottoman Bosnia did not change between 1699 and 1878, though they changed in 1718, 1739 and 1833; that Srem was given to the Croatian Banovina in 1939, when only the western part was; and that the leader of the White Eagles in 1992 was Vojislav Šešelj, though it was actually Mirko Jović.

Lampe's approach is also frequently one-sided. When discussing the civil war in Yugoslavia during World War II, for instance, he refers to the atrocities committed by the Ustashe and the Partisans, but not to those committed by the Chetniks especially in northern Dalmatia and in Bosnia-Herzegovina (not just against Croats and Muslims, but also against Serbs who refused to join the Chetnik ranks). In this context it is worth pointing out that Knin, which Lampe mentions only as the site of Ustasha atrocities, after June 1941 when it came under full Italian control became a Chetnik stronghold and remained so practically until its capture by the Partisans on 3 December 1944; these Chetniks, moreover, were not just local men but part of Mihailović's general forces fighting to create an ethnically pure Greater Serbia.

In describing the descent into war of the 1980s and 90s, Lampe is like many sympathizers with the Titoist project unable to confront the awful truth: that the Socialist Federal Yugoslav state was not the impartial guarantor of peace and equality between its six constituent republics, a Hobbesian leviathan sitting on the lid of a Balkan pressure-cooker; but was itself an expression of an unsolved national question and an actor in Yugoslavia's demise. Lampe consequently blames the decentralizing aspects of the 1974 constitution for giving the republics freedom to bring down Yugoslavia. The devolution of power to the republics, which would 'stoke the fires of ethnic self-interest and exclusivism', both weakened the federal government's ability to respond to the economic crisis of the 1980s, and gave free reign to rivalry among the republican Communist parties that 'turned into full blown ethnic politics by the late 1980s'. At the same time, Lampe describes this 'ethnic politics' purely in terms of conflicts between the national groups within each republic, as though the policies of the Yugoslav government, the Yugoslav People's Army (JNA) and the Serbian leadership had no bearing on Croatia's treatment of its Serb minority, or on relations between Muslim, Croat and Serb political parties within Bosnia.

Lampe writes of the harassment of Serb minorities by Croats and Kosova Albanians, but makes no mention of the Yugoslav People's Army's bloody suppression of Albanian protests in 1988-9 or its use to close down the Kosova provincial assembly. He writes of the mass Serb demonstrations that toppled the Vojvodina, Montenegro and Kosova governments, but omits to mention that they were organized by Milošević's police — all this 'ethnic politics' taking place well before the elections of 1990. He writes of the sacking of Croatian Serbs from the police, the administration and many firms in Croatia in 1990-91, but says nothing about the far more massive expulsion in Kosova during the immediately preceding period of tens of thousands of Albanians from the administration, the police, the institutions of education and indeed all areas of employment. Worst of all, he entirely omits to mention the fact that by June 1990 the JNA was already organizing an armed rebellion in Croatia, based on part of the Croatian Serb population, using violence against Croatian Serbs who did not wish to join the undertaking, and with the aim of annexing a large part of the country to Serbia. Lampe is equally silent about the crucial facts pertaining to the aggression against Bosnia-Herzegovina. Namely, that the arming of Croatian Serbs was followed almost at once by the arming of sections of the Bosnian Serb population; that 'Republika Srpska' was established in ethnically mixed territories; and that it was created well in advance of the country's declaration of independence. All this preparation for war, moreover, like the attack on Slovenia in June 1991, took place while the Federal government of Ante Marković — whose programme supposedly represented a way to avoid the conflict — was in office.

Furthermore, Lampe appears unaware of the contradiction in his own thesis: namely, why a conflict between multi-ethnic republics over economic resources and constitutional prerogatives should culminate in the 'civil war' transcending republican boundaries that he describes, between the Bosnian government and the leadership of the principal Bosnian Serb political party or between the Croatian government and Croatian Serb rebels. Are we talking here of an interstate conflict between the six republics, or of a series of distinct civil wars between ethnic groups within each republic?

Lampe appears unaware of the difference, claiming that in 1989-90: 'Krajina Serbs staged their own confrontations with local Croats and, encouraged by the Milošević media, began to demand autonomy within Croatia, cultural if part of Yugoslavia and political if not. A direct Serb-Croat confrontation had always threatened the very survival of any Yugoslavia, from the first such fatal intersection in 1927-28 forward.' Yet 1927-28 saw an alliance between Croats and Croatian Serbs against Belgrade, whereas 1990 according to Lampe saw an alliance of Croatian Serbs and Belgrade against Croatia. Such paradoxes are only obscured by talk of 'ethnic politics', a wholly meaningless term by which Lampe absolves

David Owen, **Balkan Odyssey,** Indigo, London 1996, 436 pp., £8.99

The first duty of any reviewer is to say whether the book under review will be of interest to the general reader. In the case of Lord Owen's *Balkan Odyssey* this poses an unusual dilemma.

On the one hand this is clearly a book for specialists in Bosnian affairs and international diplomacy. General readers will quickly weary of the blow-by-blow accounts of conferences and reports to committees, where every blow sends a shower of acronyms into the air like sparks from a blacksmith's anvil: VOPP, JAP, ICFY, UNSCR, UNPA and so on.

On the other hand, this book will hold an extraordinary fascination for anyone who is interested not in diplomacy but in human psychology. Seldom have all the syndromes of resentment and retrospective self-justification been so thoroughly exposed to public view. Not until Sir Edward Heath writes his long-awaited memoirs, will we ever have a chance to study pique on such a monumental scale.

The problem is that in order to appreciate and interpret the display of symptoms in Lord Owen's case, you do also need a specialist knowledge of recent Bosnian history. Only then will you be able to spot all the ways in which Lord Owen's account depends on factual error, false logic and sheer omission.

Self-justification comes naturally to Lord Owen: he has, one might say, a lot to justify himself about. Most commentators would agree that his entire mission in ex-Yugoslavia has been a failure, and that his attempt to bully the US government in public was cack-handed; many regard his famous Vance-Owen Peace Plan (the VOPP) as having encouraged the vicious Croat-Muslim conflict in 1993; some have criticized the methods he used to put pressure on the Bosnian Government; and a great many observers think he should have resigned or been dismissed after his VOPP was finally rejected by the Serbs.

But Lord Owen sets about his self-justification with surprising zest. His first defence against the general charge of failure is a novel one. He tells us that, secretly, he always favoured a completely different solution anyway, a solution which nobody was prepared to consider: redrawing the borders of Bosnia, Croatia and Serbia.

Actually, the redrawing of borders was being not only considered but carried out — at enormous cost in human suffering — by Serb politicians and gunmen. To justify what they were doing, those

Serbs put out bogus claims about how the borders of Bosnia and Croatia had been arbitrarily invented by Tito. Such claims are put forward also in the very first section of Owen's book. According to Milovan Djilas, Owen tells us, the borders were sometimes drawn quickly 'during a march' in the middle of the Second World War, and were 'often arbitrary'.

Any reader with an elementary knowledge of Yugoslav history will be puzzled by this: they will know that the borders were settled by a commission headed by Djilas, who at that time was Tito's right-hand man, after the war; that it spent months considering points of detail; and that it restored the historic borders of Bosnia which dated back to 18th- and 19th-century treaties.

If they look up the passage in one of Djilas's books which Owen cites as evidence for his claim, they will find that the decision made 'during a march' was not about drawing borders, but about the status of Bosnia as a republic. Nor does Djilas say that this decision was made 'arbitrarily'; it was made for good reasons, and would no doubt have been made whether marching, standing still or sitting down.

Again, discussing the Serb-held Croatian 'Krajina', another of his candidates for border changes, Lord Owen chides 'commentators' for having failed to understand that the Krajina, which included 'the Serb-inhabited areas of northern Dalmatia', had never been governed from Zagreb. He seems unaware that northern Dalmatia was never part of the Krajina, and that the entire Krajina was brought under Croatian administration as long ago as the 1870s.

Those who think these are trivial points should pause to consider the feelings of Bosnians or Croatians who had to watch the fate of their countries being influenced by a man whose head was filled with such errors — errors which happened to match quite closely the claims of Serb propaganda. The citizens of the republic of Macedonia will have similar feelings when they find Lord Owen endorsing equally false Greek propaganda claims about the printing of a picture of a 'Greek castle' on Macedonian stamps. All this from a man who chides President Clinton for his inadequate grasp of Balkan history.

But then, factual accuracy is not Lord Owen's strong point. Just a few examples of his errors must suffice here. On the question of British military involvement in Bosnia, he declares that the Government's position was strongly influenced by British public opinion, 'where there was never anything remotely approaching a majority for becoming a combatant'. The truth is that many public-opinion polls indicated just such a majority: on 15 April 1993, for example, the *Daily Telegraph* reported on its front page: 'Nearly two-thirds of people questioned by Gallup about Bosnia believe that an international force should intervene to enforce peace, and that British troops should take part.'

Lord Owen is capable of equally glaring inaccuracies even when stating what his own opinions were at the time. He insists that, as a negotiator, he was constantly emphasizing 'the dangers of inaction'; on the very first page of this book he announces that 'the killing and maiming made it impossible to justify waiting until the fighting petered out into an exhausted peace'. What he said at the time (in a public speech delivered in Dublin on 16 November 1993: see *Bosnia Report* No 2, pp. 1-2) was, however, completely different: 'As physicians and surgeons we have long been aware of the dangers of simply responding to the cry to "do something". All too often we know that an illness has to work its way through the system. As a protective mechanism the medical profession has developed the skill of masterly inactivity . . . politicians need some of the same skills.'

Again, discussing General Morillon's visit to Srebrenica in March 1993, Owen writes that he 'found himself stuck there, in effect a hostage, having been refused permission to leave by the Muslim soldiers within the enclave'. The truth, as recorded in some detail by Morillon himself, is that he was never 'refused permission to leave' by soldiers: he was detained for some hours by a crowd of women and children. He slipped past this crowd during the hours of darkness, but, on reaching the outskirts of the town, decided of his own volition to return (*Croire et oser,* pp.172-4).

Another curious error is made when Owen refers to the fact that large numbers of Serb military helicopters were crossing freely from Serbia into Serb-held territory near Srebrenica during February l995. He describes the incident as follows: 'The Russians felt that the helicopter controversy, where the UN Military Observers watching the Serb radar screen at Belgrade airport had picked up tracks of what might have been helicopters flying from Bosnia to Serbia, was designed to discredit Milošević. Investigation by experts from Contact Group countries was inconclusive.'

The truth is that 62 helicopter sorties were observed, visually, by UNPROFOR personnel in the Srebrenica area: 10 helicopters flying simultaneously on 2 February, 6 on the morning of 3 February, 15 that afternoon, and so on. They entered the area flying in a westerly or south-westerly direction, which strongly suggested that they had just crossed the Serbian border (these details are from the UNPROFOR log, printed as an annex to Security Council report S/1995/6/Add.8, and reproduced in *Globus*, 24 February 1995). The Belgrade authorities denied UN personnel access to radar screens which could have demonstrated that the flights came from Serbian territory (see the briefing note of the American mission at the UN, reproduced in the same article).

What is the significance of the fact that Owen has got these details entirely the wrong way round? The answer may be that, having set up a small, inadequately staffed monitoring mission to report on Milošević's so-called 'sealing' of the Serbian-Bosnian border, Owen found that it was criticized by the US administration for failing to notice large-scale violations (which, of course, made nonsense of the policy of trust in Milošević on which Owen's diplomatic efforts were now based). He objected to such criticisms, which he describes as having 'undermined' his monitors. Hence, perhaps, Owen's mis-remembered or revised version of the 'helicopter controversy', in which those aircraft are downgraded from real, visible helicopters to uncertain deductions from traces on a screen, and in which Milošević's friendly air-traffic controllers continue to give the UN their unfailing support.

For, in the end, the only way to make sense of this book is to look at everything it contains through the spectacles of Lord Owen's retrospective self-justification. Facts which might not reflect well on his judgement are passed over at remarkable speed. The two most important examples of this concern the two civil wars which caused so much suffering to Bosnian people: the war between Abdić's forces and the Bosnian Army in the Bihać enclave, and the Croat-Muslim war of 1993-4 In both cases, competent observers have judged that Owen may have contributed (indirectly, of course, and unintentionally, no doubt) to the fomenting of these subsidiary wars. And yet his defence is either to ignore the criticism, or to offer only the most perfunctory of replies.

In the case of Abdić, the criticism has been frequently stated, most recently by Allan Little and Laura Silber. In the summer of 1993, they say, Owen and Stoltenberg took steps to weaken Izetbegović's position on the Bosnian Presidency. 'At their invitation, Fikret Abdić emerged from a long silence in the Bihać enclave to challenge Izetbegović for the leadership of Bosnia's Muslims. The mediators [Owen and Stoltenberg] believed that Abdić would cut a deal with the Serbs and Croats on partition ... Given a boost by international attempts to bring him into the game,

Fikret Abdić declared his own state ... Another front line emerged, and war erupted between Muslims in the Bihać enclave' (*The Death of Yugoslavia*, pp. 337-9).

Owen's comment on his encouragement of Abdić is confined to a single sentence: 'We [Owen and Stoltenberg] had urged Abdić to stay in the collective Presidency and warned him that his influence would go if he broke away ... while within the Presidency his influence was legitimate and benefited from his realism.' Informed readers will recognize just how tortuously coded that final phrase is; but casual readers will be none the wiser.

On the stimulating of the Croat-Muslim war in 1993, the criticism of Owen was made by no less an authority than Tadeusz Mazowiecki, the UN Human Rights Rapporteur, who observed that the Vance-Owen Plan was acting as a stimulus to Croat-Muslim fighting in central Bosnia (see the report in *The Times,* 20 May 1993). One might think that such a serious criticism deserved a full and detailed reply. But no such reply is made in this book.

Owen admits that 'we knew, of course, that some of the boundaries of provinces [the provinces delineated by the Vance-Owen Plan] would inevitably be treated as front lines.' But his defence, which consists of only two brief points, is a feeble one. His first point is that the conflict between Croats and Muslims had already begun in 1992, with episodes of fighting in some central Bosnian towns. But episodes are not the same as full-scale war; some factors must have helped produce the shift from the former to the latter, and the accusation that the Vance-Owen Plan was one of those factors must still stand.

The second point is largely implicit: he implies that his Plan cannot have been responsible for fomenting inter-ethnic war, because the provinces did not have ethnic labels anyway. 'We were careful', he says, 'not to label any provinces Serb, Croat or Muslim, contrary to the impression given by some newspapers and commentators.' This is extraordinarily disingenuous. It is true that ethnic names were not formally added to the cantons on the official map issued with the Plan; but, as Lord Owen well knows, all parties to the negotiations understood that the basis of the Plan's territorial division was primarily ethnic, and it immediately became the normal practice of all parties to refer to the provinces envisaged by the Plan as Serb, Croat or Muslim. What makes Lord Owen's disavowal here peculiarly absurd is that he himself, a few pages later, starts to give the provinces ethnic labels: he refers to 'provinces with a clear Serb majority', 'the Muslim-majority province', 'provinces ... allocated to the Serbs', and even, concisely and conclusively, 'Serb provinces'.

One rather comical detail must also be recorded here: while accepting no blame for stimulating the Croat-Muslim war, Owen does demand credit for ending it. He tells us that a meeting which he helped to organize in January 1994 between Tudjman and Izetbegović at the German state guest-house of Petersberg 'laid the foundation for the Washington Accords three months later'. How exactly did it do that? The only comment he makes on the substance of the meeting, a little earlier in his text, is as follows: 'the Petersberg two-day meeting made no real progress and, what was worse, personal relations between Izetbegović and Tudjman deteriorated even further.' It is nice to know that Owen's magic touch did not fail him, even at that critical hour. And, of course, it would anyway have been quite wrong for 'peace mediators' such as Lord Owen and Mr Stoltenberg to end a war between Croats and Bosnian government forces: as he said on 14 March 1994, after the signing of the Washington Accord, 'it would have been very, very difficult indeed for us to have done it, without compromising our impartiality.' What he meant, quite simply, was that Mr Karadžić might have objected.

The illogicalities of 0wen's position on the Croat-Muslim war are as nothing, however, compared with the absurdity of his argument on the central theme of the book: the failure of the Vance-Owen Plan. Anyone who knows anything about the history of the war will remember that the Plan was first accepted by the Bosnian Government, then initialled by Karadžić at Athens, and then taken back to the Bosnian Serb 'parliament' at Pale, which denounced it and called for a referendum in the 'Republika Srpska'. That referendum, held on 15-16 May 1993, rejected it by 96%. During the following week, the representatives of America, Russia and other states met in Washington and agreed on a package of new proposals.

Owen's claim in this book is that the Plan was destroyed not by the Pale Serbs, but by the US Government. He blames the Clinton administration for publicly criticizing the Plan, and for raising the hopes of the Bosnian Government that an alternative strategy of 'lift and strike' would be pursued instead. In this way, he thinks, the Americans first 'undermined' his efforts, and then 'ditched' his famous Plan on 20 May.

This whole argument is both logically and chronologically absurd. The one party which might have been encouraged to reject the Plan by American talk about 'lift and strike' was the Bosnian

Government, but it agreed to sign. The one party which had reason to fear the hawkish tone of American statements, and therefore to accept the Plan instead, was the Pale regime, but it was the Pale Serbs who rejected the Plan. And how does Owen deal with the fact that their rejection was sealed by a 96% vote in a referendum, four whole days before the Washington meeting which he blames for 'killing' the Plan? The answer is marvellously simple. *He does not even mention the result of that referendum.*

Instead he insists, with the obsessive energy of a true monomaniac, that the Plan should just have been 'imposed', whether or not anyone on the ground accepted it, and that the Americans are to blame for not having agreed to impose it. This is truly breathtaking. If consent was not needed to make it effective, why had he wasted four whole months trying to get that consent? Why did he claim, in the earlier part of this book, that any suggestion about ignoring the objections of one side was 'unrealistic' (referring to a time when, of course, it was the Americans who were suggesting that Western policy should ignore Karadžić and treat the Bosnian Government as a legitimate government)?

And why does he always dismiss as naive and impractical those 'politicians, retired generals and commentators in television studios' who proposed that the West could impose a settlement on the Bosnian war by force? Did he have a practical proposal of his own for imposing the Vance-Owen Plan by force, against the wishes of General Mladić?

The answer is yes and no. He did have a plan, but it was not really his own proposal. It was, rather, a plan generously supplied to him in Belgrade by 'senior advisers' to the 'Serbian leadership'. Under this plan, a UN 'implementation force', including American and Russian troops, would have imposed order on Bosnia with the assistance of 'Yugoslav Army liaison officers'. How cross Lord Owen must have felt when this wise and practical proposal failed to gain the instant approval of those naive Americans in the Pentagon and the State Department.

Finally, in order to give the reader an idea of the general character of this book, it is necessary to say something about Owen's attitude towards the Bosnian Government and its overall moral position. His general method here is to devote many sentences to describing the wrongdoing of 'the Muslims', and then round the passage off with a single sentence pointing out that, of course, as everyone knows, the wrongdoings of the Serbs were much greater. It is a handy technique: the final sentence is always there to cover him, should anyone accuse him of playing down the crimes of the Pale Serbs, but the overall effect is unmistakable.

When he summarizes Ejup Ganić's message to the Americans as 'We are the victims', he describes Ganić as a 'propagandist'. Lord Owen, after a couple of briefings in London in August 1992, knew better. 'While the terms "aggressor" and "victim" were being brandished as weapons in a propaganda war the true situation was obviously far more complex than that dichotomy implied.' Those of us who regard the outbreak of the war in Bosnia as an act of planned aggression against the Bosnian state are 'obviously' quite wrong — so obviously, indeed, that there is no need to offer any evidence to the contrary.

At no point in this long book does Owen offer any account of how or why the Bosnian war began. He tells us repeatedly that no one is guiltless in Bosnia, and that there are no clear 'aggressors' or 'victims'? Like so many diplomats and military men, he seems to treat the war in the way that a referee would treat a football match; all his talk about guilt relates only to the good or bad behaviour of each side as combatants, once the war has begun.

The judgement that one side is indeed guilty, because it deliberately started this war, is not even considered here. But since others have made such a judgement, Lord Owen devotes great effort to trying to paint as black a picture of Bosnian Government behaviour as possible, in order, it seems, to redress the balance.

Thus he gives great prominence to an incident which happened just after his appointment as Balkan negotiator: according to a UN press release in Zagreb, two French UN soldiers were killed in cold blood by Bosnian Muslims, who made an unprovoked attack on a humanitarian convoy. This taught him, he says, to shed his illusions about the so-called 'innocence' of the Muslims.

What it should have taught him was a lesson about the unreliability of the UN press office, which, not for the first time, had rushed out a garbled version of events. A more accurate version was printed two years ago by the UN commander General Morillon, who naturally took a close interest in the fate of the French soldiers. Morillon explains that the two Frenchmen were killed 'in a convoy which was caught in a firefight between Serbs and Muslims: Muslim army riflemen, newly arrived in the region, badly controlled and over-excited in the fighting, were responsible for the deaths' (Croire et oser, p. 104). Nothing about cold blood there.

Similarly, when discussing the market-place massacre in

Sarajevo of February 1994, Lord Owen goes on at length about a UN investigation which concluded that the mortar shell had been fired from a Bosnian Government position. Dramatically, he confirms that General Rose put pressure on Bosnian ministers by threatening to reveal this finding. unless they did as they were told.

What Lord Owen does not tell us is that a second, more thorough investigation found that the first had made mistakes in its calculations, and concluded that the shell could equally have come from the Serb side. It is surely inconceivable that Owen is unaware of this second report; yet he chooses not to mention it.

Readers will have to draw their own conclusions about the overall reliability of this grotesquely vainglorious book.

Noel Malcolm

This greatly extended version of a review first published in
The Sunday Telegraph, *12 November 1995,*
appeared in Bosnia Report *No. 14 (February-March 1996)*

General Sir Michael Rose, **Fighting For Peace: Bosnia 1994,** Harvill, London 1998, 269 pp., £18

If General Rose was not a bitter and angry man before he went to Bosnia, he certainly was by the time he left. Members of the press corps there recall him (as Roger Cohen of the *New York Times* puts it) 'barking scattershot responses to questions, pouring scorn on what he viewed as America's guilt-ridden attachment to Bosnia's Muslims, muttering about Muslim plots...'. Even Rose himself now refers to the 'venomous' way he treated anyone whom he regarded as obstructing his 'peace process'. Particularly high on his hit-list were those critics in the media (including myself) who argued that his policies were, in effect, prejudicial to the Bosnian Government and (whether he intended it or not) beneficial to the Pale Serb leadership.

And now General Rose has produced a book which performs two useful services. For the General himself the benefit must be therapeutic: this volume of memoirs enables him to get a great deal of anger and bitterness off his chest. For the rest of us, the service it performs is a documentary one: it provides a wealth of evidence to show just how right General Rose's critics were. At the same time, it also supplies useful evidence of some other relevant things: his ignorance of the history and politics of Bosnia, his uncertain military judgement, and his strange confusion over the real nature of his mandate.

One of the main themes of this book is the sheer unremitting awfulness — in Rose's eyes — of the Bosnian Government leaders, both civilian and military. Vice-President Ejup Ganić is described as 'ruthless, without once demonstrating to me ... a shred of human decency', and there are sneering references to his 'high nasal voice' and his 'soft white hands'. Bosnian Army General Atif Dudaković is characterized as 'short, fat, arrogant and brutal'. As for President Alija Izetbegović, Rose simply announces, without offering any evidence whatsoever, that 'his talk of creating a multi-religious, multi-cultural State in Bosnia was a disguise for the extension of his own political power and the furtherance of Islam.'

Rose habitually refers to the Bosnian Government as 'the Muslims' (when he introduces General Divjak, he describes him as 'an elderly Serb who ... was fighting on the side of the Bosnian Muslims'), and loses no opportunity to emphasize what a cultural gulf divides these people from the Western world to which Sandhurst-trained, Paris-educated generals — and, it seems, Serb peasants — belong. When a special performance of Mozart's Requiem was held in the ruins of the National Library (a library, incidentally, that had contained hundreds of thousands of the products of Western culture, before it was targeted with incendiary shells by the Serb commanders), Rose notes that 'across the river, in their trenches, the Serb soldiers kept their guns silent and listened to the music.' After the concert, when Izetbegović goes to the trouble of thanking Rose for making the occasion possible, Rose cannot resist just one more sneer: 'I wondered if he understood the Christian sentiment behind the words and the music.' Evidently Rose has never bothered to read Izetbegović's treatise *Islam Between East and West*, which contains not only praise of Mozart, but also knowledgeable and sympathetic discussions of Christian ethics and Western art. For Rose, however, as he puts it in his opening pages, 'Bosnia's cultural inheritance is Near Eastern rather than Western European.'

At some points, readers may begin to wonder whether Bosnia is part of Europe at all — as, for example, when Rose explains that the city of Travnik 'lies astride a traditional trading route between Asia and Europe'. General Rose apparently did not think that the Bosnians belonged in Europe, even if they happened to be there in some geographical sense. Prime Minister Haris Silajdžić once complained to Rose about his description of the Bosnians as 'savages', and insisted that they were all, like Rose, Europeans. 'I refrained,' General Rose now writes, 'from replying that, in my view, after the way they had slaughtered each other it would take them at least 500 years to achieve that status.' This comment displays not only the usual obfuscation about who had actually killed whom and why ('they' had just slaughtered 'each other'), but also an extraordinary lack of historical consciousness. Had General Rose been stationed in 1945 in Berlin, or Auschwitz, or Dresden, the logic of this argument would surely have compelled him to say the same, or worse, about the Germans and the British. In which case, all of us (including British Army generals) can look forward to achieving European 'status' in a mere 446 years' time.

Do General Rose's views on the awfulness of the Bosniaks (Bosnian Muslims) extend equally to the Bosnian Serbs? Almost, but not quite. He gives some vivid descriptions of the bluster and outright mendacity of Radovan Karadžić, and describes General Ratko Mladić as a 'fat, swaggering and coarse-featured' man who thought nothing of targeting civilians and used 'trickery and intimidation' to win arguments. And yet, almost in the same breath that he calls Mladić 'brutal and manipulative', Rose insists that he 'generally kept his word if he agreed to something' — contrasting him immediately with his Bosnian Government counterpart, General Rasim Delić, who 'rarely did'. This statement about Mladić, who will go down in history as the man who promised safety to the people of Srebrenica, would be extraordinary enough, even without the fact that in the course of this book Rose himself gives four examples (on pp. 39, 71, 101-7 and 160) of important agreements which Mladić broke.

Discussing one of these incidents, involving a broken promise not to shell Goražde, Rose writes: 'Mladić was either quite mad, a liar, or completely out of touch with his army. I ruled out the latter possibility.' Whether he ruled out the first, however, is much less clear. There are moments in this book when Rose seems to imply that the Serb leaders were not fully responsible for their actions. 'Since the end of the Geneva talks', Rose comments, 'they had lapsed into a state of lunacy and self-destruction, blocking convoys and cutting off communications with the world.' (Did it not occur to Rose that the blocking of convoys was not a mad act of self-destruction, but a calculated attempt to destroy a different set of people — the people whom the convoys were meant to reach?) When he introduces the Serb leadership he explains that 'they lived in a world so far removed from reality and so full of hatred for the Muslims, that their own propaganda was contributing to their state of paranoia' — again, a depiction of people suffering from a psychiatric condition, not fully in control of themselves.

On the other hand Mladić is credited with being 'deeply religious' (apparently because he 'once told me that he prayed every day for the lives of his men'), and on two separate occasions we are informed that he wept — in the presence, conveniently, of important UN officials — over the deaths of Serb soldiers or civilians. The overall effect is to imply that the Serb leaders were not always responsible for their actions because they were slightly crazy, and that what had rendered them crazy was the strength of their genuine and deeply-held beliefs and feelings. This contrasts with the overall depiction of 'the Muslims', for whom no such potential exculpation can be constructed from the arguments of this book: they are consistently described as calculating, cunning and devious. Rose's comments on that Mozart performance are, indeed, an example of this contrast in miniature: in Rose's view, the Serb soldiers were obviously moved by the music, while Izetbegović's expression of gratitude was somehow hollow and suspect. He does not consider the possibility that, while Izetbegović may have genuinely enjoyed the performance, the Serb gunners and snipers may have been under orders to stay their fire, for fear of the bad publicity that might have accrued from disrupting the concert, maiming Zubin Mehta or killing Jose Carreras.

The deviousness of 'the Muslims' is in fact the most constant *Leitmotiv* of this book. If any readers were to rely on this memoir as their sole source of information, they would come away with the impression that the Bosnian war consisted mainly of tricks, provocations and aggressions by 'the Muslims'; that the Serb forces replied to these in self-defence; and that Western policy-makers (and Western journalists, who were in thrall to Bosnian Government 'propaganda') then unfairly blamed the Serbs for doing so.

One very prominent example of this occurs on Rose's first day in Sarajevo. As he was driven from the airport to the city centre, some nearby Bosnian Army mortars opened fire on Serb artillery positions; the UN civil-affairs adviser told him that this was a common tactic, aimed at provoking an artillery bombardment in order to strike terror and sympathy into the hearts of visiting dignitaries. Rose's writing immediately glows red-hot with furious indignation. 'Here, humanity and decency had been banished to another world in which the ends always justified the means. Obviously my first task would be to tell President Izetbegović that this grim strategy of inflicting such horrors on his own people would never succeed...' (That first sentence has gone slightly wrong: he means that humanity and decency had been banished *from* a world in which, etc. — but never mind.)

The tactic was indeed a callous one, and few observers of the war in Sarajevo would deny that it was employed from time to time. But Rose's presentation of the issue remains hugely one-sided. Of the several hundred thousand artillery shells that the Serb gunners fired at Sarajevo during those three and a half years, what proportion were sent in response to such calculated provocations? One percent? Half a percent? No one knows the precise figure, but it was certainly very small. And yet in Rose's account, this type of incident receives almost one hundred percent of the emphasis. The fact that the city just happened to be ringed with heavy artillery in the first place is more or less taken for granted.

The most dramatic example of Rose's fixation with trickery and deviousness on the Bosnian Government side concerns the marketplace massacre of 5 February 1994. As with every other shelling that succeeded in killing a large number of people in one go, this mortar attack was immediately blamed by Serb propagandists on the Bosnian Government side. (The usual argument, which had been current since the bread-queue massacre of 27 May 1992, was that the Bosnian Army had detonated a land-mine at the site; only in this way could they have guaranteed an explosion at the precise point where so many people stood. Such allegations continue to be repeated to this day, even though the characteristic 'splash-mark' of a mortar shell landing at an angle remains clearly visible in each of these cases.)

When Rose introduces this topic, he says that the first examination of the site by 'French military engineers' suggested that, because the market was almost surrounded by high buildings, 'the bomb might not have been fired from a mortar at all, but detonated in situ'. This strange claim conflicts with the most detailed previously published account of the investigation (David Binder, 'Anatomy of a Massacre', *Foreign Policy*, no. 97, Winter 1994-5, pp. 70-8), which notes that the two French soldiers who did the first analysis of the crater were in no doubt that a mortar shell had landed there — they even found its tail-fin. Two other initial analyses were made on the day of the massacre; all three agreed that a mortar had been fired, but each gave a different estimate of the direction and/or the distance. Only one of the three, made by a French captain, argued that the shell must have been fired from an area under Bosnian Army control; this report was, however, immediately given credence by many people, including General Rose. Later a team of artillery experts re-examined the evidence, and discovered that the French captain had made an elementary mathematical error. The final verdict of this team was that the mortar had been fired from the north-north-east, from a distance of between 300 and 5,551 metres. This meant that it could have come from either Bosnian Army or Serb positions: the scientific evidence was simply inconclusive.

How does Rose present these facts? When he first discusses the incident, he mentions that a team of experts eventually contradicted the claim that a bomb had been let off 'in situ', concluding that a mortar had been fired from the north-east. But he makes no comment on the question of the distance, leaving the reader completely unsure about whether the experts had reached any conclusion or not on the identity of the firers. Then, four pages later, he drops a little bombshell of his own. Describing how he put pressure on two Bosnian Army generals, Divjak and Hajrulahović, to agree to a ceasefire which he was negotiating with the Serbs,

Rose says that he threatened to reveal that 'the first UN examination of the bomb crater' had shown that 'the bomb had been fired from the Bosnian side ... or perhaps detonated in situ'. (He also said it was hard to be precise 'because the Bosnian Army had removed some of the important forensic evidence before the UN arrived': this is contradicted by Binder's account, which, based on interviews with the relevant UNPROFOR personnel, states that UN soldiers were on watch at the marketplace within five minutes of the mortar attack, that they themselves removed the tail-fin, and that there was no tampering with the crater site.)

There followed, Rose says, 'a long silence in which I saw Hajrulahović and Divjak exchange glances'. Finally Divjak agreed to take part in the ceasefire discussions; having given in to Rose's demands, Divjak now looked 'strangely relieved'. The innuendo is unmistakable: Rose wants his readers to believe that these 'glances' and relieved looks were tell-tale signs of guilt. The alternative explanation, that the two generals were bewildered by having such an extraordinary accusation thrown at them, and alarmed by the thought of the damage it could do if it were made public, is not even considered. And the reader is left completely unaware that the key difference between this 'first UN examination' and the final report lies not in the question of whether the shell was detonated in situ, but in the claim that it had definitely come from a Bosnian Army position — a claim which, in Rose's presentation, remains uncontradicted.

This incident is also important because it illustrates another of Rose's fixations: his belief that the Bosnian Government and Bosnian Army were the real war-mongers, while the Serb leaders were more genuinely interested in peace. Again and again, Rose tried to persuade the Bosnian Government to agree to local ceasefires, or general ceasefires, or demilitarizations of entire areas. His own sincerity need not be doubted: he sincerely believed that in this way he would fulfil his most essential task, which was to bring peace to Bosnia.

But what has to be doubted is Rose's willingness to make any attempt to look at the situation through the Bosnian Government's eyes. For Izetbegović and his colleagues, at that stage of the war, a general ceasefire would have meant a freezing of front lines at their most disadvantageous extent; any negotiations for a final settlement would then have taken place against the background of a de facto Serb military victory. Churchill, one presumes, would have been equally reluctant to agree to a general ceasefire in 1940.

From time to time Rose repeats the Owen-ish mantra that the peace schemes on offer from international mediators in 1994 were not very different, in territorial percentage terms, from what was eventually agreed at Dayton; this argument is then used to blame the Bosnian Government for inflicting more than a year of 'unnecessary' suffering on its people. The key difference, however, lies not in the percentages of the map, but in the political conditions of the deal and in the psychology of the situation in which the deal would have been struck. Any settlement that followed from a de facto recognition of a Serb military victory would have been negotiated by Karadžić in triumphalist mood; whatever its terms, it would then have been treated by him as merely a step on the way to complete partition. That Dayton ruled out partition (in theory), or at least put a heavy brake on the move towards it (in practice), is something that was possible only because it was a deal hammered out against a background of impending Serb defeat. Dayton does in fact furnish the justification, not the condemnation, of that attitude of Bosnian Government intransigence which so infuriated General Rose in 1994.

Although Rose seems unable to look at the situation through Bosnian Government eyes, he does display quite a good understanding of the viewpoint of the Serbs. Discussing the Sarajevo ceasefire deal with American special envoy Charles Redman, he 'explained that the Serbs had shown themselves to be more than happy to stop the fighting while they were ahead'. Later, when he was trying to arrange a demilitarization agreement for that city, he noted that Mladić was 'interested' in the idea because 'this would release thousands of troops from the trenches around the city for deployment elsewhere.' And yet he continues to present the Bosnian Government's resistance to such plans as evidence of its irresponsible war-mongering attitude.

In his failure to consider the wider context of such decision-making, Rose offers a classic example of what might be called 'football-referee syndrome'. This is an attitude adopted by self-styled peace-keepers that involves treating a war rather as if it were a football match. All talk about good or bad behaviour, about 'aggressors' or 'victims', relates only to the conduct of the players as combatants, once the match has begun; and almost the worst offence a player can commit is to carry on with the game after the referee has blown his whistle. Of course, for a referee, that a football match is taking place is just a donnée, a given fact, and there is no point in his enquiring into the reasons why those two teams came to play against each other in the first place. But a war is not like that. The question of why it was started (and by whom, and how) is not some separate, irrelevant issue; it is basic to the whole nature of the conflict, and central to any understanding of the meaning of any particular 'peace settlement'.

Even if football-referee mode were the only way in which the Bosnian war could be judged, a proper judgement along those lines would still differ overwhelmingly from Rose's: the evils committed by Serb military and paramilitary forces, above all in their campaigns of mass ethnic cleansing during the first four months of the war, vastly outweighed those for which the Bosnian Army was to blame. But many of those evils happened in far-off places such as Kozarac, Prijedor, Višegrad, Foča and Srebrenica, before or after General Rose's tour of duty; whereas the minor tricks or obstructions of Bosnian Government officials happened right under his nose in Sarajevo.

Another reason for Rose's failure to consider the wider context of the fighting can be more simply stated: he was (and has remained) extremely ignorant about such matters. His brief summary of the historical and political background, presented in the opening pages of this book, is a mass of errors, and the rest of the book is a riot of mis-spelt names, of both people and places. He says that Bosnia was never an independent state; in fact, under King Tvrtko it was the most powerful independent state in the Balkans. He says that Slovenia and Croatia were part of the medieval Serbian empire; they were not. He says that Bosnia was ruled by the Turks for 500 years; the correct figure is 415. He says that more than 500,000 Serbs were killed by the Germans and the Ustashe during the second world war; the figure he uses is in fact a total Serb death-toll, including typhoid victims, Axis collaborators, Serbs killed by Chetniks, Serbs killed by Partisans, and several other categories.

Rose's grasp of the facts is equally shaky when he turns to the immediate background to the war. He gets the results of the 1991 census wrong: the figure for Croats was not 20 percent but 17. He thinks that Izetbegović became President after an election in 1992; the election was in 1990. He says that the EU recognized Croatia and Slovenia in 1991; the recognition came in 1992. Ludicrously, Rose states that Karadžić 'had once been in prison with Izetbegović, but had split from him after he had been freed'; in fact the two men had been imprisoned at different times, and for completely different reasons — Izetbegović for his beliefs, and Karadžić for criminal fraud. Rose declares that the Vance-Owen peace plan was 'destroyed by the unenforceable demands being made by the Bosnian Government'; in fact Izetbegović signed the plan, and it was Karadžić's Serbs who rejected it in a referendum. Most bizarrely, Rose says that 'it must be remembered that in 1996, as a result of the Dayton Agreement, 250,000 Serbs left the Krajina part of Croatia and western Bosnia'; the mass exodus from the Krajina took place, as everyone knows, in the summer of 1995. It is as if General Rose, having failed to do any serious historical reading before he went out to Bosnia (the only works he specifically commends are those by Misha Glenny and Karadžić's key adviser, 'John' Zametica), could not be bothered even to read the newspapers after his tour of duty had ended.

Alert readers will have noticed that many of the errors listed above have the effect of downgrading 'the Muslims' and strengthening Serb claims. Thus the suggestion that Izetbegović was thick as thieves with Karadžić lowers the former to the latter's level, while most of the historical howlers in Rose's account have the effect of boosting Serb historic claims (about victimhood, or territorial rights) and undermining Bosnian statehood.

Similarly, when he comes to explain the actual outbreak of the war, Rose defends what is in fact — whether he realizes it or not — the central Serb propaganda claim, which is that the whole Bosnian conflict was essentially just a 'civil war'. The way in which Rose presents this case involves a thoroughly confusing use of the word 'Serbs'. First he describes the outbreak of the war, with 'the Bosnian Serbs' firing on unarmed crowds in Sarajevo on 6 April 1992. (This in itself is misleading: it was not the Bosnian Serbs in general that did the firing, but a particular group of extremists organized by Karadžić and supported by Milošević.) Then, in the next sentence, he says that 'the Serbs' were determined 'to fight to the death to prevent Bosnia establishing itself as a Muslim State'; he goes on to say that 'the Serbs' had therefore withdrawn the JNA into Bosnia. Many casual readers may think that 'the Bosnian Serbs' and 'the Serbs' refer here to the same people; but of course it was not Bosnian Serbs, but Serbia — i.e. the government of Slobodan Milošević — that had moved the JNA into Bosnia and continued to direct its actions there after Bosnia had become an independent country.

Rose has already told his readers (two pages earlier) that 'the situation in Bosnia was not simply that of one nation invading another. It was a civil war about territory in which the Bosnian Croats and the Bosnian Serbs sought to secede from the State...';

thereafter, the concept of invasion receives no further mention, and the term 'civil war' is used over and over again. And in his entire account of the origins and outbreak of the war, Rose refers only once, in passing, to Milošević.

If such an account had come from the Ministry of Information in Belgrade, one would regard it as a masterfully sanitized version of events. In Rose's case, one has to accept it as just an honest expression of his own extremely limited understanding. At the same time, however, it is possible to sense a kind of ideological pressure at work on his thinking — the ideology being not a deliberately pro-Serbian one, but rather the fixed pattern of thought of the professional 'peace-keeper'. Standard peace-keeping doctrine depends on maintaining a doctrine of absolute equivalence between the 'sides' or 'factions'; this is what is drummed into officers at staff colleges when they go on 'peace-keeping' courses. For anyone who went to Bosnia with such assumptions in his head, dismissing the war there as just (to quote Rose) 'a three-sided civil war over territory' was by far the most convenient line to take, ensuring maximum equivalence all round.

Unfortunately this doctrine of equivalence corresponded neither to the facts, nor even to the terms of General Rose's mandate. The UN Security Council resolutions which made up his mandate referred repeatedly to the status of Bosnia as a sovereign state, and to the need to respect its integrity — something which the legitimate government of Bosnia was quite properly seeking to defend. The first key task assigned to UNPROFOR by those resolutions was to help ensure the delivery of humanitarian aid; if one 'faction' was mainly responsible for blocking such deliveries, then the actions of the UN troops would necessarily be directed mainly against that side. Other key elements of the mandate concerned the so-called 'safe areas': here the UN forces were mandated by Resolution 836 (1993) not only to 'deter attacks', but also to 'promote the withdrawal' from those areas of 'military or paramilitary units other than those of the Government of the Republic of Bosnia and· Herzegovina'. In other words, the forces of the legitimate government of this sovereign state were quite clearly permitted to stay in the 'safe areas', which of course remained parts of Bosnia's sovereign territory.

Readers who depend only on Rose's book will, however, acquire a rather hazy and inadequate idea of what the mandate was. He constantly refers to UNPROFOR as a 'peace-keeping' force; at one point he sternly announces that 'our mandate was to keep the peace', although he readily admits elsewhere that there was no peace to keep. Those staff-college courses make a basic distinction between peace-keeping, which depends on the consent of all parties on the ground and derives its mandate from Chapter VI of the UN Charter, and peace-enforcement, which is based on Chapter VII and permits the use of force where consent has not been given. At one point Rose does comment, quite correctly, that the UNPROFOR mandate was largely based on Chapter VII; but because it was not a mandate to end the whole war by force, he persists in trying to squeeze it into the category marked 'peace-keeping' — a category to which it patently does not belong. The best description would be to say that it was a mandate to use force, if necessary, to carry out a number of specific tasks, most of them humanitarian-related, within a war situation.

How did General Rose conceive of his mandate? This is what he wrote in the *Royal United Services Institute Journal* in June 1995, after his tour of duty had ended: 'Once a military force has deployed in a humanitarian aid role it is precluded by its rules of engagement from acting as an occupying power, which can dictate its own political and military agenda to the parties in the conflict... It is ... only able to operate with the consent of those elements who control the territory ... A peace-keeping force designed to assist the delivery of humanitarian aid simply cannot be used to alter the military balance of force in a civil war, modify the political goals of one party or another, or even attempt to enforce the passage of a convoy — for these are pure acts of war.'

One leading expert on this area of international law, Marc Weller, discussing this statement in his authoritative study of the UNPROFOR mandate ('Peace-Keeping and Peace-Enforcement in the Republic of Bosnia and Herzegovina', *Zeitschrift für ausländisches öffentliches Recht und Völkerrecht*, vol. 56 (1996), nos. 1-2, pp. 70-177), has described Rose's opinion as 'absolutely extraordinary': after all, enforcing the passage of convoys, and taking other necessary measures to ensure humanitarian access, were precisely what UNPROFOR was mandated to do. Yet this was the doctrine for which Rose became famous: invoking America's unhappy experience in Somalia, he argued that there was a 'Mogadishu line' which must never be crossed, a line between peace-keeping and war-making.

Where exactly should that line be drawn? Those who want a clear answer to this question will certainly not get it from Rose's book. Describing his attempt, during his first weeks in Bosnia, to introduce a more 'robust' policy, he proudly relates his order that 'any illegal roadblocks or other obstacles to the movement of a convoy were, after due warning, to be forcibly dealt with' — after which, to Rose's satisfaction, 'a young French lieutenant smashed down a roadblock outside Pale with his armoured cars.' Did that lieutenant cross the Mogadishu line? Apparently not. A couple of months later, Rose even states that he 'dispatched NATO aircraft to the enclave of Maglaj at the request of [General Rasim] Delić to support the Bosnian Army.' Was such an action designed 'to alter the balance of force in a civil war'? Of course not — for that would have been a pure act of war.

As for 'acting as an occupying power', or trying to 'dictate' a 'political and military agenda to the parties in the conflict', readers may find such phrases not altogether inapposite when they consider Rose's account of how he treated the 'elderly' General Divjak (then the second-in-command of the Bosnian Army), when trying to get him to take part in a negotiation which Rose had arranged in February 1994. 'I ran past the startled sentries and burst into Divjak's office ... Seizing hold of Divjak's arm, I asked him what the hell he was playing at ... He resisted, saying that a senior officer of the Bosnian Army should not be treated like this. Putting my face close to his, I shouted at him that I represented the Secretary-General of the UN and I would not be lied to or given the run-around by the Bosnian Government ... Not even allowing him to get his coat, I bundled him into the Range Rover behind a grinning Goose [Rose's bodyguard] ... Goose was clearly enjoying this unexpected shift from Chapter VI to Chapter VII of the UN Charter — from the peaceful settlement of disputes to enforcement.'

One has to assume that the last remark, about the UN Charter, is facetious, given that the Chapter VII elements of his mandate had absolutely nothing to do with manhandling Bosnian Army generals; this is, on the other hand, one of the very few places in the book where Rose specifically invokes such powers.

The strangest aspect of Rose's presentation of his mandate concerns his treatment of the safe areas, and of the enforcement of 'demilitarization' agreements. It is a simple fact that the safe areas, as defined by the relevant UN Security Council resolutions, were not intended or required to be 'demilitarized' by all sides: Resolution 836, as quoted above, clearly permitted Bosnian Army units to remain in them. Once again, however, any readers who depend only on Rose's book will get a very different impression. At one point he quotes Radovan Karadžić as saying that the Serb offensive against

Goražde 'had been caused by the Muslims attacking out of the enclave in violation of the UN Security Council Resolution, which demanded the demilitarization of all safe areas'. Instead of immediately explaining that no such UN resolution existed, Rose blithely goes on to say: 'Karadžić always quoted UN resolutions when it suited him.'

As we already know, General Rose was very keen on demilitarizing. Once, after a heavy-weapons exclusion zone had been created (thanks to a NATO ultimatum) in and around Sarajevo, he was so angered to hear that a solitary Bosnian Army tank had been spotted inside the zone that he threatened to call down a NATO air strike on it. On another occasion, he wanted to make the same threat when he learned that Bosnian Army infantrymen were violating an earlier agreement (between the Bosnian Government and Mladić's army) to vacate a 'demilitarized zone' on Mount Igman, just to the south-west of Sarajevo.

The fact that Rose thought such threats were even legally possible must raise serious doubts about his understanding of his mandate. It is true that the NATO ultimatum of 9 February 1994 had threatened air strikes against all parties; but the legal grounding of that ultimatum consisted only of the UN resolutions, which means that the threat to bomb Bosnian Army positions was a mere flight of fancy by NATO drafters, not justified in law. (To quote Marc Weller again on this point: 'It is difficult to conceive of a legal argument which might be deployed in defence of this action.') General Rose, in any case, was acting as a UN official, not a NATO one; in calling for a NATO air strike against a Bosnian Army tank he would have needed a strict justification for his action within the UN mandate, and this he did not have.

At one point he says that if he had asked NATO to bomb the infantrymen on Mount Igman, it would have been not under the 1994 ultimatum but under some earlier NATO declaration — referring, presumably, to the North Atlantic Council statements of 2 and 9 August 1993. But the second of those statements had clearly said: 'the air strikes foreseen by the Council decision of August 2 are limited to the support of humanitarian relief.' Quite how knocking Bosnian Government soldiers off Mount Igman could be described as supporting humanitarian relief remains obscure. The most straightforward interpretation of these UN and NATO documents would suggest that Rose's mandate simply did not permit him to call down air strikes on Bosnian Government troops in such circumstances. Had he done so it would have been, to coin a phrase, 'a pure act of war'. The General would then have crossed, finally and decisively, the Mogadishu line, in order to go to war against the Bosnian Army. In the event he actually did this, albeit in a less dramatic way: he sent French UNPROFOR units to Mount Igman to carry out an 'assault' on the Bosnian Army positions, using armoured bulldozers to drive them off the mountain.

When Rose was trying to persuade NATO to bomb those soldiers, he telephoned a senior figure, General Corvault, at NATO's Naples headquarters. His account of this conversation forms one of the defining moments of the book: 'Corvault replied that ... NATO was not prepared to carry out air strikes against the Bosnian Army merely because they were in the demilitarization zone in violation of the NATO ultimatum. For the first time I was being officially told that NATO had taken sides in the war ... Sadly, this failure by NATO to act impartially was to prove terminal to the UN peace-keeping mission in Bosnia.'

The significance of this is not confined to the fact that Rose seems to have got things completely the wrong way round, accusing NATO of 'taking sides in the war' when it was in fact refusing, quite correctly, to be dragged into an act of war by him. What matters most here is the insight such comments give us into Rose's overall attitude to NATO, to American policy, and to the way that the war was eventually ended. As the book proceeds, Rose's expressions of irritation with various Americans (both military and civilian) for being 'pro-Muslim', or hawkish, or both, grow stronger and stronger. On the political side, his comments about the actions and initiatives taken by the USA are notably grudging. The first time he refers to the Vance-Owen peace plan he immediately repeats the old canard that it was 'the Americans' who 'pulled the plug' on it at the end of May 1993. (As was mentioned above, the plan was massively rejected by the Pale Serbs in a referendum, held on 15-16 May; what the Americans rejected ten days later was in fact a new proposal by Owen, suggesting that the West should just go ahead and enforce the plan on the ground, with or without the Serbs' consent.) And when Rose describes the negotiations between Bosnian Army and Croat military commanders which preceded the Washington Accord, he tries hard to divert all credit for their agreement away from the American envoy Charles Redman. ('It became clear to me that [General Rasim] Delić and [General Ante] Roso had both been briefed by their respective political masters, before the meeting arranged by Redman': apparently it has not occurred to him that those political masters were themselves acting under American diplomatic pressure.)

At the end of the book, Rose even manages to transfer much of the credit for the successes of both the Washington Accord and Dayton to UNPROFOR, in a couple of sentences from which the acronym 'USA' is conspicuous by its absence: 'It was also UNPROFOR that helped bring about an end to the fighting between the Muslims and Croats by implementing the Washington Accord. By doing this, the UN created the necessary preconditions for the Dayton Peace Agreement that finally brought an end to the war in Bosnia.'

How, then, does Rose deal with the fact that when those irritating NATO 'hawks' finally got their way, and launched a bombing campaign against Mladić's army, the end of the war followed within a few weeks? His comments on the bombing itself are very off-hand: 'the military effect of some 3,500 sorties was judged by many commentators to be negligible.' (Which commentators? He does not say; certainly he cannot mean Richard Holbrooke, who remarks that one of the American cruise missiles 'knocked out the main communications center for the Bosnian Serb Army in the west, with devastating consequences'.) When Rose returns to this theme in his last chapter, he declares that 'the NATO air campaign was no more than a useful signal to the Serbs that the peace-keeping option had been suspended and that the West was now prepared to use a greater level of enforcement than before.' But that 'useful signal' was useful precisely because it was not just a signal: if 3,500 sorties did not count as part of the reality of a 'greater level of enforcement', one wonders what would have done.

As General Rose himself puts it in his final pages, 'the peace process was suspended for a brief period and the Serbs were compelled by force of arms to accept a negotiated settlement that ended the war.' Readers should pause to savour the unintentional irony of that passage, in which it is admitted that the achievement of peace was made possible, at long last, by a suspension of the 'peace process'. And they will find that the irony becomes even more exquisite when they place that passage alongside the one quoted above, in which Rose bitterly complained that 'this failure by NATO to act impartially was to prove terminal to the UN peace-keeping mission in Bosnia.'

Rose's final chapter does at least attempt to answer the obvious question: if the war was ended successfully in 1995, why could it not have been ended, using the same methods, in 1994? His answer (on p. 239) takes the form of a list of special factors which had arisen after the political climate had 'radically changed' in mid-1995 — in other words, after his departure from Bosnia. The most important of these are the following: '1. Belgrade had withdrawn its support from Pale, reducing the risk of Serbia entering the war if the West attacked the Bosnian Serbs; 2. the Bosnian Serb Army had ceased to be militarily superior to the armies of the Croat-Muslim Federation; 3. the Americans had finally accepted the fact that a 'just' political settlement was not obtainable and that territorial concessions would have to be made to the Bosnian Serbs.'

This is not, however, the first such numbered list to appear in Rose's book. Readers who turn back to pp. 134-5 will find an analysis of the strategic situation in Bosnia made by Rose himself in May 1994, when he was less than half-way into his tour of duty there: 'It was obvious to me that there were five strategic imperatives that would persuade the Serbs to sign up to the present proposals: 1. the Serbs could no longer rely on support from the Russians; 2. their economy was suffering because of international sanctions; 3. President Milošević no longer supported the Bosnian Serbs in the war in Bosnia; 4. the Bosnian Serb Army was finding it difficult to recruit soldiers from an exhausted Serb population; 5. the military balance had now tilted in favour of Bosnia with the formation of the Croat-Muslim Federation and the growing strength of the Bosnian Army.'

Placing these two lists side by side, we see that factor 1 in the 1995 analysis corresponds to factor 3 in the 1994 list, and that factor 2 in 1995 corresponds to factor 5 — reinforced by factor 4 — in the 1994 list. As for factor 3 in the 1995 list, the willingness of the Americans to accept a less than perfect political settlement, this corresponds to the fact that, as Rose has already explained in his narrative, the American Government was backing the Contact Group plan in the summer of 1994. (In late May of that year, Rose tells us, 'I had an encouraging meeting with Redman, who for the first time admitted that the US Government might have to support a territorial division of Bosnia that was less than what the Bosnian Government wanted.') The 'radical change' between May 1994 and the second half of 1995 is, to put it mildly, hard to discern.

One qualification, however, must be added here. Although Rose clearly states that he thought the military balance had tilted against the Serb forces by May 1994 — he had noted as early as the end of March that 'the Bosnian Serb Army was beginning to lose its military superiority' — he did not draw the obvious corollary of this, which was that the Bosnian Government and Croat armies might actually win back territory from the Serbs. On the contrary, he argued throughout his time in Bosnia, and continues to argue in this book, that the Bosnian Army was so militarily hopeless that even lifting the arms embargo would not have improved its chances. Apparently the Bosnian Army officers were all incompetent, including even the ones who had been trained as JNA officers before the war, whereas those Serb officers who had also had careers in the JNA 'had been well educated by their Soviet masters in the art of manoeuvre'. This is, incidentally, yet another of Rose's historical howlers: 'Soviet masters' had had nothing to do with training the Yugoslav Army since 1948. And his general statement that 'the Bosnians, on the other hand, had received no military training' is also absurd: among the ordinary soldiers in the two armies the level of previous training, acquired through the military service that was performed by all young men in the former Yugoslavia, was precisely the same.

Some might expect an experienced British Army general at least to produce some well-reasoned observations on military matters of this kind; but his comments on these topics are at best confusing, and at worst self-contradictory. Just after his announcement that the military balance had tilted against the Serbs, he says that even if the arms embargo were lifted 'it would take many years before the Bosnian Army would be in a position to conduct offensive operations on a scale capable of delivering their political aims.' A few pages later, on the other hand, he admits that lifting the arms embargo 'might put pressure on the Serbs to agree to the Contact Group plan and map', which suggests that even if Rose did not think that a better-equipped Bosnian Army could make politically significant gains, the Serbs did. (Should we not allow their opinion at least some weight, given that they were, after all, the ones fighting the war?) And at the end of the book, when Rose discusses the 'series of strategic actions' that ended the war in 1995, he does include 'the Croat-Muslim Federation ground offensive in the west of Bosnia'. Otherwise, throughout the book, he simply repeats that the idea of letting the Bosnians defend themselves was 'militarily unwise', because the Bosnian Army 'was not militarily capable of defending itself', and that if the arms embargo were lifted 'Bosnia would be overrun by the Serbs' — those very same Serbs who had such difficulty recruiting soldiers, and against whom the military balance had so decisively tilted.

If readers find Rose's military judgement a little confusing here, they will be even more disconcerted by his geo-political pronouncements. Take, for example, his comments on Russian policy. He welcomed the sudden deployment of Russian troops in the Sarajevo area in February 1994: as he now explains, 'I realized that our common determination not to allow air strikes placed me in some kind of unholy alliance with the Russians against NATO.' So pleased was he to see them, indeed, that he brushed aside the objections of Ejup Ganić (who complained that the Russian soldiers had openly taken the Serb side, giving the Serb nationalist three-fingered sign as they drove through Pale), and told him rather briskly that 'it was not his responsibility to decide the locations of UN troops'. (There is a whiff of double standards here. Elsewhere in the book, Rose calmly states that offers of new UNPROFOR contingents from Pakistan and Turkey were of limited value because 'it was not possible to deploy Muslim troops on 70 per cent of Bosnia that was occupied by the Serbs'; indeed, the Serbs would not 'allow' such Muslim contingents even to 'transit their territory'.)

At this point in his narrative, Rose has a little dig at the Oxford historian Mark Almond, who warned in a newspaper article against the dangers of allowing the Russians into Europe's Balkan back-yard. 'Perhaps no one had told him', sniffs General Rose, 'that the cold war was over.' Three chapters later, however, Rose has changed his tune. During the crisis over Goražde, he notes, the Russian UN civil affairs adviser in Sarajevo, Victor Andreev, was 'gloomily predicting the start of a Third World War.' Rose comments that 'he had some grounds for saying this, as President Yeltsin, following NATO air strikes against the Serbs in Goražde, had refused to sign the "Partnership for Peace" deal with NATO, and had even threatened "war for ever" if the West intervened in Bosnia.' And one chapter after that, Rose's own gloom has intensified: 'I began to wonder whether the gradual slide into war that was taking place in Bosnia in the summer of 1994 might not end in a world war.' It is hard to tell which was the more absurd of Rose's opinions: his initial idea that Russian involvement in Bosnia was risk-free, or his later belief that the risk it might entail was that of a third world war.

This mention of Mark Almond brings me, finally, to an admittedly minor point: Rose's constant desire in this book to rebut comments made by several of his critics in the media, among whom Mr Almond and myself seem to enjoy pride of place. Rose was certainly a very media-conscious person; he says that he regarded the creation of a positive impression in and through the media as an absolutely crucial part of his job. (This obsession with the media is one of the things that distinguish him most sharply from his successor, General Rupert Smith, whom many observers believe to have been the more effective commander.) Readers can get some sense of the importance which General Rose attributed to the impact of the media from passages such as the following: 'In response to the growing international concern caused by the escalating number of violations [of the ceasefire agreement in Sarajevo], I simply put a stop to the daily reports of them, although we continued to brief the press on incidents that resulted in any civilian casualties. I took this decision to reduce the political pressure growing in NATO for punitive action to be taken against the Serbs.'

Some of the comments I made at the time seem to have stung General Rose to such an extent that he cannot now give either an accurate representation of what I said, or a sensible answer to it. In one passage — where he calls me, by direct implication, a 'propagandist' — he says that I described Douglas Hurd as having blood on his hands because of his refusal to take direct military action. What I actually argued was that he had blood on his hands because he had actively supported the arms embargo, thus preventing the Bosnians from adequately defending themselves. Another put-down from General Rose concerns my prediction, at the time of Jimmy Carter's intervention in Bosnia in December 1994, that any ceasefire brokered by him would hold only for a short period. Triumphantly, General Rose retorts: 'It lasted for more than four months.' In fact the ceasefire never held in one important theatre of war, the Bihać region (where, contrary to what Rose states, fighting continued between Serb forces and the Bosnian Army); and in any case the ceasefire was decisively ended by the launching of new Bosnian Army campaigns in central Bosnia, in the Majevica hills and around Mount Vlasić, on 20 March 1995 — just two months and three weeks after that ceasefire agreement had come into force.

A public figure who routinely refers to his critics as 'propagandists' needs to be sure that his own record, in respect of propagandistic activities, is squeaky-clean. But although, as I have tried to emphasize in this review, the overall sincerity of General Rose's views cannot be doubted, there are two specific issues on which an element of possibly conscious propagandizing seems to have crept in. One concerns the destruction of houses and expulsion of Serbs from Goražde. In 1994 Rose claimed that 'most' of the destroyed houses there had been damaged not by Serb artillery, but by 'the Muslims' when they expelled 12,500 Serb inhabitants from the town in 1992. In the extra chapter which I added to the second edition of my *Bosnia: A Short History*, I pointed out that this statement was simply not credible: there had been fewer than 10,000 Serbs living in the entire administrative district of Goražde (an area of 383 square kilometres), only half of whom had lived in the town itself. I concluded that 'General Rose was acting here, however unwittingly, as little more than a conduit for Serb propaganda.' Now, when Rose returns to this issue in his book, he repeats the substance of his original claim, but simply omits the false statistic of 12,500 Serbs. Perhaps he has learned, either directly or indirectly, of my comment on this bogus figure; if so, it seems strange that he should continue to repeat the same argument as before, even when he knows that the central plank of that argument was rotten.

Stranger still is his own admission about another Goražde-related topic: the alleged destruction, during a NATO air strike against the Serb tanks outside that town, of a Serb armoured ambulance. General Rose was so pleased by this visual proof of the unwisdom of air strikes that he kept a photograph of the wrecked ambulance pinned up on the wall of his office, for visiting dignitaries and journalists to see; underneath it he added the sarcastic caption, 'Nice One Nato!' Several members of the press corps were sceptical about this photo, suspecting that the story had been concocted by the Serb side. (I myself have no technical military expertise, but I can report that when I showed the photo — which is reproduced on the jacket of this book — to a Bosnian journalist who had been a soldier during the war, he immediately said that it must have been hit by a grenade. The chassis is completely intact and unbuckled, which would not be the case, he observed, if it had been hit from above by an air-to-ground missile.)

And now, astonishingly, Rose himself admits: 'I suspected that the Serb report [that the ambulance had been hit by a NATO air strike] was probably propaganda.' Yet he made use of it, in an attempt to influence key Western policy-makers who visited his office, all the same. Readers who recall Rose's account of his arrival in Sarajevo, and his furious denunciation of a 'world in which the ends always justified the means', may start to wonder just what sort of world it was that the General himself inhabited.

Noel Malcolm

This review was written specially for the present volume

Michael Sells, **The Bridge Betrayed: religion and genocide in Bosnia,** University of California Press, Berkeley, Los Angeles and London 1996, 244 pp., £15.95

This is an important and well-researched book. The author, an American Professor of Religious Studies with a partly Serb background, analyses with great thoroughness and understanding the way religion led to genocide in Bosnia, as also the way people in the West — both politicians and church leaders — for the most part systematically closed their eyes to the greatest crime committed in post-Second-World-War Europe, endeavouring to cover up with a series of futile and essentially immoral explanations about what was going on and why they could and should do nothing about it. The scale of the wider collusion in genocide has been vast indeed and, in strict terms of international law, few are the leaders of the West who could not reasonably be indicted for such collusion at The Hague.

While Sells concentrates mostly on the responsibility of Serb religion and nationalism for the genocidal crimes of 1992-95, he devotes one important chapter to the Croats, important especially for Catholics. It is chilling to realise that the worldwide preoccupation of devout Catholics with the Marian visions at Medjugorje has proceeded throughout the period when the Catholics in and around Medjugorje have been systematically murdering and expelling Muslims from their midst and destroying every historic Muslim monument they could lay their hands on. Of twenty-nine major Islamic buildings in Mostar, dating from 1552 to 1651, twenty-seven have been totally destroyed. The theme of resurgent Croat nationalism orchestrated by President Tudjman has been that Croatia is part of Europe and has, moreover, the mission of 'Europeanizing' Bosnia. This is how they did it. The Croats did not, of course, begin the genocide in Bosnia — they came in on it like jackals in the wake of Karadžić — yet their part has been steadily underestimated through the influence of a very powerful Catholic lobby in Germany and elsewhere. Despite the Pope's appeals for Bosnia, he too never clearly brought his influence to bear at the one point where it could have been effective — in publicly condemning the policy of Croatia, a policy backed to the hilt by large sections of the Church in western Herzegovina.

The central theme of this book is, however, a Serb one. One of the most depressing things about the whole Yugoslavia breakdown has been the influence of diaspora Serb and Croat groups in Europe and North America backing the extreme nationalists. While there have been many brave Serbs in Bosnia and Belgrade to speak out against the whole Serb national enterprise, there has been almost no Serb voice in Britain, for instance, which has done other than act as a defender of what in fact has been genocide. That is why it is important to note the Serb background of Sells. There has, alas, been a further religious extension of this same phenomenon: it is very noticeable that other Christians with a special interest in Orthodoxy and in ecumenical relations with the Orthodox have almost entirely failed to make their voice heard against what has been done with massive Orthodox backing. A false ecumenism has thus become a powerful factor in undermining Christian concern for justice: a defence of the good name of Churches has become more important. This is one of the reasons, one suspects, for the general decline in respect for the World Council of Churches and for circles connected with it.

Sells is quite clear that what we are talking about is 'genocide' and nothing less. That, of course, is something the establishment in the West has never wanted to admit, because it places legal obligations upon other states in a way that civil war does not. The evidence for it, however, is overwhelming, and that is where Sells starts, following on Roy Gutman's *Witness to Genocide*, Norman Cigar's *Genocide in Bosnia* and other exceedingly well-sourced books. He goes on to explore the ideological rooting of the pursuit of genocide in the myth of the Battle of Kosovo, the theme of the Christ killer, and the way the darkest side of the Serb religious and national tradition was deliberately resurrected and played upon by ecclesiastical and political leaders in the 1980s. It is important in that context to note that the Church authorities have separated from Milošević where and only where they have seen him as failing to implement their extreme brand of religious nationalism. They have never criticized Karadžić as they have Milošević. It is, therefore, futile to point to church criticism of Milošević as proof of a certain surviving conscience within the leadership of Serbian Orthodoxy. It actually indicates the opposite. It does no long-term service to Orthodoxy whatever to obscure its collusion in crimes of this order, fomented by a long tradition both religious and literary, in which *The Mountain Wreath*, a classic written by Njegoš, a nineteenth-century bishop of Montenegro, is crucial. While being no less than an instigation to the mass murder of Muslims, it has often been seen as the most central work in the Serb literary tradition.

Bosnia has provided horrific proof that, fifty years after the Holocaust, the world's promise 'Never Again' has come to mean remarkably little. One wonders whether John Major was even aware of the existence and terms of the Genocide Convention. What is certain is that almost the entire political and religious establishment of Britain, France, the United States and Western Europe in general willingly swallowed a totally false interpretation of the conflict and for three years did everything possible to ensure that the victims of genocide remained defenceless. The scale of atrocities was deliberately played down, every possible example of Muslim criminality was played up, and understanding of what was in reality a crude re-enactment of the Crusades at their worst was muddied by a constant stress upon the dangers of Islamic Fundamentalism.

Every bishop in the West who evaded doing anything to protest against the arms embargo or against a policy which ensured that nothing effective was done otherwise to stop the killers in their tracks should read this book slowly and penitentially — it might make a better retreat book than anything more ostensibly devout. If Karadžić and Mladić are unlikely ever to appear to answer for their crimes at The Hague, it is because the political leaders of the West do not want that to happen. And they do not want it because they know that the crime of genocide extends to collusion in it by people in other countries, and once a major trial was under way the degree of collusion of Owen, Hurd, Warren Christopher and many others could become only too obvious. But, at a more spiritual level, would the collusion of Church leaders not also become evident?

Adrian Hastings

This review first appeared in The Heythrop Journal, *January 1998*

Jasminka Udovički and James Ridgway (ed.), **Yugoslavia's Ethnic Nightmare: the inside story of Europe's unfolding ordeal**, Lawrence Hill Books, New York 1995, 252 pp.

Before the breakup of Yugoslavia in the period 1987-91, no adequate explanation of the national question in the country under Communist rule had been provided by any historian in any language. The Western left mostly followed the Titoist line, that national inequality had been abolished and the national question solved, and showed more interest in the system of 'socialist self-management' than in the forces that were to bring about the dissolution of the Yugoslav federation and the dismemberment of two of its constituent republics.

The outbreak of full-scale war in 1991 found the left without the theoretical tools needed to formulate a principled response. Many of its members, unwilling to blame the catastrophe on a political system that had appeared least deformed of any of the world's 'socialist states', vented their despair, ignorance and prejudice on anything and anyone but the real culprit. The war was variously attributed to endemic ethnic hatreds that had been kept in check by Tito's fatherly dictatorship; to a German conspiracy to dominate the Balkans; to a Croat propensity towards fascism; or to the impact of the international capitalist system (why this same capitalist system did not bring war to any of the neighbouring countries was never explained).

Serbia was seen as the last bastion of socialism in Europe and the misunderstood victim of an imperialist conspiracy. Since the Yugoslav national question had been solved under Communism, it followed that the Slovenes, Croats and Bosnian Muslims were not 'oppressed nations'; consequently they had no reason to seek independence or even to defend themselves from attack by Serbia, which was after all only trying to defend the Socialist Yugoslavia we all knew and loved from the machinations of the Germans, the Vatican and international capitalism.

To this day most Western socialists cannot comprehend the Bosnian or Croatian desire for independence, which they blame for the bloodshed, much as Winston Churchill once lamented how Hindus and Muslims would never have massacred each other if only India had remained within the British Empire.

Yugoslavia's Ethnic Nightmare is a collection of essays that will dent some of these misconceptions, but unfortunately confirm many more of them. In fairness to the authors, they do speak unequivocally of Serbian genocide of Bosnian Muslims, and put the primary blame for the war on Milošević's Serbia, which is unambiguously presented as an aggressor. In one of the more useful articles, Stipe Sikavica describes the role of the Serbian government and army in arming and inciting Serbs in Croatia against the Croatian authorities.

Yugoslavia's Ethnic Nightmare is a useful antidote to arguments that play down talk of genocide and aggression and thus speak of a Bosnian 'civil war' between parties bearing equal guilt, the more so since it is the work of writers from Serbia. Unfortunately, it may also be cited by leftists in the West who have always been hostile to Bosnia's struggle for survival and independence, and who now have their views confirmed by respectable members of the 'opposition' in Serbia

At first glance the book appears promising, claiming to be 'written by a team of antiwar Muslim, Croatian, and Serbian journalists and a noted Croatian historian', to be 'the first book in English to represent the voices of resistance inside the former Yugoslavia', and to ' describe the causes of the conflict from the perspective of the people who live there'.

It turns out that all the contributors, except for the editors themselves, work for institutes or 'oppositional' newspapers in Serbia, and the articles are mostly written from the perspective of a liberal, 'oppositional' Serb nationalism. This makes them unrepresentative of the views of the majority of the 'people who live' in former Yugoslavia.

Nowhere do they express the slightest sympathy or understanding for the national rights of non-Serb peoples. In their view these are not an issue, because 'the concept of self-determination' when applied to Yugoslavia was 'not only absurd but perilous' (p.6). Rather, 'the crucial issue for Yugoslavia' was 'the rights of minority ethnic groups in the republics and provinces'(p. 9). This turns out to mean only the Serbs in Croatia, Bosnia and Kosova, since the grievances of other minorities are given no space and their rights not defended.

The international community is faulted for having 'supported the right of self-determination of the former republics' (p. 15), when it should have placed its hopes in Ante Marković, Yugoslavia's Gorbachev-style reformist Prime Minister. Marković is viewed retrospectively by many liberals in the West as the man who could have saved Yugoslavia if given the chance.

Just as Gorbachev promised much but ended up using the Soviet

Army against Lithuanian, Azerbaijani and Georgian movements for democracy, so Marković presided over repression of the Albanian population in Serbian-occupied Kosova and the Yugoslav Army's attack on Slovenia. The promises of a 'liberal Stalinist' leader should not be relied upon.

Slavko Ćuruvija and Ivan Torov turn reality on its head in their discussion of Kosova, portraying the Serb minority as victims of Albanian oppression in the years before Slobodan Milošević seized power in Serbia in 1987. They write sympathetically of the grievances of Kosova Serbs, which were apparently 'ignored by both the federal and the Serbian authorities' (p.79).

They repeat approvingly the view that Kosova was granted 'excessive autonomy' under Tito, and oppose Albanian self-determination on the grounds that 'for Serbia, this would have meant the loss of a significant portion of its territory'(p. 7), ignoring the fact that this 'portion of its territory' was brutally conquered by Serbia in 1912-13 and again in 1944-45, against the will of its inhabitants.

They claim chillingly that 'in the decade before Tito's death, the Albanian population in Kosova increased from forty percent to more than eighty percent' (p. 76). Falsehoods of this kind reflect the Serb-nationalist obsession with the higher birth-rate that has supposedly allowed Albanians to 'outbreed' Serbs in Kosova, and imply that the 'proper' ethnic balance should be restored through the expulsion of several hundred thousand Albanians.

Ćuruvija and Torov, a Serb and a Macedonian respectively, make no acknowledgement whatsoever of the oppression of Albanians within their native countries. The mass meeting held in February 1988 in the Slovenian capital of Ljubljana to show solidarity with Albanian miners on hunger strike against Milošević's repression is described as an 'anti-Serb rally' (p. 101).

The authors conclude that Milošević merely manipulated Serbian fears over Kosova that were largely justified, revealing the common ground that much of the Serbian 'opposition' continues to share with its President. The editors later speak of an ethnic partition of Kosovo, between 200,000 Serbs and almost two million Albanians, as a 'creative solution' to the problem, falsely attributing the proposal to an Albanian oppositionist, while admitting it has met with 'little approval' (p. 231).

Serbian oppositionists can do and have done much better. Srđa Popović has helped demolish nationalist myths about Albanian persecution of Serbs, while Bogdan Denitch has called for the separation of Kosova from Serbia.

In his chapter on the origins of the war in Croatia, Ejub Štitkovac devotes much space to presenting the grievances of Serbs against Tudjman's regime in Croatia. Many of these grievances were justified, but Štitkovac concedes no legitimacy to the fears of Croats whose country was soon to be devastated and partitioned by the Serbian army.

Indeed, his article represents a Serb-nationalist critique of Milošević, faulted for a military campaign that 'consolidated the perception abroad of Serbs as nothing but aggressors' and 'made it possible for flagrant human-rights violations perpetrated by Tudjman's forces to be disregarded by the international community' (p. 163). Štitkovac claims that 'a half million Serb civilians had to abandon their homes to escape Croatian reprisals' (p. 163), an implausible figure given that at no point in the war did the total number of Serbs in Croatian-controlled territories even approach half a million.

Though he condemns Serbian aggression and the atrocities inflicted on Croatian civilians, Štitkovac's sympathy for Croat victims does not extend beyond the purely humanitarian level. He shares with Milošević an opposition to Croatia's right to independence, even though this right was guaranteed by the Yugoslav constitution, and though independence was the will of the overwhelming majority of Croatian citizens as expressed in a free referendum.

Most 'oppositional' journalists in Serbia still seem unable to support the democratic and constitutional rights of the citizens of other republics.

The editors argue against Croatian independence on the grounds that Croatia had not provided sufficient guarantees for the rights of its Serb minority. Had the international community insisted on guarantees, they claim Milošević would have lost his justification for the war. The insincerity of this argument is made apparent by the treatment of Bosnia. The Bosnian government gave full guarantees for the rights of its Serb citizens. This prevented neither the Serbian attack, nor a condemnation of Bosnian independence by the authors of *Yugoslavia's Ethnic Nightmare*.

Udovički and Štitkovac repeat two Serb-nationalist falsehoods: that Bosnian Serbs voted 'one-hundred percent' against Bosnian independence (p. 171); and that the proclamation of Bosnian independence was therefore illegitimate since it was a 'violation of the Bosnian constitutional principle requiring the consent of all

three Bosnian nations in far-reaching decisions such as secession' (p. 175).
In fact, the great majority of Serbs in cities like Sarajevo and Tuzla voted in favour of independence. Elsewhere both Serbs and non-Serbs were prevented from voting in the referendum on independence by the paramilitary forces of Karadžić's Serb Democratic Party, which had no constitutional right either to represent all Bosnian Serbs or to veto Bosnian independence.

Udovički and Štitkovac acknowledge that the alternative was for Bosnia to join Milošević's Greater Serbia, but believe this represented the lesser evil, though it would presumably have violated the 'constitutional principle' requiring the consent of Bosnian Croats and Muslims for a decision of this kind. They argue that for Serbs both in Serbia and in Bosnia, 'self-determination, for historical reasons, had special significance' (p. 175). It did not apparently have similar significance for non-Serbs.

Strong condemnations by several contributors of Croatian aggression in Bosnia provoke mixed feelings. Certainly Croatian President Tudjman has pursued an expansionist policy in Bosnia involving mass killings. But the facts do not bear out the editors' claim that 'the Yugoslav conflict was in fact a conflict between two conceptions of strident ultranationalism, one propounded by the Serbian regime, the other by the Croatian' (p. 9).

Milošević's goal of a Greater Serbia is supported by all the major political parties in his country, none of which recognizes Bosnia's independence or territorial integrity. His aggression against Bosnia was planned and executed uncompromisingly from the start.

Tudjman's anti-Muslim brand of ultranationalism is not shared by any Croatian opposition party, all of which oppose the partition of Bosnia. Tudjman and the anti-Bosnian faction within his regime have precisely lacked popular backing for their expansionism, forcing them to pay lip service to Bosnian independence and vacillate between alliance with Bosnia and underhand collusion with Serbia.

Unlike the *a priori* Serbian aggression, the Croatian attack could have been avoided if the Western powers had thrown their weight behind the majority in Croatia by refusing to endorse the partition of Bosnia. Instead, the Vance-Owen Plan of 1993 offered major territorial concessions that encouraged and legitimized Croat irredentism. Even so, over ten times as many Bosnians were killed through the Serbian aggression as lost their lives on both sides during fighting between Bosnian and Croatian forces.

Serbian forces today occupy territory almost equal in extent to the free areas of Croatia and Bosnia combined. One cannot help suspecting that commentators from Serbia who insist so strenuously on the equal guilt of Croatia are trying above all to shift the burden of blame, the more so since they do not mention any 'mitigating factors' for Croat nationalists as they do for their Serb counterparts.

Yugoslavia's Ethnic Nightmare makes few criticisms of the West's response to the conflict, and none of its conciliation and legitimization of Greater Serbia, or its complicity in the dismemberment of Bosnia.

The contributors object only to the recognition of Bosnia and Croatia, victims of the aggression of the very Serbian regime to which they claim to be an 'opposition'. They argue for the need to appease Serbian nationalism. If only Milošević and Karadžić had been denied the pretext for war presented by Croatian and Bosnian independence...

Mention is made darkly of the fact that Bosnia was recognized on 6 April, the anniversary of Hitler's bombardment of Belgrade in 1941, apparently adding insult to injury for the Serbs. 6 April was also the anniversary of Sarajevo's liberation from the Nazis in 1945, but this is passed over.

The West is condemned for having favoured Croatia over Serbia; this might surprise most Croats, given the economic sanctions, arms embargo and six-month denial of international recognition inflicted on Croatia following its June 1991 declaration of independence.

With the Vance Plan of December 1991, the Western powers forced Croatia to accept a permanent ceasefire just when the Serbian army was on the verge of collapse; since then they have combined threats and bribes to dissuade the Croatian regime from fighting to regain its lost territories, even while the Serbian occupiers continued to consolidate their control of these territories under cover of the United Nations.

The arms embargo against Bosnia is defended on the grounds that its acquisition of arms, combined with promises of American support, 'had become disincentives for the Bosnian government to seek peace' (p. 227). Attempts by the Bosnian government to recapture lost territories are opposed, the editors hoping that 'economic reality' alone will 'render ethnically pure fiefdoms or reservations obsolete' (p. 235). Decades of 'reality' have not, of course, ended ethnic partition in Ireland, Cyprus or Palestine.

It saddens me to have to write in this way about people who seem to be genuinely horrified at the crimes committed against non-Serbs (other than Albanians). The book is above all a testament to the failure of the Titoist project in Serbia. After forty-five years of Titoism based supposedly on the 'right to self-determination, including the right of separation', even relatively sophisticated 'oppositionists' are often incapable of comprehending the principle of national democratic rights, or making the jump from opposing Serbian aggression to supporting the rights of its victims.

Several contributors criticize the 1974 Yugoslav Constitution that increased the sovereignty of the republics and reduced Serbian control over Kosova, claiming 'pressure from Slovenia and Croatia' had led to a constitution that 'crippled' the federal government, with each federal unit 'taking account only of its own needs' so that 'none worried about the common household' (p. 75).

The current catastrophe is said to have its 'roots' in the 1974 Constitution (p. 75) — the Titoist regime is thus faulted for giving the Yugoslav peoples too much freedom. This is the fundamental misconception shared by leftists both in Serbia and in the West: granting freedom to subject peoples just allows them to destabilize the 'common household' and eventually to start killing each other; far better to deny them freedom.

There are many national traditions that give rise to such misconceptions: the Serbian tradition of 'liberating' smaller Balkan neighbours from German or Turkish influences; the British tradition of conquering large parts of Africa and Asia to 'introduce' the natives to parliament and cricket; the American tradition of burning down villages in Indochina in order to'save' the inhabitants from Communism; and above all the left-wing tradition of supporting the Red Army's 'defence of socialism' in Hungary and Czechoslovakia.

The peoples of Bosnia and Chechnya are paying the price for illusions of 'multi-ethnic empire' that prevent socialists and liberals from speaking out for the victims of Belgrade and Moscow. Peace will come to the Balkans not as a result of antiwar activism, or the avoidance of provocations to Serb nationalists, or the restoration of some form of Yugoslavia, but only when Croatia, Bosnia and Kosova are freed from occupation through defeat of the oppressor. Recent victories of the Bosnians around Bihać and at Mt Vlasić, and of the Croatians in Western Slavonia, show that this is not as impossible as it seemed a year ago.

Attila Hoare

This review (written in June 1995) first appeared in
Against the Current*, September/October 1995*

Ed Vulliamy, **Seasons in Hell: understanding Bosnia's war,** Simon and Schuster, New York and London 1994, 370 pp., £6.99

'All day long, the refugees, or deportees as they should more properly be called, had been made to run a gauntlet of fear, hate, arrogance, humiliation and uncertainty on the day that had started with them being bullied out of their homes in Sanski Most. The announcement came over the radio, Radio Sana, that the convoy was leaving, and it had been made clear that this was among the last chances. The previous night had been one of horrific violence, with gangs lobbing grenades through the windows of people's homes and firing willy-nilly on the streets of the Muslim quarters. The mosque had been blown up, all Muslim shops burned and looted, Muslims sacked from their jobs and some undamaged houses allocated to new, incoming Serb families, their names posted above the doorways. Tickets for the journey were purchased from the police, the fare payable in Deutschmarks. People could use the buses and trucks provided, or take their own vehicles. The convoy left shortly before midday.'

Substitute 'Jews' for 'Muslims', 'synagogue' for 'mosque', a German or Polish town for 'Sanski Most', and you are back in a past from which the generations born after the Second World War believed they had been permanently separated. The above passage from Ed Vulliamy's *Seasons in Hell: understanding Bosnia's war* describes only one instance of a carefully planned and coldly executed operation — habitually now described as 'ethnic cleansing', though as Vulliamy insists 'genocide inspired by the ideology of fascism' would be a far more appropriate definition — involving the two thirds of Bosnia-Herzegovina that came under occupation in the first few months of the Serbian blitzkrieg. His book is a powerful testimony to the realities of this terrible war.

What gives it additional value is that through it we hear Bosnians speak of their destroyed existence, their fears and their hopes. As the war progresses in its terrible and dehumanizing fashion, so too these voices articulate an increasing incomprehension of — and despair at — the betrayal (for this is the true word) of international law and those values which Western civilization claims to be its unique contribution to historical progress. Out of 20,000 Muslims who once lived in 'the neat and pretty town Sanski Most', only 1,000 remained by the end. Within weeks, in this way, a town that in typically Bosnian fashion had been multi-ethnic — 44 per cent Muslim, 42 per cent Serb, 8.5 per cent Croat and 4 per cent other — lost more than half its population. Some of those expelled were put into concentration camps — which Vulliamy was among the first to visit. Others were herded across mountains towards the central area under government control, or ended up leaving Bosnia altogether. Serbia's concept of the war as a racial and religious crusade — pioneered a year earlier in Croatia — established a model that came to be emulated subsequently by Croatia itself, as forces under Zagreb's control pushed from the west towards central Bosnia. Guided by similar annexationist aims, these practised the same odious policies. At some point, albeit in desperation, the Muslims in central Bosnia started to respond in kind. As a nation, they in particular faced the prospect of extinction. That they have thus far escaped their own 'final solution' has been due first to the Bosnian state's capacity for self-defence and secondly to the willingness of a limited number of countries — *not* including Britain — to offer sanctuary to significant numbers of a people that, like the Jews in earlier times, found itself thrust outside all laws or moral rules.

The great value of Vulliamy's book lies in such detailed rendering of the horrors of this war, which makes it an indispensable source of reference. Yet even such an account fails to convey fully what this violent alteration of a centuries-old ethnic and cultural configuration has done to that part of Europe. This is what Armageddon must look like. 'Seasons in Hell' is indeed an apt description. Vulliamy's angry, passionate account of the destruction of the Bosnian state and society is also explicit about the reasons for his anger. It is directed above all against the ever-deepening complicity of Western chancelleries — especially the British Foreign Office — with the perpetrators of the Bosnian cataclysm. Unlike the politicians, who not only knew what was happening and did nothing but also did their best to hide their knowledge from the public, it was journalists like Vulliamy who braved great dangers in order to tell the true story. It is thanks to their efforts that one is led to question a system of governance in which citizens are denied any say in shaping their country's response to a war that is the harbinger of a violent European future. British — and Western — handling of the war in Bosnia has revealed the fragility of what we have assumed to be a *terra firma* of international law and rules of conduct, codified in numerous conventions including the founding Charter of the United Nations. The response amounts in practice to a wilful tearing up of all such international agreements and a brazen acceptance of the principle that only might is right.

If, however, you wish to understand the causes of the former Yugoslavia's disintegration and the forces that set this war in motion, then Vulliamy is a poor guide. This is a matter of both factual and analytical weaknesses. Here are a few examples taken at random. In 1992 Bosnia did not opt for independence 'from Yugoslavia', since Yugoslavia by then was no longer in existence. The war in Bosnia was not due to Serbia's and Croatia's desire to 're-establish their ancient frontiers' (the presence of these states on Bosnian soil represented but a fleeting moment in the history of the country, as short in duration as — for example — Bosnia's incorporation of central Dalmatia), but was simply the result of a direct attack by Serbia. Moreover, as Vulliamy himself observes in other parts of the book, the policy of partitioning Bosnia-Herzegovina has always been unpopular in Croatia, as it has been with the Catholic Church — unlike the way things were in Serbia. There was no 'War of the Maps already nascent between Croats and Serbs during the 1980s'; on the contrary, only in Serbia were Yugoslavia's internal borders challenged at that time (by the bulk of its political and intellectual establishment, what is more). Croatia's eagerness to defend itself in 1991 should not be ascribed, as Vulliamy ascribes it, to some great desire to go to war with Serbia: how could it be, in view of Croatia's initial near-total lack of arms? At the start of the Serbian aggression against Croatia, not 'a few' but more than half the country's Serbs found themselves outside the self-proclaimed 'Krajina'. The four Cs found in the Serbian state emblem do not come from the motto 'Samo Sloga Srbina Spašava', but reflect a Byzantine heraldic inheritance. Dragiša Cvetković, who in 1939 signed the infamous agreement with the Croatian Peasant Party leader Vladimir Maček partitioning Bosnia-Hercegovina, was not 'a Serbian diplomat' but the Prime Minister of Yugoslavia. Nebojša Popov, once a dissident Belgrade sociologist, could hardly be described as a 'Titoist Communist'. Milošević did not become head of the Serbian Communist party after defeating Ivan Stambolić, for it was Stambolić who gave him the post in the first place. Finally, the war in Bosnia may be seen as a 'War of Maps', but it is certainly not a 'War of the *narod*', i.e. an ethnic war. In fact the schema into which Vulliamy tries to fit the wars in Croatia and Bosnia-Herzegovina is far too simple and static, further aggravated by scant knowledge of events in the former Yugoslavia prior to the break-up of the ruling League of Communists.

These weaknesses, however, should not detract from the immense value of Vulliamy's book, which lies in its urgent compassion for, and attachment to, what Bosnia-Herzegovina has signified: a multicultural co-existence of which Europe should have been proud, but which it did nothing to protect.

Branka Magaš

This review first appeared in The Tablet *on 19 February* 1995

Susan L. Woodward, **Balkan Tragedy: chaos and dissolution after the cold war,** Brookings Institution, Washington DC 1996, 536 pp., £15.16

Apologists for Communism and Western cold warriors, though from opposing trenches, tended to agree on one point at least. They saw a complete dichotomy between a-national Communism in Eastern Europe and the USSR and the national-democratic (or bourgeois-reactionary) socio-political orders that had gone before. The events of 1989-91 in this view represented a sharp break: a victory for liberal democracy and/or reactionary nationalism over Communism. In the former Yugoslavia and the Caucasus, in particular, this break was accompanied by bloody wars of succession, and former Cold War antagonists in the West have often joined in lamenting the passing of the 'Communist man's burden', whereby authoritarian but impartial Marxism-Leninism 'kept the lid on ethnic conflict'. From here it is only a short step to support for the attempts of the imperial centres, Moscow and Belgrade, to 'restore order' among the tribes. Thus Walter Laqueur, in a vitriolic anti-Communist polemic against even the most vaguely pro-Soviet intellectuals and historians (*The Dream that Failed*, Oxford 1994), did not think it odd simultaneously to praise the Soviet regime's murderous occupation of the Azerbaijani capital of Baku in 1990, stating baldly that 'the intention of Russian forces was to restore law and order'.

The ideological strait-jacket of the Cold War has been a particular barrier to efforts to understand the break-up of Yugoslavia. Those who have bothered to look at its history during World War II know well that Tito's Partisans, who brought the Communists to power in Yugoslavia, constituted a heterogenous force if ever there were one, including Croats fighting for Croatian sovereignty, Serbs fighting to unite all Serbs within a single state, and Bosnians fighting for Bosnian statehood. Alongside the original anti-fascist patriots, the Partisan ranks came to include by the end of the war former Ustashe, Chetniks and Muslim SS recruits. Yet post-war historians consistently mistook form for content, seeing in Communism the negation, rather than the uneasy reconciliation, of Yugoslavia's conflicting national projects. Since 1991, a wealth of books have appeared arguing that, once the undemocratic but anti-national Communist order began to break down in the 1980s under the impact of an economic crisis, its antithesis spontaneously and inevitably re-emerged: irrational but popular 'rival nationalisms' that plunged Yugoslavia into war. Since the war was caused by the 'collapse of Communism', it followed that it could have been avoided if only elements of the Communist Yugoslav old order had been propped up, such as those represented by Yugoslavia's reformist and centralist last prime minister, Ante Marković, or, more ominously, by the Yugoslav People's Army (JNA), seen here as a force of 'law and order'. The secession of Slovenia and Croatia, and their subsequent recognition by the EC, are regularly presented as the actions most responsible for the outbreak and prolongation of war. Although the principles of Croatian and Slovenian sovereignty were integral elements of Yugoslav constitutionalism, and although the JNA in 1991 was hardly an impartial defender of the 'brotherhood and unity' of the Yugoslav nations, writers of this ilk have persisted in viewing the crumbling Yugoslav state, stained as it already was with the blood of thousands of its own citizens, as the only bulwark against 'rival nationalisms' analysed with equal vagueness (form once again being confused with content), so that Serbian nationalism appears as just one nationalism among many, and not necessarily the worst.

Susan Woodward's book is the most extensive version to date of the approach. Writing as a one-time advisor to UN Special Envoy Yasushi Akashi, her thesis is familiar enough: economic and constitutional collapse coupled with widespread social despair created a void that the rival leaders of the Yugoslav national groups sought to fill through mutually exclusive national projects. She writes euphemistically that 'fundamental disputes' concerned 'the locus of sovereignty and of new borders that had been created by the breakup of the state' (p. 13) — in rather the same way, she might have reminded us, that the 1939 dispute between Germany and Poland over the 'locus of sovereignty and of new borders' was created by the collapse of the Versailles settlement.

Woodward's book shows how easy the passage is from identification with the centralized Yugoslav state and Army to support for Serbian nationalism. Criticism of republican autonomy vis-à-vis the Federal centre is a frequent theme, seamlessly extended to opposition to the overwhelmingly Albanian province of Kosova's autonomy vis-à-vis the republic of Serbia. Describing 'Milošević's objective' as 'to restore the constitutional integrity of the republic [of Serbia] by ending the extensive autonomy granted Kosovo and Vojvodina by the 1974 Constitution' (p. 94), she dismisses Albanian claims to self-determination on the grounds that 'their constitutional classification' — by that same 1974 constitution, presumably — 'as a nationality rather than a constituent nation made them ineligible for such rights' (p. 106). She subsequently criticizes the EC's call for the restoration of Kosova's autonomy in 1991, 'which was the very problem of the 1974 Constitution that Serbia had spent the 1980s attempting to reverse' (p. 182). This contrasts sharply with her treatment of the Serb minorities in Croatia and Bosnia and, by implication, Croatia's and Bosnia's own claims to 'constitutional integrity'. She writes, for instance, that in the summer of 1990 the 'Serbs in the *krajina* (border) region of Croatia and Bosnia were beginning to arm in self-defense' (p. 148). And again, referring without comment to the wholly bogus claim that Serbs owned 65% of land-holdings in Bosnia, she writes that 'the Bosnian Serb army under General Mladić pushed instead to fill in the patchwork quilt of these land-holdings to make contiguous, state-like territory', which was 'intended to ensure the survival of the Serbs as a nation in this area' (p. 269). Woodward is particularly ready to defend the JNA, which in the course of 1991 had 'come to the defense, not only of the Yugoslav border, but also of civil order and of minorities during violent clashes between Croats and Serbs in Croatia in the spring' (p. 165), and which 'continuing into September 1991' had been attempting 'to provide such a neutral buffer between Serbs and Croats, particularly in eastern Croatia, so as to dampen the fighting and create cease-fires' (p. 257). She neglects to mention that this 'neutral buffer' had been arming Serb extremists within Croatia since the summer of 1990, since its true intention, as Yugoslavia's last minister of defence General Kadijević has publicly admitted, was to establish new borders for an expanded, Greater Serbia.

Woodward's apologies for the Serbian side contrast with her treatment of Croatia and Slovenia. One of her favourite arguments is that Milošević's claim to be the 'protector of Serbs wherever they lived was the logical equivalent' of the 'identification of Slovene sovereignty and the defense of Slovene human rights' and was 'based on an equally legitimate but alternative concept of a nation' (p. 133). Indeed Radovan Karadžić's political project simply involved 'transferring the Slovene precedent (of the right of nations to form states within a state and, if they wish, to secede) from the republics to the constituent nations of federal Yugoslavia. His aim was to legitimize the sovereignty of Bosnian Serbs within Bosnia' (p. 211). Elsewhere, Woodward claims that Slovenia 'was not a state' (p. 164), and that in recognizing the independence of Slovenia and Croatia the EC was 'not only creating new states but dissolving an old one — Yugoslavia' (p. 250). Quite apart from whitewashing the

Serbian aggressive campaign, such statements reveal an extraordinary ignorance on the part of this self-proclaimed expert on the nature of federations in general and the Yugoslav federation in particular. In fact, Yugoslavia, identified by Woodward solely with the central state and army based on Belgrade, was specifically a federation of six republics and two provinces; within it Slovenia and Croatia functioned as sovereign nation-states, with the right of veto over the central bodies' decisions.

Woodward not only defends Serb nationalism's aspirations in principle, but repeats some of its most grotesque claims: 'The effect in Bosnia-Hercegovina of demographic changes and emigration in the 1960s and 1970s, for example, was to complete the process begun with the genocidal campaign in 1941-44 of reducing the Serb population from a majority to a minority' (p. 213); 'From the mid-1980s on, both Austria and the Vatican had pursued a strategy to increase their sphere of economic and spiritual influence in central and eastern Europe, respectively' (pp. 148-9). Indeed, Austrian and German support for the Republic of Croatia's independence was 'an extension of the German idea of citizenship through blood alone (*jus sanguinis*) and the impossibility of ethnically heterogeneous states — ideas that had been at the core of fascist ideology' (p. 206), as if Milošević's 'alternative concept of a nation', Karadžić's quest for 'the sovereignty of Bosnian Serbs within Bosnia' and General Mladić's work on 'filling in the patchwork quilt' were not precisely driven by the ideology of blood and soil.

By contrast with Germany's and Austria's evil intentions, Russia's view on the Yugoslav issue had little to do with pro-Serbian bias, 'but grew instead from its understanding of the issues at stake as a result of its more similar experiences in the twentieth century and contemporaneously in dealing with the national question' (p. 205): presumably Woodward is referring here to Russia's 'similar experiences' with the Chechens and Crimean Tartars. Despite the enormous wealth of scholarly works cited and almost a hundred pages of notes, Woodward repeats Serb-nationalist falsehoods that no serious scholar would entertain for a moment. One prime example is her claim that the HDZ regime in Croatia 'adopted the historical symbols of Croatian statehood (coat of arms and flag) that had last been used by the fascist state in 1940-45' (p. 120); in reality, as every student of Croatian history knows, the red-cornered chequerboard that adorns the Croatian flag today was used by the Socialist Republic of Croatia within Yugoslavia, but *not* by the

Ustashe. Another is her allegation (p. 236) that Serbian attacks on hospitals were provoked by the Bosnians and Croatians themselves, in order to win international sympathy — a serious charge for which she neglects to provide any sources.

Susan Woodward has written a long, turgid and repetitive work whose seemingly scholarly style and pretence of objectivity mask effective acquiescence in Serbian war aims and a dislike of Germany, Austria and Croatia that borders on hatred. Another main dimension of Woodward's thesis concerns the way in which the Germans and Americans in turn supposedly sabotaged international attempts to resolve the conflict. This line of argument presents few surprises for anyone familiar with the similar themes emanating from British and French official sources throughout the wars of succession in former Yugoslavia. What makes this book unique, however, is its revelation of the degree of ideological sympathy for Serbian nationalist aspirations in the highest echelons of the UN operation in the very countries suffering the effects of Serbian aggression.

Attila Hoare

This review first appeared in Bosnia Report, *no. 15*
(April-June 1996)

Warren Zimmermann, **Origins of a Catastrophe**, Times Books, New York 1996, 270 pp., $25

Warren Zimmermann arrived in Belgrade on 9 March 1989, a few months after Serbia had seized direct control of three out of Yugoslavia's eight federal territories (Vojvodina, Kosovo and Montenegro), destroying the country's constitutional framework in the process. Yugoslavia was visibly falling apart; with the recognition of Slovenia and Croatia in January 1992 it would finally cease to exist, though the official certificate of death — symbolized by its removal from the United Nations — has thus far been withheld. By the time Zimmermann was recalled home on 12 May 1992, the JNA had attacked and retreated from Slovenia, Serbia had occupied a quarter of Croatia, and Milošević's armies were conducting a genocidal war in Bosnia-Herzegovina. In January 1994 Zimmermann resigned from the State Department, citing its passivity in Bosnia-Herzegovina and its personnel policy. *Origins of a Catastrophe*, which appeared after the Dayton Agreement had been signed, describes the three years he spent in Yugoslavia and offers his views on why it fell apart.

The approach of the Bush administration, which Zimmermann took with him to Belgrade, was encapsulated in the formula 'unity and democracy'. In its original formulation, 'unity' was made conditional upon 'democracy': 'we could only support the country's unity in the context of progress towards democracy; we would be strongly opposed to unity imposed and maintained by force.' In late 1989, however, the emphasis was reversed: 'unity without democracy meant Serbian or military dictatorship; democracy without unity meant war. Democracy and unity were inseparable Siamese twins of Yugoslavia's fate. The loss of one meant the other would perish.' In its new formulation, this was not so much a policy as a puzzle, since it contained no answer to the real problem: how was Yugoslavia to be democratized while Belgrade was preparing for war? In the absence of a counter-force capable of stopping Serbia's unfolding aggression, the policy of keeping Yugoslavia together while at the same time encouraging its democratization became mission impossible. In the event, by pursuing Yugoslavia's unity rather than supporting Slovenia and Croatia in their demands for either the country's confederal transformation or its peaceful dissolution, the United States helped ensure its violent break-up.

Zimmermann implies that this policy change was made on his advice. Soon after his arrival he sent a cable cautioning Washington 'not to equate decentralization with democracy or centralism with authoritarianism. These equations might have described the Soviet Union, a ruthless dictatorship from the centre. But they did not describe Yugoslavia.'

What equations did describe Yugoslavia at this point in time? Zimmermann knew that, unlike the Soviet Union, Yugoslavia was a polycentric state — that it functioned as a real federation, and in some important fields as a confederation. What he never understood, however, was that its comparatively higher democracy derived precisely from the fact that political power never condensed in Belgrade — in the central bodies of the Federation — as was the case with the Soviet Union. Like so many ambassadors before him, he viewed Yugoslavia through the spectacles of the capital city. Wrong at all times, this was a particularly grave handicap in the second half of the 1980s, when that city was transformed into the bastion of an aggressive Serbian nationalism. Zimmermann's error, in fact, was uncritically to accept the view then prevalent in Belgrade — not just in the freshly purged League of Communists of Serbia, but also among the latter's domestic critics — that Yugoslavia's problems derived from the weakness of the Federal bodies; and that the constitutional empowerment of the provinces and republics (other than Serbia: Zimmermann registers no complaints about the extension of Serbian power into Kosovo, Vojvodina or Montenegro), far from being a precondition of Yugoslavia's stability and democracy, was little more than a capitulation to ethnic nationalism. The premise that Yugoslavia was destroyed by republican nationalism forms the central message of Zimmermann's book. It stands, however, in sharp contrast to another — and far better established theme: that it was Milošević backed by the JNA who, in wishing to dominate Yugoslavia, ended up by destroying it. For indeed, Yugoslavia's grave-digger was not rampant nationalism as such, but the unchecked armed power of Yugoslavia's largest republic.

Zimmermann's other, equally serious, failure was to register the extent to which Milošević's assault upon the constitution had made the Federal bodies illegitimate and inoperative. At the level of the Yugoslav Presidency, which was also commander-in-chief of Yugoslavia's armed forces, Serbia now had four votes in place of its earlier one. It was four times more powerful than any other republic, indeed as powerful as all the other republics put together. And it was backed by the Army. These were the real equations describing Yugoslavia at this point in time, and they erased the whole preceding period from 1945 on: the Yugoslavia Zimmermann had known during an earlier posting no longer existed. It was this sudden redistribution of power within Yugoslavia that plunged the country into crisis, rendered it unstable and placed its survival in question. Zimmermann, however, never mentions this seminal moment in Yugoslavia's break-up. He writes that 'the Slovenian and Croatian declarations of independence [in June 1991] cast Yugoslavia into a political and constitutional limbo', whereas the country had already entered such a limbo in 1989, with the forcible closure of the Kosovo assembly. No return to constitutional order — to the status quo ante Kosovo — could be achieved without a confrontation with Milošević. If the other republics shied away from this, it was because of his support in the JNA, which at the time of Zimmermann's assumption of ambassadorial office was already policing Kosovo on Serbia's behalf. In this situation, seeking greater autonomy from Belgrade was a logical choice and an essentially democratic one.

For reasons that remain unclear, Washington was ready to accept the redistribution of power in Serbia's favour. Rather than insisting that the state of emergency in Kosovo be lifted, it reduced the problem to its human-rights dimension. Zimmermann headed the US delegation to the Conference of Security and Cooperation in Europe, where Yugoslavia — criticized, on account of Kosovo, as the country with the worst human-rights record outside the Soviet Union — 'had gotten off lightly' thanks to the Americans. As ambassador, he was irritated by the efforts which US Congressmen Robert Dole and Tom Lantos were making on Kosovo's behalf, leading to Congress's adoption in November 1990 of a resolution to withhold financial assistance to Yugoslavia until its treatment of the Albanian population improved. Zimmermann protests in his book that this largely symbolic act made life harder for the Yugoslav Prime Minister Ante Marković, but the book shows that his dissent went much deeper, since he accepted one of the central tenets of Serb nationalism, that Serbia had special rights in Kosovo. He writes, quite inaccurately, that Kosovo is to Serbia what Jerusalem is to Israel and that 'the Kosovo issue [...] may have to be settled one day by some sort of partition'. Rebecca West, whom Zimmermann greatly admires, may be responsible for this. Reading Zimmermann's book, one is struck by how little he knew or sympathized with other Yugoslav republics and nations, in comparison with Serbia and the Serbs.

Yet Kosovo's fate was not a sui generis problem. The state of emergency which the Yugoslav army had imposed in Kosovo was

emblematic of the whole new mood in Belgrade. A year before
Zimmermann came to Belgrade a self-appointed 'Military Council'
made up of the JNA's high command, meeting in secret, had
concluded that Slovenia's precocious democracy amounted to a
counter-revolution. The Army's subsequent arrest and trial, in
defiance of the Slovene leadership, of several young journalists was
a provocation: the JNA was testing the waters for a military
takeover. When, in February 1989, practically all of Slovenia,
including its Communist leadership, publicly protested against the
state of emergency in Kosovo, it was in the knowledge that Slovenia
could be next in line for 'Kosovization'. Kosovo also provoked the
first demand that Slovene soldiers should leave the JNA: the
Slovenes did not wish to be associated with what one of the arrested
journalists described as 'state terrorism in Kosovo'. Yet
Zimmermann, talking to Milan Kučan soon after his arrival, found
himself bewildered by the Slovene leader's concern with Kosovo.

In the Yugoslavia being forcibly remodelled by Milošević,
democracy demanded decentralisation if it were to avoid break-up.
Unity and democracy, far from marching in harmony, were heading
in opposite directions, and the US ambassador was left clutching at
straws. 'In the seething cauldron of ethnic rivalries, Yugoslavia
needed a leader who could deal with the growing economic crisis
and at the same time appeal to Yugoslavs to stay together and build
a democratic society. Amazingly, a man who represented all these
qualities found himself the new prime minister of Yugoslavia in
March 1989.' Although Zimmermann knew that the post of
Yugoslav prime minister in fact wielded little authority, 'we in the
embassy worked as hard as we could on Marković's behalf and did
achieve a high public level of US political support for the embattled
prime minister'. Financial assistance, on the other hand, was not
forthcoming: 'Yugoslavia did not look like a good bet', indeed
'Yugoslavia looked like a loser'. Marković's room for manoeuvre
was strictly circumscribed by Milošević. When, in late 1989,
Milošević imposed an economic embargo against Slovenia because
of its stand on Kosovo, Zimmermann told Washington that 'the
odds against Prime Minister Marković's success were lengthening'.
And although the State Department's estimate was that Marković
was more likely to fail than not, the US ambassador continued to
encourage him until the ambitious prime minister, instead of
supporting Slovenia's and Croatia's calls for confederation, came to
believe that, by calling for countrywide elections for the Federal
assembly on the basis of one-person-one-vote, he could strengthen

the authority of his office and thus save Yugoslavia. Both Zimmermann and Milošević gave him support in this, but it was only logical that Slovenia and Croatia would block a constitutional innovation that was little more than grist to Milošević's mill. When Zimmermann writes that, as a result, 'Yugoslavia perished without its citizens ever being permitted to cast their votes as Yugoslavs', he only shows his profound misunderstanding of the nature of the Yugoslav federation. Sounding a surprisingly Marxist-Leninist note, he blames the abysmal electoral performance of Ante Marković's Alliance of Reform Forces on its inability 'to tap into the sympathetic reserve, reflected in the polls, among workers and peasants'. Later, however, after he had given up on both Marković and the Yugoslavs, he admitted that 'tragically, Yugoslavs never saw themselves as a nation'; that Yugoslavia had 'congenital defects': 'it was a state, not a nation. Few felt much loyalty to Yugoslavia itself.' To judge by this book, Zimmermann never quite managed to work out whether the Yugoslavs were just born nationalists or whether in 1990 they were simply deluded by their leaders — or even tricked by a small and secretive bunch of extremists.

Yet, if the Yugoslavs had a chance to vote for Marković at all, this was due to democratic change in Slovenia and Croatia. Their leaders' decision to let people choose their government was part of their strategy of national self-defence: they responded to the JNA threat by reaching for the powerful weapon of democratic legitimation. Zimmermann writes that the Croatian Communists hurried into elections because they feared a popular overthrow on the Czech model, but this is not true. In Croatia popular wrath grew almost exclusively in reaction to the Croatian leaders' passivity in the face of Serbia's aggressive interference in Croatia. Zimmermann informed Washington that Milošević was driving the Slovenes towards separatism and the Croatians towards nationalism, but in his book he omits to say that the choice which the leaders of those republics faced at the end of 1989 was between being removed by their own people or by Milošević (in a repetition of the model applied earlier in Vojvodina, Kosovo and Montenegro). Indeed, well before the elections Serbia was engaged in destabilizing the governments in Croatia, Bosnia and Macedonia, using the tried and tested formula. In the middle of 1990, a few months after the elections, it yielded its first result when the main communication link between northern Croatia and Dalmatia was cut at Knin by men armed and trained by the JNA. In the plans that the JNA made in early 1990 for the overthrow of the now non-Communist governments, the same methods were to be applied in Macedonia and Bosnia-Herzegovina, in conjunction with an outright military subjugation of Slovenia and Croatia. By declaring itself neutral in the conflict between Serbia and Slovenia-Croatia, Washington effectively aided the forces of aggression and war.

On the eve of the Slovenian and Croatian elections of April 1990, the State Department sent a cable to its ambassadors in Europe stating that it was up to the citizens of Yugoslavia to decide their form of government. This is precisely what the citizens went on to do. In reality, however, their choice had been rejected in advance, since Washington's preference for Yugoslav unity far outweighed its commitment to democracy. The 'instruction cable' contained also a warning to European governments that 'the elections might bring to power those advocating confederation and even dissolution', and that they should 'avoid actions that could encourage secession'. The maxim that democracy in Yugoslavia was welcome only if served unity ensured that the electoral results first in Slovenia and Croatia and later in the rest of Yugoslavia would be qualified as anti-democratic and denounced as 'nationalism'. 'In bringing nationalism to power, the elections helped snuff out the very flame of democracy they had kindled', writes Zimmermann. Again: 'The paradox of the Yugoslav elections in 1990 [was that], in bringing democracy to birth, they helped to strangle it in its cradle.' In reality, of course, there was no paradox: it was not the elections that strangled Yugoslav democracy, but the JNA's use of force against democratically elected non-Communist governments. Zimmermann's description of Washington's warning as 'prophetic' would be much more credible if the cable had contained also information about the Army's intention to go to war. He omits to say that at the end of April 1990 the JNA high command had sent a secret order (unknown to all but the Serbian leaders) to the commanders of the military districts to disarm all the Yugoslav republics except for Serbia and Montenegro, by seizing their Territorial Defence weapons.

Following Marković's débâcle, the United States was left with no other policy but, as Zimmermann writes, to wait for Armageddon. And whereas it may be true that Washington never actually condoned the use of force against Slovenia and Croatia, its public and persistent disapproval of their moves towards independence, including the imposition in May 1991 of a unilateral US arms embargo, served only to confuse the Yugoslav actors. Each of them believed that the West had given them a mandate of sorts. The hapless Marković, entrusted by the West with saving Yugoslavia, realized after the elections that this could be achieved only by force; but when he sought to make a deal with the JNA, he was warned by James Baker that: 'if [he] resorted to force, Marković's support in the West would be threatened', since the JNA was 'not to be trusted'.[1] Slovenia and Croatia, relying on Western advocacy of democracy, claimed their countries' independence in the name of a clearly expressed popular will. The JNA attacked them on the assumption that Washington's preference for Yugoslavia's unity gave it a green light. Serbia, whose armed expansion into Kosovo had been accepted and whose arming of Serbs in Croatia and Bosnia-Herzegovina had provoked no international outcry, had no reason to think that, with the might of the JNA on its side, Greater Serbia was an unrealistic proposition. When Baker came to Belgrade 'armed with a statement committing all thirty-three countries [of the OSCE] to unity, reform, human rights, and a peaceful solution of the crisis' but nothing else, the Yugoslavs were left in no doubt that the United States would not use force to stop Serbia and the Army. The republics were left to fend for themselves as best as they might.

Of the three republics attacked, the ones which fared better were those that managed to raise an army to fight the aggression. These forces had to be created in secret, under embargo, and practically overnight. Bosnia was the last to do so, and only after the aggression against it had begun. Zimmermann notes coolly that 'Izetbegović, unlike Tudjman, had done almost nothing to build a Bosnian military force'. Indeed, Izetbegović went on believing almost to the end that he could rely on the Army, although 'he and I knew that the JNA was unlikely to accept his civilian authority since it didn't accept Bosnia's independence'. The Americans knew as early as May 1991 that the JNA was arming Radovan Karadžić, but not only did they do nothing about it, they did not even warn Izetbegović. In early 1992 the US ambassador 'detected no inkling on [Izetbegović's] part of the massive aggression that the JNA, together with Milošević and Karadžić, was mounting against him'.

[1] However, General Kadijević told his staff prior to the intervention in Slovenia that the Army had the support of the United States and the Soviet Union and 'real support' from Britain and France (a summary of the speech is given in Janez Janša, *Pomaci*, Zagreb 1993, pp. 128-9). General Marijan Čad, whose 4th Corps based on Rijeka took part in the operation, claims they were told it had been 'agreed between General Kadijević, prime minister Marković and American secretary of state James Baker' (*Globus*, Zagreb, 19 December 1993).

Zimmermann also omits to mention just how much the United States, through the medium of Cyrus Vance, had contributed to the firepower of that aggression. Vance arrived in Croatia in late 1991 to negotiate a permanent cease-fire as part of the 'Vance Plan'. Finding the Croatians laying siege to the JNA barracks, in order to prevent the Army guns being used against their cities, he told Zimmermann of being 'appalled by this shabby treatment of professional soldiers' — this even though the JNA had been targeting mainly civilians and conducting ethnic cleansing, had totally destroyed Vukovar and was now busy shelling Dubrovnik. During the negotiations Vance insisted on 'treating the JNA with the same degree of respect that he treated the Croatian government', despite knowing full well that the JNA was by now an instrument of Greater Serbia. One consequence of Vance's respect for this army was that, in addition to being permitted to remain in control of one quarter of Croatian territory, it was allowed to withdraw from the rest of Croatia with the bulk of its weapons. From Yugoslavia's only jet-refitting facility located in Zagreb, the JNA took 42 aircraft, 32 aircraft engines, and 3,500 tons of equipment. The evacuation of the JNA base at Šibenik alone involved 2,100 vehicles carrying 12,000 tons of matériel. Altogether, the JNA took from Croatia 300 tanks, 280 APCs and 210 aircraft, as well as tens of thousands of tons of equipment and supplies.[2] Some of these weapons were immediately turned against the Croatians, some were left in the areas under Serbian occupation, some were taken to Serbia. The great bulk, however, was transferred to Bosnia, together with 'professional soldiers' freshly released from Croatia (one of these soldiers was Ratko Mladić). This military power was used in Bosnia with devastating effect. It should be recalled, also, that this transfer of weapons to Serbian control took place in the context of an arms embargo imposed by the Security Council in September 1991. No wonder Zimmermann found General Veljko Kadijević singing the praises of Cyrus Vance in early January 1992, a few months before the JNA moved against Bosnia. 'There are two roads', Kadijević told the American. 'You can follow the road of Germany with its early recognition policy; that road leads to bloodshed. Or you can follow the Vance road, in search of a comprehensive political solution; that road leads to peace.' Appalled by this transfer of weapons to Bosnia's enemies, Izetbegović asked that UN peacekeepers be sent to Bosnia as well, but the United States refused to support this

2 Norman Cigar, 'Croatia's War of Independence: the parameters of war termination', *Journal of Slavic Military Studies* (forthcoming) [pub. 1997].

request. Zimmermann, to his credit, did so — but, as he admits, not as hard as he should have.

Unprepared for the war, Bosnia was to be mercilessly laid to waste, the bulk of its population turned into refugees and the Muslim component exposed to genocide, its territory partitioned. In view of what happened to Bosnia and Zimmermann's own anguish over the US response, you would think that *Origins of a Catastrophe* would include some reflections on the value of organized self-defence. Far from it: much of Zimmermann's passion is devoted to castigating Slovenia and Croatia for attempting to raise their own armies in order to withstand the coming attack. Thus in late June 1991, when the JNA was already busy truncating Croatia, Zimmermann complained that the Croatian president 'was itching to use his growing Croatian army against rebellious Serbs. [I] warned Tudjman that the United States would give no support to the militarization of his republic. Democracy would be the best guarantee of Croatian security.' The proposition that Croatian security and democracy was linked was true enough: Croatian Serbs would not have joined the rebellion in quite such numbers if Zagreb had not provoked them, especially in Eastern Slavonia. Tudjman's anti-Serb policy undermined both Croatia's democracy and its defence effort. The proposition is largely invalidated, however, by the imputation that in the summer of 1991 the main threat to Croatia's security came from its defective democracy, rather than from Serbia's designs on its territory. Far from itching for action, Tudjman did not in fact wish for war and believed it would not happen. He remained convinced to the very end that Slovenia would not be attacked and, after it was, that Croatia would not. After Croatia too was attacked, he firmly believed that the war could be ended by negotiating with Belgrade. Such was his commitment to a negotiated settlement that, for the sake of it, he persistently neglected Croatia's defence needs. This is shown by his repeated and outright rejections — in December 1990, June 1991 and July 1991 — of the defence plans which the Croatian generals submitted to him; by his passivity in the face of the JNA attack on Slovenia; by his unwillingness to authorize, until it was almost too late, the seizure of JNA garrisons and arms depots; by his giving Serbia time to reconstruct its army after the JNA's débâcle in Slovenia; by his belated decision, in September 1991 after Croatian military commanders faced with the loss of all Slavonia threatened to rebel, to permit the creation of an army (ZNG was not an army but a substitute for it); by his refusal to name Serbia the aggressor and declare a state of war between Croatia and Serbia; by his insistence that Stipe Mesić stay on in Belgrade even after Croatia was attacked; by his readiness to accept ceasefires at — from the point of view of Croatia's defence — the most inopportune moments; by the alacrity with which he accepted the (for Croatia) unfavourable Vance Plan; etc. It was not Tudjman's militarism that was the problem, but rather the reverse: Croatia's military weakness at this stage only encouraged Serbia's aggression. Despite his protestations, Zimmermann knew that Croatia was militarily not ready to take on the JNA, for he also warned Tudjman that independence could cost him territory. In his book he draws up a lurid and wholly inaccurate picture of Croatia's military readiness on the eve of the JNA attack. Its government, he writes, was 'dominated by people whose inclination and expertise were in clandestine and military affairs', while 'Croatia's police and the military probably did add up to an army larger than the armies of Belgium, Canada and the Netherlands, Portugal, Austria, or Sweden'. And when the Croatian government tried belatedly to defend its cities and population by laying siege to Army barracks and military depots, Zimmermann joined Vance in defending the aggressor: 'Despite its depredations [such as committing war crimes on a large scale], the Yugoslav army remained a proud institution that the Croats were trying to humiliate.'

Despite considerable evidence to the contrary and inverting cause and effect, Zimmermann argues that the Army had 'lost its bearings with the 1990 elections', and that it was the 'rise of Slovenian and Croatian nationalism and separatism' that led it to abandon its 'firm opposition to nationalism' and become the military arm of Serbian nationalism. His sympathy for the JNA derives, it seems, from his perception of it as a 'constitutional protector of Yugoslavia'. Yet the Yugoslav constitution, while obliging the Army to defend Yugoslavia against external enemies, specifically prohibited it from interfering in internal political disputes, except by consensus of all eight federal partners — which was never reached. His book is peppered with various bogus claims for the legitimacy of JNA action in Slovenia and Croatia. 'The JNA's concerns', he writes of the time when the Yugoslav army was threatening those two republics, without approval from any legitimate Yugoslav body, 'were not imaginary. Yugoslavia was still one country, with one constitutionally approved army. Federal law was on the JNA's side. Moreover, the growing republican armies gave every indication of being hostile.[...] The Yugoslav Army had a point in its desire to prevent the proliferation of armies in the still-sovereign state of Yugoslavia.'

The operational plan which JNA drew up for its action against Slovenia involved 400 tanks and 25,000 men; its aim was, after sealing the country's borders, to take control of Ljubljana prior to installing a new Communist government run from Belgrade by Milošević. In Zimmermann's view, however, it was Slovenia and not the Army that initiated the war, by taking control of customs posts on its western borders — though this act involved no violence at all. Echoing Kadijević, he treats Slovenia's assertion of control over its borders as an attack on Yugoslavia's territorial integrity: 'in a lightning manoeuvre the Slovenes had in a few hours moved the borders of Yugoslavia, stable for half a century, a hundred miles to the east'. 'It wasn't accurate', he writes, springing to the defence of an army now in free fall, 'to talk about a JNA "invasion" of Slovenia, since the JNA was in its own country. Its troops were, quite normally, stationed in camps in every Yugoslav republic.' The JNA was, if anything, the victim: 'The not very heroic Slovenian (and later Croatian) tactic was not to take on the JNA directly, but to lay siege to JNA barracks and try to starve the soldiers out.' And, to complete the picture, Slovenia's resistance was in fact not democratically validated at all: 'the most extreme faction in a coalition [forming the majority in the Slovene parliament] provoked a war by stealth without even informing key Slovene leaders.' The Slovenian resistance — which would pass any democratic test in terms of popular mobilization and the modalities of its organization — Zimmermann dismisses outright as '[Slovene Minister of Defence Janez] Janša's war': 'Janša's war had alienated the Slovenes permanently from Yugoslavia.' In his book *Pomaci* (Moves), Janša writes how, on 26 June 1991 when Slovenia was celebrating its independence, 'the American military attache arrived incognito in Ljubljana so that he could be directly present at "the show".'

Slovenia's and Croatia's declarations of independence were a moment of truth not for Yugoslavia, which was already gone, but for the West. Zimmermann takes some of the credit for the State Department's next cardinal error: 'I had backed, and in fact helped to create, the US policy of non recognition of Slovenia and Croatia.' Even though by abandoning Slovenia the JNA had given up on Yugoslavia, even though the Federal government and presidency were no longer functioning, and even though the JNA had become a purely Serbian force and was engaged in a dirty war in Croatia, Washington stuck by the failed policy. Zimmermann strongly disapproved of the decision of Carrington's commission in the autumn of 1991 to treat Yugoslavia as non-existent, and of the growing trend in Europe — especially in Germany — towards the recognition of the six republics. Instead, while urging the European Community to defer recognition, 'the State Department encouraged my proddings of republican leaders to find a formula for living together'. When, in late December 1991, the European Community decided to recognize Slovenia and Croatia, the US embassy in Belgrade continued 'carrying out the full range of diplomatic business while being officially accredited to nobody'. The 'diplomatic business' involved, among other things, encouraging the Bosnian president to go to Bonn to plead against recognition of Croatia. For Bosnia this would have been a grave strategic error, since recognition of Croatia's borders amounted also to recognition of two thirds of Bosnia's borders. Although, on meeting Genscher, Izetbegović failed to raise the subject, this did not prevent Tudjman from using Izetbegović's stance on Croatian recognition against prominent Bosnian Croats, as well as against domestic critics who protested his intent to divide Bosnia with Serbia. The old erroneous argument that recognition would bring about war (when, in fact, war had preceded recognition in Slovenia and Croatia) was again trotted out, this time against Bosnian independence. On learning in late December 1991 that Bosnia too would seek international recognition, Zimmermann's comment was: 'This premature push for independence was a disastrous political mistake, since Serbia, Bosnia's vastly more powerful neighbour, now had the pretext it needed to strike.' Given, however, that as he himself writes 'Milošević and Karadžić had been embarked for nearly a year on a comprehensive strategy to tear away two-thirds of Bosnia and incorporate it into Serbia' , there was in reality little point in Bosnia waiting.

And so the US diplomatic gyre went on, describing ever smaller circles. Gone was the insistence on unity and democracy, on democracy for its own sake, or on the evils of nationalism. The Americans now backed the Lisbon conference, at which Bosnia's ethnic partition was for the first time endorsed as a solution nobody knew to what. Though the plan was rejected by the Bosnian assembly, Zimmermann encouraged Izetbegović to accept anything the European Community was ready to endorse. Only after Karadžić had rejected the Cutilheiro plan and declared his own republic, when all easy options were gone and Bosnia was sliding unprepared into a bloody war, did Zimmermann recommend to

Washington that Bosnia be recognized: 'Now the EC had recognized Croatia and Slovenia, Izetbegović's Bosnia was threatened with isolation in a Milošević-dominated "Serbo-slavia".' This was March 1992, three months after the EC's decision. The argument that recognition meant war no longer applied: 'Western recognition did not provoke that aggressive strategy, nor would the lack of Western recognition have deterred it.' On the contrary: 'early Western recognition, right after the expected referendum majority for independence, might present Milošević and Karadžić with a fait accompli difficult for them to overturn.' And in case Milošević were tempted nevertheless, 'we could offer him that recognition [i.e. of Serbia-Montenegro as the sole successor to Yugoslavia] in exchange for his recognition of the territorial integrity of the four other republics, including Bosnia.'

And this is just about how far things have got: Serbia has recognized the territorial integrity of the other four republics (that of Bosnia only conditionally), while believing that it will inherit Yugoslavia's seat in the United Nations. Between the US recognition of Bosnia and Serbia's recognition of Bosnia, however, lay the genocide.

'For three years of the Bosnian war', writes Zimmermann, 'the Western countries had attempted to rebuff the Serbian aggressors, bloated by their use of force, without making them fear that force would be used against them. Western diplomacy was reduced to a kind of cynical theatre, a pretence of useful activity, a way of disguising a lack of will. Diplomacy without force became an unloaded weapon, impotent and ridiculous.' He himself came out in favour of air strikes against Serb targets in Bosnia in July 1992: 'My view was that the Serbs were acting in the belief that NATO wouldn't react. Indeed, no other conclusion could be drawn from the West's past actions.' And he now believes that NATO should have used force already at the end of 1991, to stop the JNA shelling Dubrovnik; even that, in retrospect, it might have been better to have supported Yugoslavia becoming a confederation, albeit this would probably not have saved it in the end. Zimmermann thus deserves credit at least for his readiness to concede that he and his superiors made mistakes.

But the real charge to be levelled against the West is not that it was unwilling to use force against the Serbian aggressors. As the history of the Yugoslav wars of succession shows, Slovenia and Croatia proved perfectly able — despite Western disapproval — to defend themselves. They lacked weapons at first, but soon equipped themselves by taking them from the JNA or purchasing them abroad. The arms embargo made things more difficult, but in the end made little difference. A multinational conscript army, the JNA started to fall apart as soon as it attacked Slovenia. Slovene, Croat, Albanian, Muslim, Macedonian and even Serb and Montenegrin recruits deserted, surrendered or simply refused to be drafted. Slovene and Croat officers joined their republics' defence and most other non-Serbs left as well. Macedonia and Bosnia stopped sending fresh recruits into the army. The war was unpopular in Serbia and Montenegro, and became more so as Serb and Montenegrin casualties began to mount. The break-up of the JNA wiped out Serbia's military superiority. Slovenia and Croatia, with tacit Bosnian support, achieved this without a shot being fired by NATO. And although Serbia remained superior in military hardware, the two republics had the winning advantage of their troops' high morale: they were fighting on home ground.

The problem lay not in Western reluctance to use force, but in the fact that the West essentially took the Serbian side from the start. Whatever Zimmermann may claim, the threat to Yugoslavia and to regional stability came not from the democratic demands of Kosovo, Slovenia or Croatia, but from the undemocratic and militaristic regime in Belgrade. Rather than invest in democracy, however, Washington chose to appease that regime. In 1989, it bowed to the Serbian threat of war and supported Yugoslavia's unity unconditionally. Two years later, instead of breaking the political impasse by recognizing Slovenia and Croatia (and, in Croatia's case, insisting on safeguards for the Serb minority), it allowed Belgrade to do so by recourse to war. Rather than being punished, Serbia was rewarded for its attack on Slovenia with half the weapons held in that republic by the JNA. Six months later, when Serbia faced military defeat in Croatia, the West intervened to save it by offering Croatia international recognition in return for acceptance of the Vance Plan. Since human and material destruction was greater in Croatia than in Slovenia, Serbia's reward was proportionately greater: it got most of the weapons held by the former JNA in Croatia, and swathes of Croatian territory adjacent to the Bosnian border. The Vance Plan — whose first step was highly appropriately initialled in Sarajevo — greatly facilitated Serbian military preparations for the assault on Bosnia.

Moreover, by building upon 'realities on the ground', the plan accepted the logic that had led Milošević to create the Serb 'republics' in Croatia and Bosnia-Herzegovina; and that also led

Tudjman, in advance of 1995, to the corollary view that the re-integration of the UNPA areas into Croatia could durably be secured only by removal of the Serb population from that area of Croatia. By opening the issue of Croatia's borders, it sent the message that Bosnian territory too was up for grabs. In the subsequent negotiations between Tudjman and Milošević on how to divide Bosnia, Croatia's occupied territory was one of the bargaining chips. In the late summer of 1992 Serbia indeed gave back to Croatia the southern portion of the latter's coast, in return for Croatian-controlled northern Bosnia — with more barter to come. True, Zagreb and Belgrade had begun to haggle over Bosnia three months before the outbreak of the war; but the actual business of Bosnia's violent dismemberment proceeded only after the Vance arrangement was in place in Croatia. Had Serbia been defeated and disarmed in Croatia before the Vance Plan was in place, i.e. before the consolidation of 'Republika Srpska Krajina' and the Serbs' isolation within it, most of these Croatian Serbs would have remained in Croatia, while the nascent Republika Srpska, which was no more than a military outpost of Serbia, would have collapsed. The resulting new balance of power in the former Yugoslav area would have provided the basis for a just settlement and lasting peace. Western policy ensured, however, that the war, rather than ending in early 1992, would continue for another four years — and end in a settlement that was not just and could not bring durable peace.

Serbia was rewarded for its aggression against Bosnia-Herzegovina even more generously than it had been in Croatia, in proportion to the scale of destruction and the genocide committed. The United States supported every proposal for Bosnia's ethnic partition from first to last, dissenting occasionally only on details. Unlike with Slovenia and Croatia, whose geopolitical locations had allowed them to break the ban on import of weapons, in the case of Bosnia US support for the arms embargo and persistent disapproval of all Bosnian efforts to organize self-defence contributed positively to the dismemberment of the republic's territory and people. Disarmed and then kept unarmed, Bosnia was hardly in any position to bargain. Its outright partition was prevented only by the fact that, despite the embargo and with little diplomatic support (one should not forget here the valiant efforts of the US Congress to provide some) — i.e. under the most terrible conditions that any country has ever faced — it managed to create an army. The Washington Agreement was a direct result not so much of US diplomacy, as Zimmermann claims, as of this army's defeat of Croatian forces (which showed little will to fight outside Croatia). But when the new balance thus created led at the end of 1995 to a fresh threat of military defeat for Serbia, Washington again stepped in to prevent it. The Bosnian government was now threatened with total diplomatic disapprobation and political, economic and military isolation if it did not recognize a Republika Srpska covering half of Bosnia-Herzegovina.

The themes that dominate Zimmermann's book — inter-Yugoslav disputes; the role of nationalism in the country's break-up; nationalism's nefarious effect on democracy; the treacherous and dishonest behaviour of local leaders; the excellency of the US diplomatic service; UN and US humanitarian efforts; the relevance of the NATO use of force in Bosnia — are in themselves of limited importance. The only thing that ever mattered was which side Washington would take in the political and military dispute between Milošević's Serbia and the rest of Yugoslavia. Zimmermann's book allows a glimpse into the reasoning that produced the original decision to appease Belgrade, with all its fateful consequences. Had Washington supported democracy instead, the war would probably not have started; or, if it had, it would have ended long ago. Bosnia-Herzegovina would have emerged from Yugoslavia's break-up 'uncleansed' and territorially intact. The aggression designed to redraw old political and ethnic borders did originate from within Yugoslavia, but it succeeded only because it had the permission of the greatest power on earth. Herein lies the true origin of the Yugoslav — and the Bosnian — catastrophe.

Branka Magaš

This expanded version of a review first published in Bosnia Report 17 *(November 1996-January 1997) was prepared for the Balkan Institute in Washington and published by it in* Balkan Monitor, *February 1997.*

INDEX OF AUTHORS, EDITORS AND CONTRIBUTORS

Page references in roman type are for authors and editors whose books are listed in Part One; those in italic type are for contributors to volumes listed under another authorial or editorial name; those in bold type are for authors or editors whose books have been given a longer review here.

INDEX OF TITLES

Page references in bold type are for works given a longer review